UNIVERSITY OF NEBRASKA PRESS: LINCOLN AND LONDON

Ancestral Voice

Conversations with N. Scott Momaday

Charles L. Woodard

Manufactured in the United States
of America

The paper in this book meets the
minimum requirements
of American National Standard for
Information Sciences –
Permanence of Paper for Printed
Library Materials,
ANSI Z39.48-1984.

Library of Congress Cataloging
in Publication Data
Momaday, N. Scott, 1934–
Ancestral Voice: conver-
sations with N. Scott Momaday/
Charles L. Woodard.
p. cm.
Includes index.
ISBN 0-8032-4749-4 (alk. paper)
1. Momaday, N. Scott, 1934–
Interviews. 2. Authors, American –
20th century – Interviews.
3. Indians in literature. 4. Indians
of North America.
I. Woodard, Charles. II. Title.
PS3563.047Z464 1989
813'.54 – dc19 [B] 88-19089 CIP

TO SARAH

CLW How would you characterize your deepest voice?

MOMADAY It is lyrical and reverent and it bears close relationship to Indian oral tradition. That is my deepest voice. It proceeds out of an ancient voice. It is anchored in that ancient tradition.

Contents

ILLUSTRATIONS

Works by
N. Scott Momaday

Photographs

Introduction

For years he has been telling his essential story, in poetry and prose, in public performances, in recorded conversations, and by painting and drawing. He is the storyteller of whom he often speaks. The man made of words.[1] And this identity of his, this word being, has become increasingly definitive, fuller, and more nearly complete.

I first met N. Scott Momaday in 1974. Having read and reread *House Made of Dawn*, and then the rest of what he had written, I went to Stanford to discuss the dissertation I would eventually write on his works. In our first meeting, I was surprised by his voice. It was naturally, conversationally, the voice of his writings. Conditioned as I was to the typical distance between the spoken and the written word, I was surprised by the literate resonance of that voice, and it surprises and interests me still.

Out of those first conversations, and my ongoing responses to the story Momaday tells, and my growing interest in his visual art, this book has been created. Its conversational ingredient has been increasingly popular in modern times. Typically combining elements of the journalistic interview with the much older genre of imagined dialogues, writers and writers, or writers and scholars, have created for magazines, journals, published tapes, and books what might be called literary conversations. Momaday has been an occasional subject for this form. Because of his reputation and his verbal skills, short conversations with him have been published in a variety of forums during his career and have demonstrated the worth of this approach to his works.

In this longer work, however, in addition to asking familiar quesions to create a contextual foundation, I have endeavored to ask new questions, or to ask familiar questions in new ways. It is important to understand that Momaday means to tell one long story, as he has said on several occasions.[2] Therefore, what might seem to be merely repetition to the casual observer is usually changed, heightened, and refined in subtle ways. From book to book, and through his poems and paintings and essays and conversations, he is exploring and developing the story he means to tell.

To understand N. Scott Momaday, one must also understand the variety and fullness of his artistic expression. One must understand that he creates variously in a variety of artistic modes out of the integrated and integrative awarenesses that are his cultural heritage. So I have included Momaday's writings, paintings, and drawings with our conversations and my essays, to demonstrate the variety and importance of his art and to appropriately punctuate the text. Most of his own works are similarly punctuated.

The conversations in this book occurred in 1986 and 1987. In 1986 we were in Tucson in May, in Aspen, Colorado, in August, and in Santa Fe in November. In Tucson we met in Momaday's office at the University of Arizona and in his home; in Aspen we talked in his quarters at the writers' conference at which he was featured; and in Santa Fe we conversed in hotel living rooms near the Plaza. In each case we discussed a variety of subjects, and the topical conversations in this book are combinations drawn from all of those discussions. In October 1987 we spent several days in the Black Hills of South Dakota and traveling west to Devils Tower and the Big Horn Mountains in Wyoming. We wanted to spend time together, and to experience again some of the migration landscapes we had discussed in our earlier conversations. We have also had occasional telephone conversations as this book has developed.

My conversations with Momaday have been informal and enjoyable, the talk of old friends. He warms to such talk and, conversely, he tends to withdraw from academic interrogations. Consistent with his cultural traditions, he obviously enjoys discussion and is uncomfortable with argument. His responses to questions are typically indirect—metaphorical or anecdotal. Artful. Traditional. Out of his enthusiasm for the oral tradition, he clearly views what he says about his art as a part of his art rather than separate and "critical" in the scholarly sense of that word. So he chooses his words carefully, and he will not be moved from the tone and mood of his essential voice. And sometimes he chooses not to speak, or to say very little. I have left those moments in the text. They are also responses.

The conversations are lightly edited, for grammatical consistency, and I have added some transitions. The task was not difficult, because Momaday's careful responses are often almost textually complete. He was not involved in the editing process, but he has reviewed the completed text to verify its factual particulars.

In recalling our conversations, I see N. Scott Momaday in a variety of postures and attitudes. He is leaning back in his chair, relaxed, thoughtful, nodding, listening easily. He is talking, his tone frequently interrogative, opening his hands as he speaks. And he is laughing, suddenly, his head thrown back, his deep voice reverberating. He is a likable and provocative companion, and one is both relaxed and attentive in his presence. One is comfortable, but also alert to change. During a discussion of illusion and reality, this exchange occurred:

CLW What masks do you wear these days?

MOMADAY That's a very difficult question. The masks anyone brings to a given situation are probably innumerable. I have acquired identities which are my masks. I am a writer. That is a mask. I am a teacher. That is a mask. I am a bear. That is certainly a mask. I am many things, and in order to be any of those things at a given moment, one puts on a particular mask. Masks have to be understood as realities. They are not meant to confuse realities or to depart from reality. To the contrary. They are useful in presenting the reality of the moment.

CLW Masks are more commonly viewed in a negative way.

MOMADAY I suppose so. But I don't think of them in that way at all. One can mask the reality of something, but in the process another reality is presented, and very often it is a more appropriate reality for that moment.

The sections of this book are arranged in a sequence that roughly parallels the progression of Momaday's life. The first section, "The Center Holds," explores his individual and tribal identity, his process of becoming and coming to realize who he is. The second section, "Into the Sun," focuses on the individual and the tribe in the larger context of migrations across landscapes, and examines the evolution of the nomadic spirit. The third section, "Wordwalker," concentrates on the articulation of experience, from the oral traditions Momaday inherited to his own speaking and poetry and prose. His paintings and drawings, and the relationships of those creations to his writings, are the subjects of the fourth section, "The Vision Plane"; and the fifth section, "And Infinity," is more broadly philosophical and speculative. The essays that precede the conversation sections address each general topic more specifically, providing additional background information and creating contexts for the conversations. The final section, "Tsoai, Tsoai-talee," is an experiential conclusion.

It is difficult to communicate the complex equation that is the storyteller and his environment. Inevitably, there is loss. Gone are the gestures and movements, the facial expressions, the more delicate tonal nuances, the subtleties of the silences, the word-weaving pace. Although I have attempted to arrange and edit the conversations in ways that will most fully reveal the voice and the personality of my subject, I have included as internal indicators only occasional notations of laughter and several silences where I believe those to be essential to an understanding of certain exchanges. Otherwise I have relied solely on the language of my conversations with N. Scott Momaday. He is the man made of words.

ACKNOWLEDGMENTS

Sarah, my wife, contributed many hours of efficient intelligence to this book. We are ourselves together.

Jack Marken, my friend, made the original suggestion out of which the book has evolved, and generously contributed conversation time and resource materials as it progressed.

South Dakota State University gave me the sabbatical leave during which I began the work, and provided additional financial and resource support as it progressed.

From beginning to end, N. Scott Momaday was, as he has been since the day we met, unfailingly patient and generous-spirited.

BOOKS BY N. SCOTT MOMADAY

The Complete Poems of Frederick Goddard Tuckerman (editor), 1965

The Journey of Tai-me, 1967

House Made of Dawn, 1968

The Way to Rainy Mountain, 1969

Colorado: Summer, Fall, Winter, Spring (with photographer David Muench), 1973

Angle of Geese and Other Poems, 1974

The Colors of Night, 1976

The Gourd Dancer, 1976

The Names: A Memoir, 1976

The Center Holds

The predatory bird circles wider and wider, away from his owner's control, at the beginning of William Butler Yeats's "The Second Coming":

> *Turning and turning in the widening gyre*
> *The falcon cannot hear the falconer;*
> *Things fall apart; the center cannot hold;*

Cause and effect, Yeats seems to be implying. Loss of control of the world will be followed by chaos. But the traditional first American would view that beginning scene quite differently than did the Irish poet. First, the traditional would view the original "control" of bird by man as a perversion of natural relationships. He would say that it is inappropriate to gain such control "over" things. He would say that control begins and ends with self. One realizes one's self, centers one's self, and offers one's self. One exists cooperatively and coequally with all created things. Individual control, self-control, contributes to collective control, balance, and harmony. The natural order. Therefore, the traditional first American would not understand the anxiety about the perversion of systems reflected in the rest of the poem. He would identify those artificial constructs, those man-made control systems, *as* the problem.

N. Scott Momaday is in many ways such a traditional. His life has been a long process of imagining who he is, and the process is ongoing. The result is a man with an unusual degree of self-interest. But his self-interest should not be confused with egoism. He is not self-absorbed. His interest in the rest of creation is intense, and he has many obvious enthusiasms and a keen sense of humor. He simply believes in self-discovery and self-control rather than in dealing authoritatively with things and events outside of himself. He invests himself in the world, without seeking to control it.

To understand specific aspects of the man and the artist, it is important to understand the essential elements of his process of self-discovery. He was the only child of educator parents. From early childhood, it was apparent to him that his parents valued education, and the development of bicultural skills, and very physical and emotional understandings of cultural and spiritual origins. So he attended a variety of schools: one-room reservation day schools, church schools, and a military academy. And he lived among various peoples and cultures: his Kiowa relatives and friends, white people in towns, and traditional southwestern tribes. And he was told stories.

Out of the many stories the boy heard, two remain especially important. One is the story of the arrowmaker, the man who saves himself through language. The arrowmaker is a man who dares to speak in a moment of crisis—a man who risks himself in words in order to overcome an enemy. The boy learned from that story the importance of applying words to the world. He would come to believe that humans are beings made of words and that he could realize himself, and communicate himself, through language. He would come to believe that he could create his world in words, and that through words he might even transcend time and have perpetual being.

The other story that is essential to an understanding of the boy and the man is his story of Devils Tower, the Rock Tree of the Kiowa people. The man remembers that the tree came into being because a boy turned into a bear and pursued his sisters, who climbed upon a stump, which grew suddenly and carried them into the sky to become the stars of the Big Dipper. From this story, the boy acquired the essential words of his being. In the aftermath of visiting this crucially important cultural place, the boy acquired, ceremonially, his Kiowa name. He became Tsoai-talee, Rock Tree Boy.[1] He would come to believe that he is, in significant ways, the boy of the story. He would come to believe that the story forever connects him and his people to each other and to the seamless, intricately related physical world, and that it identifies his being and his circumstance within that world.

But N. Scott Momaday is a traditional who also has many modern enthusiasms. He is clearly bicultural, and he seems comfortable with that. One of the best examples of this cultural duality is his enthusiasm for the legend of Billy the Kid, a legend he has been celebrating and exploring for years through his writing and painting.[2] He is the Indian looking into that story, and he is the white gunfighter looking out. He appreciates the irony of that juxtaposition, and he enjoys the comedy of it. His clearly defined identity permits him to make such leaps without fear of seeming to contradict himself.

Nor does Momaday believe that there is contradiction in his refusal to be cause-oriented. He simply chooses not to be political, and he has said repeatedly that he will not accept the role of spokesman for the Indian people. Yet in many ways he is a spokesman, implicitly, as he re-creates the traditional world. As he dramatizes the idea of being Indian. As he dramatizes the great moral and ethical and environmental values of imagining that idea. As he continues that long process of imagining the Kiowa culture and values that are at the center of his being.

CLW Has the way to Rainy Mountain been difficult for you?

MOMADAY No. I would not say that it has been difficult. It has been fascinating, and something which is really fascinating is not difficult. There are sad, sad parts of the journey. For my people, the journey ended in sadness. In loss. But it has been a very pleasant experience for me, because it has filled my imagination. It has been a pilgrimage full of joy.

CLW What about the rest of us? Do you see more or less interest in cultural identity these days?

MOMADAY More, I think, than there was several decades ago. Along about the 1960s, it seems to me, there was a revival of interest in cultural being. After I wrote *The Way to Rainy Mountain*, a number of people came up to me and said, "Oh, this is wonderful, that you are able to look back into your ancestry to this degree. We wish we could do that." It hadn't occurred to me that most people can't do that. But just about that time, there was a growing interest in that sort of thing. I think it is still there, and may be still growing. We have such things as roots, after all, and there seems to be a great hunger to discover and understand those roots, those origins, in many people these days.

CLW But what are those people to do? Those people who, as you say, can't go back that far in time? Those who cannot re-create enough of their pasts to discover their cultural legacies?

MOMADAY Well, I think that they must imagine who they are and where they come from. Having the facts at hand is less important, in my opinion, than is having the desire to satisfy one's curiosities through imagining. And we also need some great mystery in our origins. That is, I would not like to know everything about my heritage. I want to be absolutely free to imagine parts of it. The facts are not very important. The possibilities are everything. When I look back, I see infinite possibility, and that's exciting to me.

CLW You have angles on other cultures and traditions, other racial legacies, in addition to your Kiowa past. Would it be possible for you to create your identity out of those other cultures and traditions?

MOMADAY Well, to some extent. I know about that part of me which is descended from a Cherokee great-great-grandmother, and about my ancestors who were European—English and French. In *The Names,* I pay some attention to that side of the family. But I'm not moved as much to understand that as I am to understand my Kiowa heritage. I think that's because my Kiowa heritage is quite exotic, and it represents to me a greater challenge in certain respects.

CLW Do you think that further exploring of your other tribal pasts would confuse your Kiowa identity in any way?

MOMADAY I don't think so, because the Kiowa identity in me is very strong now and secure. I think that there was a time while I was growing up when I might have lost my sense of Kiowa heritage, but that's no longer so. It's so deeply entrenched in me now, or I'm so deeply entrenched in it, that I don't worry about that. I'm Kiowa, and I'm going to die Kiowa. [Laughing.]

CLW You're convinced that you're going to die?

MOMADAY Oh yes, it'll happen. [Both laughing.]

CLW So you have chosen to be Kiowa. What of your mother's relationship to her Cherokee ancestors? Was her identification Cherokee? Or was

Faces, 1987, graphite and wash, 11 inches x 14 inches

it more broadly Indian? Was "Cherokee" a representation of something larger which she was attracted to?

MOMADAY I don't think her identification was specifically Cherokee. She knew that a distant relative was Cherokee, but I don't think that meant anything to her particularly. "Indian" was more important in her life than was the idea of being Cherokee.

CLW She did not imagine a Cherokee identity to the extent that you have established your Kiowa identity?

MOMADAY No. No. I don't think so.

CLW And so that is a difference between you, isn't it?

MOMADAY Yes. A circumstantial difference.

CLW Why do you say circumstantial?

MOMADAY Well, she wasn't in the same position to know the Cherokees that I was in to know the Kiowas. I came much closer to that culture and its traditions than she did to the Cherokee culture.

CLW In your essay "A Vision beyond Time and Place," you used the term "cultural nearsightedness" in reference to some elements of contemporary society.[3] Could you explain what you mean by that phrase?

MOMADAY [Laughing] No.

CLW And I had such high hopes for that question.

MOMADAY [Laughing] Well, then let me say this. I do really believe that some people today are not sufficiently concerned with the past. We live in a world that is very immediate, and we are too often all caught up in the now—what is happening now. Goodness knows it is easy to do that, and we are encouraged, I think, at every turn to lose sight of the past and the things that brought us to where we are. To who we are. I deplore this human condition. I think that there is great value in looking into the past. One can understand himself much more completely if he has a sense of his heritage.

CLW Why are we encouraged to lose sight of the past? Because we can be manipulated more easily without tribal history?

MOMADAY Well, I'm not sure that there's necessarily an intent to isolate us. But in our age, the emphasis is placed upon the immediate present, and so much is going on. There have been great revolutions—technological revolutions—and the mass media have burst upon the scene, and that's a lot to deal with. It is easy to get caught up in that, and to become so concentrated upon the present that the past and the future are simply ignored. I can see that there are great dangers in that. When we lose sight of the past, the loss is significant.

CLW What did your parents teach you about cultural identity?

MOMADAY I suppose a great deal. But it was so consistent and so pervasive in my upbringing that I probably couldn't enumerate lessons that they taught me. I learned a lot from their examples. When I was growing up, my parents and I were on a number of occasions in situations where we were outsiders looking into particular cultures. Jemez being the prime example. I took it all for granted as a child, but when I think back on it now, I wonder how it was possible to fit so easily into such situations. I was a child when I went to Jemez. I was twelve years old. Of course, children usually get along more easily in many situations, or so it seems, and are quite adaptable. So I thought nothing of it. My parents may have had a very different idea of their position in relation to the cultural realities of Jemez Pueblo. But in any case, they conducted themselves very well, and so their example was certainly affirmative. Maybe just by imitating them I crossed cultural barriers that I'm not even aware of now.

CLW So moving was for the most part an advantage to you?

MOMADAY I think it was entirely fortunate. One hears talk about how terrible it is for a child to move about and lose his friends and continually enter new situations—how demanding that is—but I certainly did not think of it in that way then, and I don't think of it in that way now. I'm convinced that it was good for me to experience so many different places when I was growing up. It was an important part of my education. So I have no misgivings about that at all. I can't presume to say that such mobility would be good for all children. I would hesitate to move my own children about like that. But, maybe because of my temperament, it was a very good thing for me.

CLW But why was moving especially good for you?

MOMADAY Being an only child might have had something to do with it. I spent much of my time alone or in the company of my parents when I was little. I didn't even have close playmates a lot of the time. But that was by no means a sad thing for me. I didn't mind. I think possibly my solitude encouraged me to develop my imagination. It may have been finally a very good thing for my writing.

CLW And you don't recall feeling threatened by drastically new circumstances?

MOMADAY No.

CLW No new-kid-on-the-block experiences?

MOMADAY I don't remember anything like that. I was basically shy, and it must have been hard for me on certain occasions to venture out into new circumstances, but I don't remember that. If I had negative experiences, they apparently didn't make much of an impression upon me.

CLW Do you recall the first books you loved?

MOMADAY Not readily. Not until about the age of twelve or thirteen.

CLW And then?

MOMADAY Then I discovered the joy of reading. We were living at Jemez, and I was bedridden with a strep throat. I was very active, and being in bed was torture. Then my father announced to me that he was going to Albuquerque to get some groceries or something. He said, "What can I bring you?"and I said, "Well, bring me a book." I didn't have anything in mind. He said, "What kind of book?"and I said, "I don't know—just something that will help me to pass the time." And he brought me *Smoky, the Cowhorse,* by Will James. And that was my first insight into the miracle of reading. That book was a wonderful experience. I couldn't put it down, to use the old cliché. As soon as I finished that book, I read everything that Will James wrote as fast as I could lay my hands on it. Those were perhaps the most important reading experiences of my life.

CLW What was it that fascinated you about those books?

MOMADAY Well, I was a boy with a horse, and the kind of life that Will James wrote about appealed to me very greatly. I think because of my setting. I was in the Wild West and very much enamored of Billy the Kid legends and stories of cowboys and horses. So the James books simply appealed to me very greatly at that time in my life. I was twelve or thirteen years old.

CLW What about poems, early on?

MOMADAY Well, my mother wrote poetry at one time, so she talked to me about it. I can remember her reading poems to me. Longfellow and such things. But I didn't have a real idea of what poetry was about until much later.

CLW What masks did you bring to Jemez?

MOMADAY Ah. All the masks that I had acquired in my childhood. I brought Billy the Kid to Jemez, and I brought the little Kiowa boy who lived with his grandmother at Rainy Mountain. I was an adolescent when

I came to Jemez, and adolescents have interesting masks. I think I was head over heels in love with Faye Emerson and Elizabeth Taylor in those days, and so some of my masks were determined by very emotional raw materials. That's not a very good answer, but it's a difficult question. The masks anyone brings to a given situation are difficult to describe.

CLW You attended several Catholic schools?

MOMADAY I did. Some.

CLW What effects did those have? Did you receive any kind of parochial conditioning that you can identify?

MOMADAY I can't think of any lasting effects that the Catholic schools might have had on me. The Catholic schools I attended were not distinguished centers of learning. Among the worst teachers I've ever had were some nuns with very poor preparation in teaching their subjects. I can't think of any particular marks the Catholic schools might have made upon my life.

CLW Did those schools refuse Indian culture? Did they deny it?

MOMADAY For the most part they did. Yes. I think that there's a strange and insidious kind of duality in such situations. Of course the Catholic church could not approve of the Indian religion, but it certainly was aware of the Indian religion. It could not accept or condone it. Consequently, there was always a religious tension in the pueblos. When I was living at Jemez I was aware of that tension, and of course reflected it in *House Made of Dawn*.

CLW Why did you choose to attend a military academy?

MOMADAY That was a very practical decision. I had run out of schools. I had gone to second-rate schools because I lived in remote areas. I wanted to go to college—that was an expectation on the part of my family and on my part—so there came a time when my parents and I sat down and decided that I should have something closer to college preparation than I was getting. So for my senior year, I went through catalogs and picked out a military school in Virginia. I went there to graduate, and I think it was a good decision. I was exposed to teaching that was better than I had had before.

CLW Were there any negative effects?

MOMADAY Well, it was hard for me. I don't think that's a negative effect, necessarily. I was challenged, and I had not acquired any good study habits. I didn't know how to study. I still don't know how to study very well, but I learned a little bit about it there. It was a good experience in that sense. But it was very hard. I was pressed and under stress there because the challenge was great. I had to compete in a way that I had not had to before.

CLW Would you object to having a child of yours go to a military academy?

MOMADAY Ah . . . [Laughing.]

CLW Lore could now go to Annapolis or West Point or the Air Force Academy?

MOMADAY I wouldn't object to it on principle, but I do think that the military academies have gone downhill. Augusta, the one I went to, is no longer in existence. It was a very old school founded by a Civil War veteran. And quite a distinguished place, as military academies were a generation or two ago. But I don't think they are as good in the 1980s as they once were.

CLW Why not?

MOMADAY I think that there is less interest in them than at one time, especially in certain areas of the country. Years ago, military-school experience was thought of as good for young boys. That certainly was the prevailing attitude when I went to Augusta. I thought of it as being something that was good for one to do. I think my parents thought of it as a good way of adding some discipline and order to my life. But I don't think many people think of military school in that same way now. I think that the popularity of such schools has fallen off in recent times. So I would have questions if my child wanted to go to one. But on principle—no—I don't object. If Lore wants to go to Annapolis and she can swing an invitation, I'll back her.

CLW You wouldn't be concerned about the militarism of such a place?

MOMADAY No. No. I don't think so. I don't think it takes hold, really. It didn't in my case. I mean, that was never the best part of it for me. The military. That's not what it was about. Though certainly there are people for whom that is what it is about. I think it depends upon what you bring to it.

CLW The best part of it for you was what? The discipline?

MOMADAY Well, the teaching was pretty good, as I said. And I do think that the uniformity of that life has some benefits. There was a tremendous sense of camaraderie there. I got very close to my roommates and to other people who were living in the same situation. We were all doing the same thing at the same time, and that made for a loyalty and a camaraderie that was new to me. And I think that can be a beneficial thing. As I look back on that year, I think it was good because it enabled me to become independent in a way that had not been required of me until then. I was well away from home and that was very hard, especially at the beginning. But once I got used to it, it was okay, and I think I came away from the experience a little bit better. That's about all I can say about that. It was not the most important time in my life, but it was okay.

CLW Was there anything out of your Indian culture that precipitated your going to a military school? There is that Indian tendency to serve, and to be involved after the fact with service organizations and ceremonially at powwows, and so forth.

MOMADAY No. At least, if there was such a thing, I was not aware of it at all.

CLW But that is characteristic, isn't it?

MOMADAY It is. It is.

CLW A great irony, but characteristic.

MOMADAY That's right. Probably the most patriotic people I know are Indians. Ironically.

CLW Those ceremonial events with flags and uniforms at powwows are very emotional for me. Because I think of the awful irony involved. The intensity of those ceremonies increases my feelings of regret for historical wrongs.

MOMADAY I certainly know what you mean.

CLW After college, you taught for a year at Dulce, New Mexico. Who would you be if you'd remained there? I ask that because you talk about the experience pretty nostalgically, and you've said in various ways that you might have stayed there.

MOMADAY I can't imagine staying there as a possibility. Though you're right, I did love the time I spent there. But if I were still there, I'd be principal at the school, maybe, and I'd be married to a Jicarilla Apache girl and we'd have thirteen children. Maybe I would be a writer and maybe not. I don't know. That was a very interesting time in my life. More important to me than the military school, for example. I was becoming an adult when I went to Dulce. It was a wonderful environment. A wonderful place in which to live as a bachelor earning four thousand dollars a year. It was a great experience. I think I grew a lot in that year's time. I was in a very fortunate situation. Well away from distraction and temptation. Lots of time in which to write, and I used it well. I think back upon that as a very happy and productive time in my life.

CLW But you can't conceive of being there now?

MOMADAY I can't conceive of having remained there. It's not in my temperament to remain in a place of that kind. I think eventually I would have run out of incentives. You know, I'm a Kiowa, so I'm a nomad, and I like to get around. Dulce would have inhibited me, I think, had I stayed there long enough.

CLW What would you want to be if you could not be a writer and painter?

MOMADAY I would like to be an actor. I admire what actors do. And there is in me an impulse to act. I think that if I had pursued an acting career, I might have been successful at it. It's something that interests me a lot. I have the opportunity in my teaching and in my public speaking to indulge some of this interest. Speaking is a similar activity and I enjoy it very much. It enlivens me in various ways. So I think it might have been possible for me at one point to bend my life in the direction of acting.

CLW But not anymore?

MOMADAY No. I'm too much committed to other things now.

CLW What leads you to believe that you might have been a successful actor?

MOMADAY I think the impulse that I was talking about probably requires a certain frame of mind. A certain degree of intrinsic interest. I have those attitudes and interests. I always have had.

CLW Did Yvor Winters, your teacher at Stanford, come as close to you as anyone has?

MOMADAY Hmm. I guess I would say yes. Yvor Winters perceived my situation more clearly than anyone else ever has on certain levels. He understood my cultural and ethnic situation very clearly. He expressed that understanding to me in letters. He certainly understood, more clearly than anyone else has, my literary potential. And as a friend, he probably saw as deeply into my personality as other people have. He was a very perceptive man and a very close friend. And we came close together in a short time. It's amazing to me how close we got to be in the years that we had together. And when he died it was a very great loss to me. He knew me. [Silence.] I can't explain that, but there it is.

CLW A matter of the combination, perhaps? What you were in relationship to what he was?

MOMADAY Something like that.

CLW There are such formulas.

MOMADAY A star-crossed kind of coming together. A destined meeting, I think.

CLW Destined? Really?

MOMADAY Oh, I think so. I'm a strong believer in destiny. And yes, I think that it was ordained. I don't mean to imply that it was something terribly unique and exclusive. I think it happens to people all the time. You meet someone in your life who sees you for what you are and who advises you, who stands in a position to change your life. And I do believe that certain things happen because they are meant to happen. I realize that in one sense that's a very dangerous thing to say, but to me it is no accident that Winters and I came together, as it was no accident that Billy the Kid and Pat Garrett came together in a much different kind of relationship. Those things are not accidental to me—they seem to me to be arranged in some pattern, like the pattern of the universe. It was no accident that the boy turned into a bear at Devils Tower, or that the girls became the stars in the Big Dipper. Those things are not determined on the basis of chance. They are destined.

CLW Is there also chance?

MOMADAY Sure. There's chance. But chance is much less interesting to me than destiny, though it may be of equal importance.

CLW Speaking of Devils Tower, what of your bear identity?

MOMADAY There is much to be said about that. My Kiowa name, Tsoai-talee, means "Rock Tree Boy," and it is, of course, associated immediately with the rock tree, what is now called Devils Tower. It is the sacred place in Kiowa tradition, and it is the place where the boy turned into a bear. I identify with that boy. I have for many years. And I have struggled with my bear power through those years. I think I have come to terms with it. I feel good about it. *Set*, my work in progress, is about the boy who turns into a bear, and in a sense I am writing about myself. I'm not writing an autobiography, but I am imagining a story that proceeds out of my own experience of the bear power. It is full of magic. But sometimes the bear is very difficult.

CLW Why?

MOMADAY Because his power is wild. He is hard to control. Bears are always

Eight children were there at play, seven sisters and their brother. Suddenly the boy was struck dumb; he trembled and began to run upon his hands and feet. His fingers became claws, and his body was covered with fur. Directly there was a bear where the boy had been. The sisters were terrified; they ran, and the bear after them. They came to the stump of a great tree, and the tree spoke to them. It bade them climb upon it, and as they did so it began to rise into the air. The bear came to kill them, but they were just beyond its reach. It reared against the tree and scored the bark all around with its claws. The seven sisters were borne into the sky, and they became the stars of the Big Dipper.[4]

hard to control. They don't give themselves easily to any domination. They are dominant. They are equal to man's dominance. A friend who writes about bears and lives with bears part of the year in Glacier National Park once said to me that a grizzly bear is the only creature equal to man in dominance. I believe him. He said that you can go among lions and tigers and be sure that you have an edge, but when you go among grizzly bears you know that you are on equal terms at best. So the bear is very hard to control.

CLW What does he threaten to do?

MOMADAY Take me over. Dominate me. I don't know if I understand the equation entirely, but it is so real to me that understanding is almost beside the point. I am a bear. I do have this capacity to become a bear. The bear sometimes takes me over and I am transformed. I never know precisely when it is going to happen. Sometimes it becomes a struggle.

CLW Do you think of the bear as sometimes separate from you? Or is he a permanent part of your being?

MOMADAY Let's go all the way back to the Kiowa story of the boy who turns into a bear. I think a bear was in that place. When the boy ventured into the bear's territory, the bear took him over, entered into the boy, and the boy became the bear, and threatened his sisters, as the story has it. We are told that the sisters were saved from the bear, but we're told nothing about the bear thereafter, or the boy. My notion is that the boy and the bear are divisible. That after the end of the story, the bear remains and the boy remains and they come together now and then. The boy becomes a boy again and becomes a bear again, and this goes on and has gone on through the centuries, and probably in every generation there is a reincarnation of the bear—the boy bear. And I feel that I am such a reincarnation, and I am very curious about it. The way I deal with it, finally, is to write about it—to imagine it and to write a story about it. All things can be accepted, if not understood, if you put them into a story. It is exactly what the Kiowas did when they encountered that mysterious rock formation. They incorporated it into their experience by telling a story about it. And that is what I feel that I must do about the boy bear.

CLW How old is your recognition of the bear potential in you?

MOMADAY I probably had the realization when I was about twenty-five years old.

CLW Do you recall what precipitated that recognition?

MOMADAY No. Not at all.

CLW Thereafter, did certain things in your past make more sense to you?

MOMADAY Yes. Understanding that I have a close relationship to the boy of the story from which my name proceeds accounts for a great deal. I can see things in terms of that realization more clearly than I could see them before. Not that I understand them, necessarily. But I can see them and I can see connections and I can account for them. From things that have happened to me. It is all very much a mystery, as it ought to be. But at some level, it is absolutely true.

CLW Is it conceivable that you could permanently separate yourself from the bear?

MOMADAY I hope not. It might happen, but I think it would be a sad thing if it did. Maybe it will. Maybe that's what eventually happens if one lives long enough. Maybe it has happened to other reincarnations of the boy bear. This bear power is dormant in me now, and has been for some time. I would not like to think that it might not come back. Because there is some kind of fulfillment in it. When I am most aware of my bear aspect, I am most alive. That's one thing that I can say with great conviction. I'm never more alive than when I'm really in touch with my bear power.

CLW How many times in your life has the bear surfaced?

MOMADAY I wouldn't have any idea. But a significant number.

CLW What happens, typically, at those times? How does the bear feel?

MOMADAY It is difficult to describe. There are manifestations of many kinds. There is an energy, an agitation, an anger, perhaps. A power that rises up in you and becomes dominant. The feeling is unmistakable. And you deal with it in various ways. You become very spiritual. You feel a greater kinship with the animal world and with the wilderness. You feel strong when you're most in touch with this bear. You become very intense in your work. And in your life. You accelerate your activity—writing, painting, whatever. You tend to be reckless, careless, self-destructive. You drink too much. You drive too fast. You pick on guys bigger than you are. [Both laughing.] All kinds of things. You become a magnificent lover, storyteller—it's just a great burst of vitality.

CLW But you have also implied that the feeling is threatening.

MOMADAY Yes. It is threatening because the bear is destructive. When he is really upon me, I feel threatened by that destructiveness, and I feel capable of destruction. It is possible for the bear to destroy the boy. The combination is potentially very destructive, just as in the story. The boy became the bear and his sisters were threatened with immediate mayhem. They were greatly imperiled. I would not like to turn into a bear and go with murderous intent after my sisters. That's a frightening thing. I think that the boy must have been beside himself with whatever it was when he found himself transformed and moving toward the destruction of his sisters. I'm sure that he was aware of it, and I'm sure that it must have torn him apart in some ways. But there was nothing he could do about it. And so I sense that when I'm in touch with the bear there is a great potential for disintegration.

CLW But it is worth the risk?

MOMADAY I think so. Worth it because it is so invigorating. And because it enables me to raise my imagination to a higher level than I ordinarily can. It is very creative.

CLW How long does the power last?

MOMADAY I have been very conscious of the power over a period of months. As long as five or six months, maybe.

CLW Does the power go away suddenly? Or by degrees?

MOMADAY Suddenly. Yes. Sometimes I think it goes without my knowing it. It can take a day or two for me to realize that it's gone. But it recedes quickly.

CLW Do you feel relief or regret then, or do you have mixed feelings?

MOMADAY I think there's a certain sense of loss that is exhaustion. I then have to wind down and it is difficult to do. It's not with regret. That is, when it goes, I don't yearn for it particularly. But I'm a little disoriented, in the aftermath of the experience, I think.

CLW Learning about the bear, thinking about it, writing about it, is a process of self-discovery, isn't it?

MOMADAY Yes. Yes. I think that if I can come to know more than I do about the boy who turned into a bear, through the imaginative process of writing about it, I will know more about myself. And I suppose that's as good a motive for writing as any. I'm curious about the story, but my curiosity stems directly from the fact that I am involved in that story. My name proceeds from that story. I have being in that story somehow, and I am curious to know as much as I can about it.

CLW And there have been multiple reincarnations of that bear spirit?

MOMADAY Hmm. Yes. I think there have been many reincarnations of the boy bear across time. I simply happen to be a current one.

CLW Are there currently other such reincarnations, do you think?

MOMADAY Not to my knowledge. But who knows. [Laughing.]

CLW It would be amazing to discover one, wouldn't it? Then what would you do?

MOMADAY I can't begin to imagine what that might mean.

CLW Say, at the same writers' conference, for instance.

MOMADAY I would be disappointed, I think. [Laughing.]

CLW Why?

MOMADAY Well, my goodness. I'd have to rethink the whole thing. [Laughing.] I'd have to make room for another whole story.

CLW Are you mindful of the bear power these days? Even though it is as you say, dormant?

MOMADAY Yes. In fact, I'm working with the memory of it as I write *Set*. There are times when I remind myself of the power, but I don't think that means that it's not dormant.

CLW Has the writing of *Set* called it forth in any way?

MOMADAY When I try to think of the bear power of which I'm writing, it reminds me of the bear power in myself. But the writing hasn't brought it forth in any perceptible way except through memory.

CLW Do you regret the dormancy of your bear power?

MOMADAY Oh, no. No. I'm rather grateful for it. It gives me time to rest. I'm getting ready for the next surge. [Both laughing.] No, I think it comes and goes and that's the way it ought to be, and there's no regret in that.

CLW Is "the next surge" inevitable?

MOMADAY I expect a next surge. I don't know if it's inevitable. I suspect that it is. I suspect that sort of power does surface inevitably. It does express itself because that's its nature. But I wouldn't be surprised to find that there are instances in which it goes and does not return. You lose the power.

CLW What other creatures are you especially interested in?

MOMADAY Dogs interest me a great deal. And hawks and eagles. I find almost any wild creature interesting. I don't identify particularly with any of them except the bear. The dog is perhaps second. Dogs and coyotes go way back in time, and have a long relationship with my people. There are a lot of stories about dogs. And in many of those stories, dogs are talking. That's an important thing to remember.

Self Portrait with Leaves, 1987, graphite and wash, 11 inches x 14 inches

CLW What about horses?

MOMADAY Dogs and horses are closely related, in my mind. The horse, as you know, was called "Big Dog" by certain Indians in early times. And dogs were horses for the Kiowas before the horse came along. They were beasts of burden. I believe that the people who came across the land bridge had dogs with them—dogs pulling travois. So the dog is an ancient animal and a fascinating creature.

CLW How do you feel about cats?

MOMADAY [Laughing] I'm not quite indifferent to cats, but they don't play a large part in my mind. I have a cat at home. A lovely creature. Black. And I rather like it. But it doesn't excite my interest as much as my dog does. Or as much as dogs in general, or horses.

CLW But dogs surrender more of themselves than cats, don't they?

MOMADAY They do. Because we encourage them to. They respond to encouragement easily—more readily, I think, than cats do. But there are people who do not encourage that kind of response in dogs, and I have seen those dogs. The dogs that my grandmother had when I was little were not pets in the sense that my Airedale is a pet. And the sled dogs in Greenland are not pets. I think that the cooperative relationship between man and the dog is older and in many ways more interesting and vital than the idea of pets.

CLW You have a higher regard for those more independent dogs?

MOMADAY I have a higher regard for those dogs because those dogs have a higher regard for themselves. Their independence matters to them. And they work—that's their life. They have a purpose. My Airedale has no purpose that I can see. [Laughing.]

CLW Why do you have him?

MOMADAY He exists for my pleasure. [Laughing.] But I'm going to fit him to a travois one of these days.

CLW You just referred to the Bering land-bridge crossing in a matter-of-fact way. How do you know that it happened?

MOMADAY It is part of my racial memory.

CLW What do you mean by that term?

MOMADAY I think that each of us bears in his genes or in his blood or wherever a recollection of the past. Even the very distant past. I just think that's the way it is.

CLW You think it's a genetic imprint?

MOMADAY Yes. I suppose I'd say that.

CLW What evidence of that do you have in your own experience?

MOMADAY Well, I've seen it in a lot of old people, particularly my kinsmen, my Kiowa relatives. I'm sure it exists in every culture. I've known old people who bear what one of my friends calls "the burden of memory," and it's not simply memory of what happened in their lifetimes. It goes far beyond that. In the case of the Kiowa, it's a remembering of the migration. A remembering of coming out of the log. A remembering of crossing the Bering land bridge.

CLW And you bear that burden of memory?

MOMADAY Yes. Yes.

CLW You have a primordial memory?

MOMADAY Oh, I think everyone does. Yes. It's probably more pronounced in small, closely defined ethnic groups, but yes, I think I have it and I think you do.

CLW Is that burden more pronounced in older people?

MOMADAY That's where it's most in evidence, I think. But it's also present in young people. It's not something you acquire in your lifetime. It's a given. You come into the world with it.

CLW How does the word *burden* apply?

MOMADAY Well, the friend I quoted had written an autobiographical narrative. I read it just at the time I was beginning *The Names,* and so we were talking about this business of writing autobiographical narrative. He talked a great deal about the burden of memory—the burden of the memory of bad things as well as the memory of good things. Memory can be a burden. Sometimes it's not easy to bear, but it is what you must deal with. It's your subject.

CLW Do you see that as an ongoing experience of yours? Drawing from not only your personal memory but also from your racial memory?

MOMADAY Yes. Oh yes.

CLW Are you always doing that?

MOMADAY Yes. I don't see how one can avoid doing that, but it is conspicuous, or more in evidence, in situations such as mine, because my past is a pretty closely defined ethnic experience and I have a hold on it. I can tell you about my people—not the individuals beyond, say, three or four generations, but the people as a whole—from the time they entered into the Great Plains and even before that through mythology. That hollow log. I don't know where it is. It could be in Asia. I have a sense of the Kiowas' existence as a people from the time they lived in

Asia to the present day. I think I'm lucky to have that sense. I'm sure that most other people don't have it as closely integrated into their experience as I do. It's important to me, and I'm fortunate that it defines me as it does. There are times, Chuck, when I think about people walking on ice with dogs pulling travois, and I don't know whether it's something that I'm imagining or something that I remember. But it comes down to the same thing.

CLW Why are you fascinated by the legend of Billy the Kid?

MOMADAY That's a good question, and I don't know if I know the answer. I think it might be because I grew up in New Mexico and heard about Billy the Kid from the time I was very young. He became a fascination, and continues to be that for me. Perhaps increasingly so. I'm now probably one of the authorities on Billy the Kid. I've thought so much about him. I have traveled through his territory and have written imaginatively about him on several occasions, and I am writing about him now in *Set*. In this novel, one of my characters fantasizes about Billy the Kid in nearly the same way that I did when I was a child. So it's something that has become a part of the life of my mind. I would be someone else if I didn't think a lot about Billy the Kid.

CLW What of the irony of that? Your writing of the Indian boy imagining riding with the white cowboy hero? The irony is part of your enjoyment of the legend, isn't it?

MOMADAY Oh yes.

CLW Billy the Kid is really in many ways antithetical to the traditional Indian world. At least in some popular imaginings. The white cowboy hero.

MOMADAY That's it. That's the thing that provides the irony, the vitality. It is a contradiction. Billy the Kid is opposed to one part of my experience—to the Indian side of me. He's diametrically opposed to that, but at the same time he's very much a reflection of the world I love. The Wild West. He's as much a reflection of that as is, say, Crazy Horse. Those two aspects—those oppositions—are the essence of Billy the Kid, and they give his story a particular vitality, it seems to me.

CLW You have also characterized your life with Billy the Kid as "strange and true." Can you say something about the origin of that phrase?

MOMADAY Well, we've just identified the strangeness of it. The true part of it is that I believe that the imagination is as much the truth as any other

Billy the Kid, from *The Billy the Kid Suite*, 1984, ink and watercolor on Arches paper, 23 inches x 30 inches

part of our intelligence, and certainly my imagining of Billy the Kid from the time I was small into the present is real and true. True in a special sense, to be sure, but true.

CLW Is it safe to say that Billy was killed by Pat Garrett?

MOMADAY Yes. He was killed by Pat Garrett.

CLW You are certain?

MOMADAY I was there. [Laughing.]

CLW Then again, you said in a Santa Fe column that maybe it was all someone's imagination.[5]

MOMADAY You were asking me about the historical reality. Yes. I think there is no doubt that Billy the Kid was shot dead by Pat Garrett on July 14, 1881, in Pete Maxwell's house in Fort Sumner. Beyond that there are other possibilities, but that seems to be the historical reality. [Both laughing.]

CLW Is revulsion any part of your reaction to Billy the Kid?

MOMADAY Revulsion?

CLW Yes.

MOMADAY Hmm. No. I'm sure that he was in his corporeal being a thoroughly unlikable person, and I'm sure that he couldn't be trusted very far, but I don't find him repulsive. I think of him as a very exciting and highly entertaining sort of man. For my purposes, you know. I certainly understand how other people might think of him in negative ways.

CLW Why is he more exciting than other legendary westerners—Doc Holliday, Wyatt Earp, Bat Masterson—any of those other legends? What is so particularly exciting about Billy?

MOMADAY Well, I think it's the way in which I think of him. I think of those other people, too. I think of Bat Masterson and Jesse James and other people, but Billy the Kid seems to me to be a more original man than those other people. I think of him as being colder, less influenced by the world around him. To me, Billy the Kid is like a shark. His principle of life is self-preservation. He doesn't usually think of other people. But that makes his occasional human gestures much more striking. As a case in point, the other day I was writing about Billy's escape from the Lincoln County Courthouse. And in the course of that writing, I also wrote about Sister Blandina Segale. About her account of two meetings she had with Billy the Kid. The account of the second meeting, when he was in jail in Santa Fe, is really touching.

Sister Blandina had met him briefly four or five years before, and she didn't think that he would remember her. She came into this dark room where Billy was literally chained to the floor. He was shackled hand and foot and he was chained in a prone position on the floor, and when she came into the room, he looked up at her and said, "I wish I could place a chair for you, Sister." And in this scene that I was writing, I dwelt for a moment upon what she must have meant to him, this European woman of the cloth who was so far removed from his experience of life that he must have thought of her as an untouchable. But I went on to say that when Billy made his escape—when he drew a gun in the Lincoln County Courthouse—nothing, nothing would have stood then in his way. He would have put bullets in the eyes of Sister Blandina if she had stood in his way at that moment. That's what distinguishes him from all the other western characters that I imagine.

CLW Which is the basis for my question about revulsion. Isn't there at that last moment something altogether negative about him? He would have put bullets in her eyes to escape. What of his absolute coldness at that moment?

MOMADAY I don't make any moral judgments about that. I simply think of him as being that kind of creature. God knows he's an aberration—a mutation of some kind. And certainly there is a negative side to that. But it's not one that I feel one way or another about. It's as if I'm looking at a shark—deadly, mindless—in whom is the irrevocable and inexorable impulse of life. What do you do with that? Is that good or bad? I don't think one can say.

CLW How do you reconcile that with his gentility? The human sensitivity of wanting to place a chair?

MOMADAY There's no reconciliation. You see, one of the things about Billy, too, that separates him from some others is that he had this curious inexplicable sense of chivalry, and it was apparently very highly developed in him. He was like Sir Galahad in certain ways, particularly with respect to Sister Blandina and to other women. He was a perfect gentleman.

CLW So chivalry was conditioning in him rather than feeling?

MOMADAY I would guess so. Yes. But there are all kinds of stories about women and their attitude towards Billy the Kid. When he was killed, a Navajo servant in the Maxwell house came out and poured out her

Stone, 1976, graphite and wash, 23 inches x 30 inches

wrath on Pat Garrett. She thought of Billy the Kid as her son. There are many such stories. There is Anita Maxwell. He was supposed to have been in love with her, and she obviously thought a great deal of him. She cared for him. She gave birth soon after his death, and there's a lot of speculation about that. She was married to another man soon after Billy died, but there are people who think that maybe the child was Billy's.

CLW You are especially interested in the idea of his being expressionless.

MOMADAY I've made a lot of it.

CLW And that interest appears elsewhere in your writing, in other characterizations. I think also of the dancers in *House Made of Dawn*. And of the albino at times. Is the expressionless condition a special interest of yours?

MOMADAY Well, I'm very interested in expression, in the ways people express themselves, whether it is facial expression or gestures of the hands or, of course, speech. So when I find someone who is expressionless, that fascinates me. And I've had experiences of that kind. Perhaps the most striking one was in Russia at the Bolshoi Theater. One night I was sitting with a friend, and an Asian man with a beautiful woman came into the row in front of us and sat one seat over. I was chatting with my friend, and I said something that triggered a reaction in this man, this bald, thick Asian man, who turned around and fixed me in a gaze that reduced me to dust. He looked at me as if he were memorizing my face. And he looked at me for what seemed an interminable time, and then he turned back. [Laughing.] And as he looked at me, I could not read anything. It was a deep, deep look, but it was not to be divined, and my friend just looked at me and said, "What did you do to that man?" I said, "I don't know." [Laughing.] But I know what he did to me.

CLW And what he is still doing.

MOMADAY Yes. When I wrote "The Strange and True Story of My Life with Billy the Kid" for *American West*, I had that experience in mind. When the drunk intervenes and Billy fixes him in his gaze. The drunk is reduced—he withers away, as I say. I have often thought, What was it that I saw in Billy's eyes at that moment? Could it have been sorrow, or at least a hint of sadness? But then I realize that I saw nothing. Nothing at all. Billy was the only man I have ever known in whose eyes there was no expression whatsoever.

CLW You're interested in the integrity of that? The absolute quality of it?

MOMADAY Yes.

CLW And you're glad you didn't confront the man at the Bolshoi Theater? You're glad you didn't go up to him in the lobby and draw him out?

MOMADAY Yes. I might have reduced the mystery to sense, and that would have been a lesser thing.

CLW On the subject of mystery, do you still participate in traditional ceremonies?

MOMADAY Yes. But not regularly. I go to Indian ceremonies as I can. It's not something that I feel the need to do religiously now, but I still enjoy going to the Gourd Dance, for example, though I haven't been in several years. It's something I tell myself I'm going to do every summer, but things have gotten in the way in recent years. Maybe this summer.

CLW You are a member of the Gourd Dance Society?

MOMADAY Yes.

CLW What does that mean to you?

MOMADAY It's a great honor. It's one of the two remaining soldier societies in the tribe, and very old. There are a good many members—over one hundred, at least. And I take pride in my membership in it. It's a way of restoring myself in the spiritual dimension of the tribe. Although I haven't gone recently, I think of myself as a gourd dancer, and I mean to go when I can.

CLW How do you feel when you participate? How are you affected by the dance?

MOMADAY Well, I become irresistibly aware of my Indianness when I dance, and I perceive the power of that identity, that belonging, as I do not perceive it in other situations. The Gourd Dance is very compelling. When I'm dancing, I get caught up in it and am transported, in some sense. I think everybody feels the same way—that's the great attraction of it to the Indian. You know, he can place himself in that current of sound and motion and by means of that—that affirmation—he can be really close to the center of his cultural world. It's an ineffable experience, finally. I wish I could tell you how I feel when I dance. It doesn't start out as affirmation. It's in Oklahoma in July. It's apt to be humid and very hot and we wear blankets, and it's not very comfortable to begin with. But once the movement starts and the drum starts gathering momentum, reaching a certain pitch, you get deep into the motion of the dance, and that feeling is indescribable. It's wonderful. I've not found that feeling elsewhere. I know why those warriors danced before they went out on raiding expeditions. It is a great way to gather yourself up, and you feel very much alive.

CLW What part does music play in your life? You talked about contemporary music quite often in your class this semester.

MOMADAY Well, I think it is important to me, but music as such is something that I know very little about. I like to hear music. And I'm very much interested in American folk songs. That's an area that I could get into if I had the time. But I'm not a student of music or of songs, in the academic sense.

CLW Why your particular interest in folk music?

MOMADAY I think because American folk music reflects a lot of things that are intrinsic in American culture and history. We're getting close to the pulse of the American imagination when we encounter those old ballads and folk songs. I love to hear them. Some good portion of my record collection is made up of American folk music.

CLW You are a folk singer of sorts in several of your poems, aren't you? I'm thinking of things like your poem called "Billy the Kid, His Rocking Horse: A Lullaby."

MOMADAY Well, certainly one could think of it in that way. Billy the Kid is an appropriate subject for folk songs. For folk tales.

CLW And in "He Encounters a Player at Words," Pat Garrett says, "We'll dance a jig and dine on shoat, / And you shall be my billy goat."[6] That's also folk music, isn't it?

MOMADAY Yes, I guess you can call it that.

CLW I think if you extended the poem a few more verses, it could become quite popular.

MOMADAY I'll think about that. [Both laughing.]

CLW Would you say something about the legacy of humor in your cultural background?

MOMADAY I think humor is extremely important in all Indian cultures. I've never found an Indian community without that ingredient. Indians like to laugh, and they place a great premium on wit. For Indians, the joke is certainly an ancient institution. The story that turns on a humorous element is everywhere. When Indian people get together, there's always laughter. But it's a kind of humor that is not easy for other people to understand. Indian humor is so distinctive. I think that even if it could be translated, much would be lost in the translation.

CLW Can you characterize it in any way?

MOMADAY I don't think so. It's so various that it would be difficult to characterize. There are too many aspects to it. But I can give you a few examples. We're all familiar with the trickster stories. The trickster is a scapegoat character. He is a very interesting personality because he's often very wise, and yet he gets himself into impossible situations all the time, and frequently the joke is on him. He bears the brunt. But that is only one example of Indian humor. It flourishes over a very wide scale.

CLW You grew up hearing Saynday stories, stories about the Kiowa trickster, from your father?

MOMADAY Yes.

CLW Does that cultural legacy of humor influence your work?

MOMADAY I'm not sure that I know the answer to that question, but I hope very much that there are influences. I admire so much not only the Saynday stories but the whole oral tradition that I am sure that those things are reflected in my work somehow. But I'm so close to my own writing that I probably am not in the best position to see what those reflections are. I hope they're there, because the Saynday stories, like the warrior stories, are highly imaginative and well made. Like the best literature, they deserve to be preserved for their own sake. Such preservation is the best thing that anyone can wish for in his writing.

CLW What are the implications of the Saynday stories?

MOMADAY Saynday is in the Kiowa culture a trickster figure, like those in other cultures, and he is very important in a number of ways. Some of them very ironic. He's a comic figure—at least on occasion. And he's possessed of supernatural powers. He can transform himself into other beings, other things. He's very creative. He's a creator. He incorporates symbolically all of the good and all of the bad elements in Kiowa life, and probably in human life. He's capable of very good deeds and very bad deeds. So he's a universal figure.[7]

CLW Is he all of us or apart from us?

MOMADAY Yes. [Both laughing.]

CLW Why do you suppose that Indian humor has been so little recognized by the majority culture? And so little understood?

MOMADAY It's probably been kept a secret. It's one of the strongest elements of language within Indian cultures, and it's probably jealously preserved.

CLW An intent to exclude? In-joking?

MOMADAY I think so. Maybe most cultures defend themselves in certain ways in their languages. Like the songs of black slaves. Those were very important to the slaves and full of meaning that was exclusive, and I think that the Saynday stories are of the same order. Maybe oral traditions as a whole are exclusive, but certainly the humorous element is one of the chief manifestations of a defensive attitude. Humor is really where the language lives, you know. It's very close to the center, and very important.

CLW Why?

MOMADAY Maybe because it's so wide in its appeal. Any Kiowa can communicate with any other Kiowa on the level of humor. It may be more difficult at other levels, even though we're talking about the same language and the same culture. Humor, it seems to me, is more accessible than are other areas of human experience.

CLW What about humor in your writings? And play? In the last lines of *The Way to Rainy Mountain,* you refer to "the feeling of play." How important is play in your art?

MOMADAY I like to play with words, and I think a lot of what I write is playful. Much of my work is a play upon words and play in the element of words. In *The Way to Rainy Mountain*, the old woman Ko-sahn talks to me about the sun dance. She tells me that it began with an old woman who brought dirt in to place on the dance ground in the sun dance lodge, and then sang. And a part of her song had to do with play. She sang, "As old as I am, I still have the feeling of play." And I was greatly taken with that, and decided that it's really a central part of the Native American attitude towards life. One doesn't ordinarily think of the sun dance as play, but if you observe Indian ceremony, there is a lot of play in it. A lot of laughter and joking and an attitude of playfulness, and it was there in that one-hundred-year-old woman, Ko-sahn. I think that's what she was talking about when she was talking in turn about the old, old woman of the sun dance. That's an important thing, and I think I deal in it. Not always consciously, necessarily, but it's a part of my attitude. It shows up in my work.

CLW Can you give me some examples of where you think it's most evident?

MOMADAY Well, the things that come immediately to mind are things that I've just been working with in *Set*. There's a lot of wordplay in that book, and there's wordplay as well in *The Names*, and a number of situations in which people are being playful. In that book, I wrote about Lupe Lucero, the little boy at Jemez Day School. One day the governor of the village comes up and speaks to Lupe in his native dialect and asks for my father. Lupe considers for a moment, and then he looks up at the governor and he says, "I'm sorry, my friend, but we speak only English here." I appreciate that little story. There's a lot of that sort of thing in *The Names*. To some extent, there's that sort of thing in *House Made of Dawn*. When Abel's horse lies down in the river and Abel has to get up and walk out with his shoes creaking and swishing water, that's funny. Indians would read that and find it very funny. They'd laugh a lot.

CLW That's interesting. I think humor is a dominant element in *The Names*, but I hadn't thought of it much as far as *House Made of Dawn* is concerned. Can you think of any other examples of humor in that novel?

MOMADAY Well, there's the whole court business where there is such a play upon words and words are the dangerous element. The narrator comments that the white men are trying to enclose him in words. Disarm him with words. There are words all around him. And of course, Tosamah makes a lot of puns. Not puns in the ordinary sense, but he plays with language a lot. He says things like, "Due process is a hell of a remedy for snakebite." There's quite a bit of that in certain sections, particularly in those that have to do with Tosamah.

CLW "Be kind to a white man today"?[8]

MOMADAY Yes. Take a white man to lunch, or something like that.

CLW Would an Indian reader be likely to laugh at elements of the court scene?

MOMADAY Yes. Where Tosamah remarks upon the court scene—I think Indians would find that funny. When he tells what happened to Abel—this poor longhair who gets himself in trouble. "Look what they did for him," he says. "They deloused him. They gave him an education and free room and board, and how does he pay them back?" I think an Indian would find that funny.

CLW The implication is that whites would not. Why do you think that is?

MOMADAY I think there's a clear distinction between Indian humor and white-man humor. Indians do have a very in-joke humor. They have their own jokes and their own humorous situations. And as we've said, their humor tends to be exclusive. Half the time, whites who overhear Indians saying things that break Indians up can't see anything funny at all. I don't begin to understand that entirely.

CLW Do whites tend to be more literal, in your experience? Or is that an unfair generalization?

MOMADAY I'd have to think about that, but my impulse is to say yes. They probably take things more literally. And more seriously, too.

CLW Can you give me an example of what you mean?

MOMADAY Well, I was in Washington recently and I spoke at the Smithsonian on a panel which included several other Indian people. Afterwards, some of us went out to dinner and a party. At the party we were all sitting around a table. Only Indians. And it was an hilarious evening. I just sat there and laughed because I could see into the humor, but I can imagine that a non-Indian sitting at that same table would have been concerned for our sanity. He would not have understood the current of humor that was running through the place. That's happened to me many times. I perceive it, but I don't really know how to explain it.

CLW I don't suppose you recall a "for instance" of the humor at the party you just described?

MOMADAY No. And "for instances" don't work. Even if I told you verbatim what someone said that made everybody else erupt in laughter, it would be meaningless.

CLW The humor is dependent on context, in other words.

MOMADAY Yes. And it is infectious. If you said the same thing outside that context, it wouldn't have the same force. I remember one man particularly who, if I heard rightly, and remember rightly, was a judge in Oklahoma. He was retired. A very dapper man with white hair. I've forgotten what tribe he belonged to, but every time he opened his mouth, the rest of us started laughing. And he may have had the best time of all. It wasn't that he was being especially witty or brilliantly funny. It was just that he understood the context of that situation so well that he knew how to make us laugh and he took great delight in it, as did the rest of us. He was just a wonderful kind of trickster figure or funny man in our presence, and his sense of timing was superb. I don't know. It may be possible for somebody to investigate that phenomenon. Analyze it and explain it. But I wouldn't know how.

CLW Didn't that man's success at making you laugh have much to do with his storytelling attitude? His tone of voice and manner? His timing? His sense of who his listeners were and what they would react to?

MOMADAY Yes. Absolutely. My father had that very Indian sense of humor, and so I grew up close to it. I can remember when he used to have other artists out and they would work together at Jemez. Then they'd go up to the mountains, and they'd take me with them. Quincy Tahoma used to come. You'd hear Quincy and my father laughing in the little studio where they worked, and then they'd take me with them up to the mountains and cook steaks. They could go on for a long time about burned steak. Just talking about how they liked burned steak, black steak. And it was very funny. It sounds silly when you try to talk about it, but on the spot it was hilarious.

CLW You also seem to be implying that what you're talking about is cross-tribal. You could be among other Indian cultures and share that same sense of humor? It transcends tribal distinctions?

MOMADAY Yes. As on the occasion in Washington, when I think probably no two people who were at the table were of the same tribe. But they were all Indian, and they all shared that same sense of humor.

CLW Quick change of pace—why do you like cooking?

MOMADAY It's relaxing and creative. It's fun and food tastes good.

CLW Do you cook symmetrically or organically?

MOMADAY I cook evangelically. [Both laughing.]

CLW I can't go on to the next question.

MOMADAY There's a lot to say about that question. We could do a separate book on that. Including some menus and recipes.

CLW Do you have a favorite recipe?

MOMADAY No. Yes. I think I do. I have my own recipe for posole, and I think it's my best cooking accomplishment to date. Posole, as you may know, is a winter stew that is popular in the Spanish-American villages of

New Mexico. It's made with dried corn and pork. Bones, really—knuckles. It can be rather bland, but the Indians in New Mexico mix into it a chili con carne. My recipe is a very good one. I cook the chili con carne separately and serve it on the table, and you mix it to your own taste. It's wonderful on a cold night.

CLW How do you react to violence?

MOMADAY I think the answer to that has to be very complicated. I am violent. Or I can be. I have been at times. I understand violence. I understand that it can happen. On the other hand, I'm opposed to it. It sickens me. If I see gratuitous violence, I'm repulsed by it. There's a lot of violence in films, as you know, and I sometimes react to that violence with disgust. But I do understand that it exists, and that people are capable of it.

CLW Couldn't one argue that any violence is gratuitous?

MOMADAY Ah. Yes.

CLW Would you?

MOMADAY No. [Laughing.]

CLW Why not?

MOMADAY Some of it is reactionary. Some of it is provoked. So it is not gratuitous then. It is a response. And one can be violent without wanting to be, I think.

CLW How do you mean that?

MOMADAY Well, I mean I think there's such a thing as losing one's temper and becoming irresponsibly enraged. Then one can do things that in one's normal condition one wouldn't ever dream of doing. That happens. And I think that one can be provoked to violence. And I would not call that sort of violence gratuitous. It's a reaction to provocation. Motive and emotion.

CLW Is violence ever creative?

MOMADAY Oh, I would imagine that it can be. I might have a hard time thinking of an example, but why not?

CLW I think of what you told me about your bear power. That potential for destruction. You said that the potential destructiveness of it is also creative.

MOMADAY Yes.

CLW So bear power is volcanic but productive?

MOMADAY Yes. One can sometimes create beauty by resorting to violence. One can react violently and beautifully to something at the same time.

For example, a lot of horsemanship is essentially violent. Using energy and using spurs. Bullfighting is violent, but it can also be beautiful. It's an artistic form predicated in some measure upon violence. The chicken-pull at Jemez. Violent and disgusting. Yet also beautiful, if taken from another point of view.

CLW Have our violent impulses remained pretty much constant across the long range of time? Or are human beings becoming more violent?

MOMADAY You would know more about that than I, I think, having been to war, where violence is protracted and magnified. But I don't think that we are moving more in the direction of violence. I think it is something that has always been a potential in us and comes to the surface in individuals. It has much to do with individual temperament, in my opinion. Billy the Kid was a violent man. And certainly there were violent men all around him. I don't think that we are more prone to violence now than we were in Billy the Kid's time or in Attila the Hun's time. But the expression of violence is very dependent upon the situation. In war, for example, violence escalates because mob psychology is involved. But I think that was always so, and is not any more so now than it was in the past.

CLW Here's a more pacifistic question. You told the interviewer for the American Audio Prose Library series that one of your great advantages is your dual vision.[9] Your familiarity with both the white and the Indian worlds.

MOMADAY You have all this evidence amassed against me, don't you?

CLW I certainly do.

MOMADAY You're going to tell me what I told other people and then ask me a parallel question. Right? [Both laughing.] Hoping for a contradiction?

CLW You're on to me. My question is, Is that cultural duality ever a disadvantage?

MOMADAY Hmm. I suppose. You know, that's a good question. I don't know that I've ever thought about that before. But my reaction to it is yes, I suppose it must be a disadvantage at times. For no other reason than that it is a complication. Having two choices or two ways of doing or proceeding or seeing can be an impediment to action, I suppose. But I think that's far less important than the advantage. The advantage of having two perspectives or two points of view.

CLW Can you think of an example where it might be an impediment? What about the contrasting explanations for the origin of Devils Tower?

MOMADAY Yes. I suppose that's about as good an example as I can think of. There are at least two ways of explaining the existence of Devils Tower. Two predominant ways. One is the geologist's explanation of its development, its formation. And obviously that is a logical explanation, and it has a truth of its own. But I also see the other explanation as being equally true, and so there you have a rift between the mythological truth and the scientific truth.

CLW Isn't it also true, though, that the dual explanation would be more problematic for the scientific side than for the mythological side? Would the traditional be as uncomfortable with the scientific explanation as the scientist would be with the mythological explanation?

MOMADAY I don't know. I just don't know about that.

CLW We'll allow a great silence in this part of the book. [Both laughing.]

MOMADAY Space. White space. [Laughing.] The reader is invited to fill in the blanks.

CLW How do you feel about the term "Indian" these days?

MOMADAY Fine. I use it all the time. I don't find it derogatory or inaccurate. "Hb

MOMADAY American Indian."

CLW Do you prefer it to "Native American"?

MOMADAY I think I do, finally. I see very little to choose between them. And I use both, but I think I'm more comfortable with "American Indian." It may be because I grew up hearing it, using it, writing it.

CLW I think that sometimes whites are apprehensive about the term "Indian."

MOMADAY I think that's because they imagine that Indians might be offended by being called Indian rather than Native American, or vice versa. But I don't think Indians feel that way. It doesn't matter much to them. They call themselves Indians. Most of them that I know, anyway.

CLW Do most of them you know call themselves first whatever tribe they are?

MOMADAY No. I don't think they do unless pressed. Most Indian people I know think of themselves first as Indian.

CLW When do you think that changed?

MOMADAY It's changed in my lifetime. It relates in some way to the decline of the reservation system. More Indians have crossed the boundaries of their reservations and more have begun to think of themselves in what we might call pan-Indian terms. When I was small, and growing up on reservations, the Kiowas thought of themselves as Kiowas and the Jemez people thought of themselves as Jemez and the Apaches thought of themselves as Apaches. Then, later in my life, when I went away to school, I encountered other Indian people off their own reservations, and those tribal distinctions became less important than the one central identity which is Indian. And with the rise of powwow power, if I may coin a phrase [laughing], young Indian people became much more willing to exchange information and traditions than they were at one time. And this, too, leads to a sense of being Indian first.

CLW And you, too, are inclined to think of yourself as Indian before you think of yourself as Kiowa?

MOMADAY With the difference that I very early had to think of myself in pan-Indian terms because I never lived on my own reservation. The Kiowas don't have a reservation as such, so I wasn't born on a land base with which I could identify or with which I had to identify. I moved away from Kiowa country when I was very young and grew up among other Indian peoples, and so in a different way I thought of myself as Indian rather than Kiowa. Of course, I've always thought of myself as Kiowa, too. But I think it was incumbent upon me to make that transition earlier than most Indian youths do. So I'm an exception in that sense. I had a different kind of experience than a child who grows up on his reservation has.

CLW You told me years ago that you feel in some ways closer to the Navajo than to other people.

MOMADAY I feel very close to the Navajo. I lived on the Navajo reservation growing up, at a critical age. I lived among the Navajo at a good time in my life, when I was young and gathering all sorts of experience and information to myself. I feel very close to the Navajo because they were like family to me when I was little. Even now, when I go among them, I feel at home. I feel that I have some investment in that community and that landscape, and I love the Navajo spirit. They have a great generosity of spirit. They are very good to be with.

CLW They are particularly generous?

MOMADAY I think so. Yes.

CLW I wonder why.

MOMADAY I do too. I can't account for it, but it is a definitive aspect of their culture. They are very generous and easygoing and dignified. They are in great possession of themselves. More so than the other peoples I know. Isak Dinesen found great nobility in some African people, and I feel that way about the Navajo. There's a great nobility in them.

CLW Does *House Made of Dawn* bear down on you in any way because of its success? Because of the standards it raised? Did it create pressures?

MOMADAY Yes. I think so. Particularly right after it was published. It's probably not the best thing for a man in his thirties to win a major prize like that. It was all on the basis of that one book, and when I did win the prize, it placed pressure on me. I thought, What do I do now? I don't know to what extent it was a deterrent to subsequent writing, but I'm sure it was a deterrent. Especially in the first two or three years.

CLW Is it fair to say that it created not only artistic pressure but personal pressure? Since you were so quickly recognized as a leading figure and a spokesman for your people? Didn't that make life more difficult for you in some ways?

MOMADAY Yes, it did. However, I had the good sense from the very beginning not to take on the responsibility of speaking for the Indian. I think that was an expectation on the part of many people. But I turned that off pretty quickly, I think. When I was asked if I was speaking for the American Indian, or if it seemed to me that the question assumed that I was doing that, I was quick to say, "No, I'm not. What I'm doing is mine. It's my voice and my ideas, and I don't want you to think that I'm the political spokesman of a people. I don't want to be that, and I don't think I'm entitled to be that. I can write about the Indian world with authority because I grew up in it. I know a lot about it, but I would be the last person to say that my opinions are anybody else's—Indian or not. I don't write in that vein—out of any sort of conviction of that kind."

CLW You must have received criticism for that stance, though?

MOMADAY I think a lot of people were disappointed that I wouldn't assume the role of spokesman. Yes.

CLW Yet the irony is that in your writings you are a spokesman. You recreate the traditional Indian world and the values of that world, and

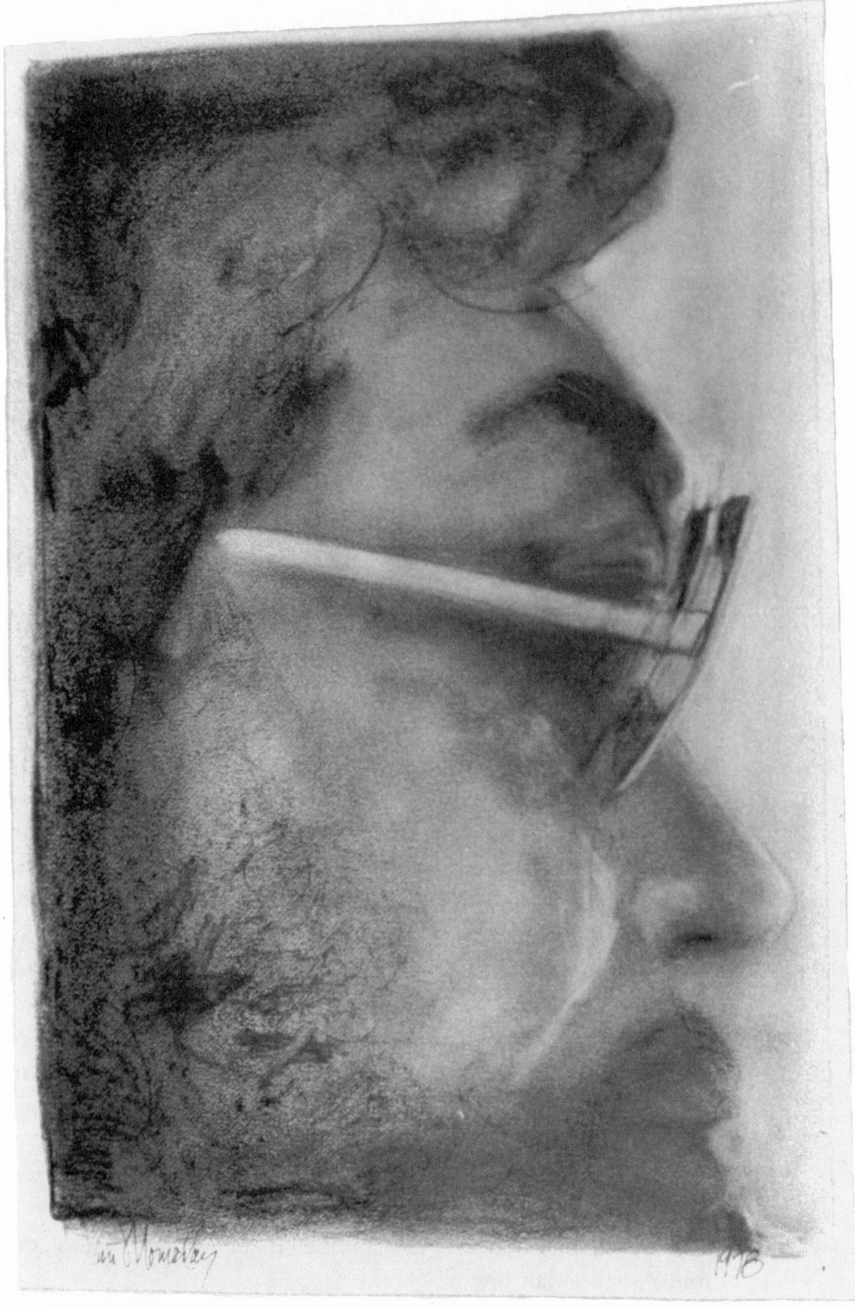

Self Portrait, 1976, graphite and wash, 23 inches x 30 inches

representative statements are implicitly and sometimes explicitly there.

MOMADAY Well, that may be so. Almost all writing is political, if you come right down to it. But my writing is not motivated by political considerations. It's not that I want people to derive moral or social or political lessons from what I write. But that is sometimes the expectation. I've encountered people who were very disappointed and upset because they thought that I was presenting the Indian world too positively. I remember once when I was in Hamburg, and spoke to a group of German writers. This woman came up to me afterwards. She was herself a novelist and a very attractive and articulate woman, and she was almost incensed that I had painted an optimistic view of the Indian world. She thought that I was lying when I was talking about the beauty of the Indian world and the Indian's appreciation of that beauty and my happy childhood as an Indian. She wanted to hear horror stories. There's a lot of that kind of expectation.

CLW Maybe it has something to do with the misunderstanding of what you mean by the word *Indian?* In your essays about land ethics, for example, you talk about the evolution to an environmental attitude—the creation of a values system.[10] You call the attitude you admire "Indian," but aren't you talking about cultural accomplishments, cultural ideals, rather than generalizing about all contemporary individuals and circumstances? Maybe that woman was taking you specifically and literally, when you were speaking philosophically and figuratively?

MOMADAY I think so. What interests me, though, is the quality of the expectation. This woman, this German novelist, had some sort of vested interest in the dark side of the American Indian experience. She would have loved for me to say that I had grown up in deep poverty, and had been abused in many ways by many people, and persecuted because of my Indianness, and gone to boarding schools and been forbidden to speak my native tongue, and all of those things which you know have happened. But she had put them into some sort of pattern and didn't want to see anything else. So when I was talking about the good things in my Indian experience, she was offended.

CLW Why do you think she had a vested interest in the dark side, to use your term?

MOMADAY Maybe because she wanted to write about it, or because she needed the Indian as an example of persecution for her own value system. I don't remember exactly what the context of my remarks was, but I have an idea that I was saying that in some ways the situation for Indians is better now than it was one hundred years ago. And I think she didn't want to hear that there have been any improvements. She wanted confirmation of this black-and-white picture that she cherished. And I think her attitude is widespread.

CLW I agree. Yet the negative things are also in your writings. They're certainly there in *House Made of Dawn,* and you summarized them in places in *The Way to Rainy Mountain*. They're certainly acknowledged, identified, defined.

MOMADAY Yes. I think they are. As they have occurred in the course of human history.

CLW But don't you also intend to nurture the idea called "Indian," which you have often said is a very good one? One of the main points you make early in *The Way to Rainy Mountain* is that many negative things happened and yet that's not the focus of the book. You call the negative things "idle recollections, the mean and ordinary agonies of human history."[11]

MOMADAY That's right. Those negative things are real. But it is at least as important to know about the positive things. And to celebrate them.

CLW Still, there are mixed reactions to those positive things. I've used some of your essays in classes and community groups. When some people read what you have to say about the Indian's idea of himself and what can be learned from that, they immediately translate it to the particular and say, "Aha, that's not true, because we know Indians who aren't like that. Let us tell you about some Indians we've known." Which is altogether beside the point, isn't it?

MOMADAY Yes. That's exactly right.

CLW On the subject of foreign reactions to you, tell me about your experiences in Russia in the spring of 1974, when you were visiting professor of American literature at the University of Moscow. Who were your students there?

MOMADAY They were graduate students in American literature. They were all writing theses in American literature, and they all spoke English very well. And I had about a hundred students to whom I lectured once a week. And I consulted with them at times on an individual basis. They were fighting for teaching positions in the Soviet Union. All of them wanted to end up in Moscow and very few would, so that competition was really keen. They were very bright and industrious and tense.

CLW Tense?

MOMADAY Because of the competition.

CLW Were they creative?

MOMADAY Yes. But I didn't really see into that. I wasn't involved with reading their dissertations, so I really didn't have a sense of their writing. I was simply lecturing to them and answering questions about American literature. I'm sure that some of them were very creative.

CLW Were they curious about your cultural frame of reference?

MOMADAY Extremely.

CLW What did they make of that?

MOMADAY Well, I don't really know. Again, I have the sense that they were somewhat surprised, because they had been fed the line that all American Indians are extremely deprived and persecuted. I'm sure they're still told that. But I didn't fit that notion. I think they were expecting a far more negative report than I gave them.

CLW So you disappointed them in certain ways?

MOMADAY Yes. I'm sure I did. Had I the good sense to live up to their expectations and paint very dark pictures of America, things might have gone more smoothly—I don't know.

CLW Are you in contact with anybody there yet?

MOMADAY Yes. Not many people, I'm sorry to say, but I did make one very close friend there, and we have stayed in touch as far as possible. It's not always easy to exchange mail with someone in the Soviet Union.

CLW You were recently inducted into the Oklahoma Hall of Fame?[12] Who of the other members do you think of first?

MOMADAY I find Jim Thorpe's presence there the most worthy and inspiring. I know that you admire athletic talent. So do I. Thorpe was a superb athlete, by any standards, and his talent was absolutely raw. He had no training to speak of until he was already a man. I would love to hear what a nutritionist of our time might have to say about his diet as a boy and a young man. How old was he when he first put on track shoes? What was happening in his mind and heart? It must have cost him something to excel so visibly; it is not the Indian way. He must have performed his deeds under a bit of tension, in mind of the innate modesty of his culture. But he performed them, as you say, relentlessly. He brought the old Indian warrior ideal to bear upon the athletic field. It was, is, a thrilling, brilliant thing to see, even in the mind's eye.

CLW How are Indian peoples doing these days, in your opinion?

MOMADAY I don't know. I have to some extent lost touch with the contemporary Indian world. It's been a long time since I've lived on a reservation, although in Arizona I'm reasonably close to reservations. But I really haven't kept up with contemporary affairs. My sense is that the Indian is about in the same position he was in during the fifties when I was fairly close to his world and observing it more closely than I do now. I think things are very slow to change in that world. And in one way that's good, because many of the traditions are still very much intact. In another way it's bad, because the things that ought to change don't. And it's been that way for a long time. My sense is that it's still that way and will be that way for a long time to come.

CLW How have you been affected by being a father? Has it affected your writing?

MOMADAY I don't think that I know the answer to that. I feel good about being a parent. I recommend it. It is a fulfilling experience. I believe that people who know what it is to relate to their own children are richer in some ways than most of those who do not have children. I think parenting must have a profound effect upon my work. And upon my life. I feel very good and in a sense more nearly complete because I have children. I'm not sure how that experience translates into my writing or my painting, but I'm certain that it's an influence.

CLW Children give us fresh perspectives, don't they? Opportunities to look at things in new ways?

MOMADAY Yes. You know that as well as I do. Children remind us of how we saw the world at one time, and then we stop and catch our breath and understand that those ways of seeing the world are still very good. In the process of time and experience, we tend to lose our freshness of vision, and children bring it back to us. That's very good.

CLW What about the particular experience of fathering daughters? An experience which we share.

MOMADAY Well, unlike you, I can't make a comparison. [Laughing.] But I can say that fathering daughters is a deeply satisfying thing, and I believe that fathers and daughters are wonderful combinations. I feel very close to my daughters. I think I felt especially close to them when they were young and learning and finding their way. I feel close to them now that they are older, too, but I think the relationship is especially vital when the child is small. There is great hope in that relationship.

Into the Sun

There are many journeys in the writings of N. Scott Momaday. In *House Made of Dawn* there are restless displacements from villages to cities, and questing movements across the surfaces of the earth, and long, ritualistic runs, and migration memories. In *The Names* there are frequent references to nomadic experiences and impulses, and the book concludes dramatically with factual and imaginative descriptions of journeys. In *The Way to Rainy Mountain* the central focus is, of course, on movement across time and space; and that movement is again a strong element in *Set*, the novel in progress. Additionally, many of Momaday's essays discuss migration experience and explore the implications of movement.

There have also been many journeys in Momaday's life. He moved frequently with his parents during his childhood, and they centered themselves on several southwestern landscapes across which he could move in imaginative play. In adulthood, he has chosen to live in a variety of places and has traveled often and widely, most recently to his wife's native Germany, where he occasionally lectures and exhibits his paintings, and from where he travels to other places. He travels often in this country as well, lecturing and exhibiting.

All of this would seem to be consistent with modern restlessness and the frequent displacements of modern life. Americans, especially, are on the move, sociologists tell us, and for them there is usually no turning back. The typical response to the idea of return is often some paraphrase of Thomas Wolfe's melancholy assertion that one cannot "go home again." That sense of loss, of irreversible movement forward, of the price of movement, of the price of linear "progress," is dramatized by Robert Frost in "The Road Not Taken." The speaker is stopped at a crossroads and must choose one "way." Although he forlornly hopes to return eventually to that physical and emotional place, it is quite clear that he will not. "Yet knowing how way leads on to way," Frost's speaker tells us, "I doubted if I should ever come back." One sacrifices where one has been for where one is going. Severing one's "roots" is simply the price one must pay.

Yet N. Scott Momaday pays no such price, nor have his people, traditionally. That is because Momaday also has a strong sense of place and an intense belief in the sustaining permanence of origins. Throughout his life and art, he has emphasized the importance of having an intimate knowledge of one's own landscape. He has dramatized that importance in many ways, but nowhere is the idea more eloquently presented than it is in *The Way to Rainy Mountain*, where he declares that a person "ought to give himself up to a particular landscape in his experience, to look at it from as many angles as he can, to wonder about it, to dwell upon it."[1]

This idea of the importance of place is therefore not contradicted by Momaday's nomadism. In his world, as was the case in the traditional world of the nomadic tribes, one departs and returns. The journey is not linear and permanent, as is so often true of modern displacements, but circular and, in interesting ways, continuous. And no version of the essential journey is complete until the return is made. Often the return is physical, as it was with the tribes that moved with the seasons, spiritually and in pursuit of game, returning always to their origin places, to their native grounds. One returns to one's native landscape whenever possible, to renew oneself. But the return is as importantly spiritual, and can be accomplished through the oral tradition. One can circle back imaginatively to one's origins. One can actualize those origins through storytelling. That is the "way" of Momaday's *The Way to Rainy Mountain*. In that book, his grandmother's grave is "where it ought to be." It is "at the end of a long and legendary way," a phrase that is, in several ways, a summary statement of the book.[2] In an important sense, Momaday and his people have never left the seventeenth-century Yellowstone area from which they began their long migration. In a very real sense, through tribal memory, they have not left the mouth of that hollow log out of which they emerged to begin their journey.

But how does one actualize the past fully enough to retain one's origin places? Momaday's response to that question is delivered near the end of *The Names*. "The events of one's life," he declares, "take place, *take place*."[3] That is, human experience has definition and permanence only within the larger context of the physical world. One understands one's past, retains one's past, through recollections of symbolic physical events. One imagistically recalls the world, with all of its implications and attendant meanings. One is connected through those recollections. That idea is beautifully summarized in *The Way to Rainy Mountain* when Momaday concludes the story of Devils Tower by speaking of the seven sisters who became the stars of the Big Dipper. "From that moment, and so long as the legend lives," he says, "the Kiowas have kinsmen in the night sky."[4]

So N. Scott Momaday is a physical and philosophical traveler, a nomad whose life is movement and whose art is a steady progression through time and place to the origins that define him and his people. Beginning with the roughly contemporary *House Made of Dawn*, he has journeyed steadily back through his writings in a creative and definitive celebration of origins. In doing so, he has demonstrated the power of those origins, and he has also demonstrated the power of place.

CLW You spend a great deal of time traveling. What effect does that have on your sense of self?

MOMADAY That's a good question. I love to travel. Travel is very important. And I think it is natural for me to travel. After all, I'm descended from a nomadic people. The Kiowas have always loved to roam over the earth, and so do I. I've been very fortunate in recent years to travel widely, and I have loved every moment of it. If I could give any gift in the world to my children, I think travel would be what I would give to them.

CLW So your love of travel is that old restlessness in the blood you describe in your father?

MOMADAY I think that has something to do with it. It's hard for me to stand still sometimes. I want to go, and I'm happiest when I can go. If that mood is upon me, to stifle it is a terrible thing.

CLW What's your favorite way to travel?

MOMADAY By train. I love to sit in a train and look at the countryside go by. It's comfortable. I especially like the trains in Europe, which are, as you know, very efficient. You can get almost anywhere you want, and can read, or get up and walk around if you want to—at the same time you're covering distances. It's wonderful.

CLW How have you come to know the land?

MOMADAY By getting into it. I said something to that effect in *The Way to Rainy Mountain*, in talking about riding.[5] I used to ride a horse all over the Jemez country. In those days, I took what I was experiencing for granted. But afterwards, I realized that I had penetrated that landscape and that I knew more about it than it ever occurred to me that I would. It was a matter simply of fitting myself into it. I think that's the way you get to know the land best. Most of what we know about landscape is, in my opinion, superficial. I've traveled over much of the earth, but I don't truly understand those places I have briefly seen. You have to spend time in a place, and come to know it as it changes in the hours of the day and in the seasons of the year. And if you put yourself into it, it absorbs you and you come to know it and depend upon it in numerous ways. In spiritual as well as physical ways.

CLW Have you involved yourself in any of the landscapes of other parts of the world?

MOMADAY Well, in addition to the Southwest, I know something about the plains, by virtue of having lived there as a child. I was born there, in fact. And the plains area interests me because it is such a unique landscape and essentially mysterious, I think. Mysterious in a different way than, say, New Mexico, which is full of canyons and high mountains and wonderful plateaus. The plains area is a sea of grasses and it is vast. That vastness is what interests me most. You know, when the Kiowas migrated down onto the plains, that must have been one of the great psychological adaptations that man has made to the land. The Kiowas had to learn how to live on those plains, and that could not have been easy. That landscape was completely different from what they had experienced, and they had to commit themselves to it. I think about that frequently. I like the plains area for that reason. I think it is a demanding, challenging landscape. It requires a great deal of strength. At least at one time it did.

CLW Is it the distance which is especially intimidating? The feeling of isolation?

MOMADAY I think so. Of course, the Kiowa were nomadic people, so distance was always in their minds. It was perhaps their most ancient adversary. How to get from here to there. They were always moving and mobile, yet when they came upon the plains, that sense of much greater distance than they had known must have nearly overwhelmed them.

CLW Yet excited them, too? Because they were nomads?

MOMADAY Yes. That was it. Especially after they acquired the horse. That was the best of all worlds. They had severed themselves from the ground and they could fly on horseback across unlimited distances. Like the story of the Kiowas who went to Honduras, just on a raiding expedition.[6] Enormous distances were traversed easily.

CLW When you said that, I thought of a fairly common theme in the literature of the white European westward movement, the theme of great loneliness. There was a fear of distance. Through characters such as Beret in Rolvaag's *Giants in the Earth*, we learn of the maddening effects of being isolated on seemingly empty expanses. And history reveals that many pioneers were driven back by the magnitude of those distances. All of that space was just too much for them. It was insoluble and ominous. Those people were, in Coleridge's words, "alone, alone, all, all alone, alone on a wide, wide sea," and sometimes that terrified them.[7] We don't find that reaction in what we know of the experiences of the plains tribes, do we? That same reaction to open spaces and great distances?

MOMADAY No. I think that psychologically the plains Indians were better equipped to deal with that than were other people. Perhaps that was because of their long prehistory. They had been here for thousands of years, and they had already experienced some of the spaciousness of the continent. Whereas Europeans even five hundred years ago had so thickly settled Europe that distance was measured in a different way. One has a different sense of space in Europe. Europeans were coming from closely settled places, and suddenly the North American continent extended before them, it seemed, to infinity. That had to be intimidating.

CLW Perhaps the Kiowas also had a racial memory of greater distances? The long distances of an earlier migration?

MOMADAY Yes. Coming down the west road from Canada, for example. That would do it. That would give you a sense of distance.

CLW Do you think that perhaps they still carried with them the stories of that journey?

MOMADAY Oh, I think it's inevitable that they did.

CLW So that those first distances were a part of their mythology as they came down onto the plains?

MOMADAY Yes. I think their stories could have carried them back even into the tremendous distances of central Asia. To the steppes. Even those places could have been remote in the minds of my people.

CLW Do you remember those distances?

MOMADAY Sometimes I imagine that I do.

CLW Why do you imagine that the Kiowas finally moved down out of the mountains into the plains?

MOMADAY There are many possibilities. For one thing, I think it was in their nature to move and travel, and so they did. And we've talked about destiny and fate. I think the Kiowas might have been meant to do what they did. I think that they might have been following an irresistible impulse when they moved onto the Great Plains, but beyond that I can't say. I don't know what the impulse was. Perhaps you account for it with words like *nomadism*. But I think visions might also have been involved.

CLW And so those migrations, those journeys into the sun, might have been responses to visionary experiences?

MOMADAY Yes. Vision quests, perhaps.

CLW You have written of the Kiowas moving along the eastern slope of the Rockies in the rain shadow. They found shelter there, and game. But did they ever, to your knowledge, move back up into the mountains for periods of time? Was there any significant return to the mountains? Or were they always plains people after that first coming forth?

MOMADAY They were always plains people who kept the mountains in view. I don't think they went back into the mountains to live. But I've always thought it was interesting that of all the places on the plains, they finally settled in view of the Wichita Mountains. It's as if they remembered their existence in the mountains and they were somehow more comfortable with the mountains in view. But after they entered upon the northern plains, they were consistently a plains people.

CLW Thinking about the allure of mountains, which is sometimes evident in your works, I wonder if they weren't tempted to return.

MOMADAY I'm sure they were. That must have been a real part of the adjustment. They must have had to cope with blood memory. With the racial memory of life in the mountains. Because that life had to be terribly important to them.

CLW When you think of the Kiowa journey, do other journeys come to mind? Or do you think of it in a pretty singular way?

MOMADAY Well, the first thing that comes to my mind is, of course, the longer migration of which this journey was a part. The migration into North America from Asia. But I don't think of any other journeys, specifically. That one, to me, is one of the great imaginative things of all times. Those hunters coming across the Bering land bridge into North America following game. I like to think about that. And I think of the Kiowa migration as being an extension of that. It's the same journey. But the Kiowa migration is almost historical. It can be defined in terms of landscape, route, and time, whereas the other one cannot. The older journey is much more obscure, but also fascinating.

CLW You recently told a South Dakota public television interviewer that during the Kiowa migration described in *The Way to Rainy Mountain,* adversity was raised to an abstract and universal plane.[8]

MOMADAY What do you suppose I meant by that?

CLW I'm not sure. That's why I'm asking. [Both laughing.]

MOMADAY Well, I think what I must have had in mind was that the hardships of that journey became universals. One can think of the hungers and the cold and the war with distance on that journey, and one can apply those things to human experience in general.

CLW Experience to measure all subsequent experience by?

MOMADAY Yes. And previous experience, for that matter. So one can think of the Kiowa migration as a symbolic expression of all adversity, of all such adventures of man pitting himself against the world. Yes. That's a good thought.

Hunter, 1985, ink and wash, 22 inches x 30 inches

CLW You also mentioned in that interview that there is a difference between the Kiowa idea of history and the modern definition. What did you mean?

MOMADAY Well, the Indian in general has a different idea of history than have the rest of us. This is very clearly demonstrated by his calendars. Things like the winter counts. We moderns think of history as a succession of events, but the Indian doesn't think that way. He has a different idea of what is important historically. For example, in one of the Kiowa calendars, there is, as I say in *The Way to Rainy Mountain*, the theft of a horse.[9] There is the Pawnee boy who is a captive of the Kiowas and who escapes and takes with him the best horse in the tribe. I have come to understand enough about the Indian idea of history so that I understand that this was a profound moment in the Kiowa experience. The loss of that horse was a crucial thing. It affected the whole well-being of the people. But we in western civilization would not think of it in the same way. So a horse was stolen. It was a fast horse. A good hunter. So what? Other things were more important that year, surely. But not in the Indian mind. I'm sure that nobody much cared about the boy's escaping. It was the fact that he took the horse that was really the important thing. So one can conclude that the Indian's focus upon history is more essential, in the sense that there is one event for the winter of 1854, say, and one event for the summer. By isolating those two events, the Indian can formulate a whole idea of history.

CLW It's a matter of putting symbolic moments in sequence?

MOMADAY Yes. Yes. Thus the Indian's writings, I think. His pictographs and other representations.

CLW Maybe that's a more informative way of understanding history?

MOMADAY I think it's at least as effective, or can be. And maybe it's a better way. It's certainly a time-proven and useful method.

CLW It's essentially the way a creative writer remembers history, isn't it? Symbolic moments? There are historical novels, of course, but in creative writing there's frequently more emphasis on emblematic recollection than on linear exploration.

MOMADAY Yes. That's right.

CLW In writing *The Way to Rainy Mountain*, were you ever frustrated by that Kiowa idea of history? Were there times when you wanted to create transitions or discover connections, and you couldn't?

Dog Horse, 1987, graphite and wash, 11 inches x 14 inches

MOMADAY Yes. The oral tradition of the Kiowas is the record of the migration, and there are a lot of gaps. I came to many places where the trail ended, and I had to pick it up at a later place, and there was nothing in between. Anytime you deal with a literature that's as tentative as the oral tradition of the Kiowas, you find many fragments, and it is frustrating sometimes. The origin myth of the Kiowas has it that they came into the world through a hollow log. It's a beautiful idea, a wonderful idea, and it accounts for their name, the name they gave themselves, *Kwuda,* "the coming out people," but there are a lot of questions. Where did they come from? What's on the other side of the log? We don't know. There is the possibility that at one time the story was larger than it is now, and that at one time maybe the Kiowas knew what was on the other side of the log. So there are frustrations of that kind—numerous frustrations.

CLW And also points at which imagination saved you? The experience of writing about the old woman Ko-sahn comes to mind immediately. Were there other such moments in the process?

MOMADAY I took liberties of that kind, if that's what we should call them, only in the prologue and the epilogue—not in the text itself. Well, maybe to some extent in the personal reminiscences—the personal voice. But in response to the larger question you're asking, yes, the imagination gets you through a great deal. Every writer is forced to rely, at some point, on the imagination. The skill with which he can do that determines his success as a writer. I can take credit for setting down those Kiowa stories in English, in *The Way to Rainy Mountain*, but I didn't invent them. The imagination that informs those stories is really not mine, though it exists, I think, in my blood. It's an ancestral imagination. It's important to understand that dimension. But in the secondary materials and in that third voice, which is a personal reminiscence, I brought my own imagination to bear.

CLW There are similarities between the Kiowa and the Lakota accounts of the Devils Tower story. How did that come about?

MOMADAY Well, I think that probably there was an original story about Devils Tower in which a bear figured. It might have been a Kiowa story or a Sioux story or a Crow story, and in the way that comparative mythologies evolve, it was retold by different tribes, each in its own way. That happens. I've told those stories in *The Way to Rainy Mountain* to various Indian peoples, and sometimes they say, "Ah yes, we have that story. We have that story." It differs in this particular or these particulars, but it's recognizable as the same story. But somewhere there's a first story about Devils Tower, and where it originated we probably will never know.

CLW What of the possibility that it originated separately and distinctly in each of those cultures? Same story?

MOMADAY I think slight. It would be one of the great coincidences of all time.

CLW What if that's simply the right story for that circumstance? What if that's just *the* story of that place?

MOMADAY Hmmm. I suppose that's possible. There are two levels of truth here. And it depends upon which one we're concerned with. There is the comparative-mythology answer to that question, which is yes, there was one story. One storyteller's creation. And it has been disseminated among various peoples. And each tribe thinks of it as its own. Then there is, of course, the reality that the rock was a tree, and that the boy turned into a bear, and that the stars and the Big Dipper were once Kiowa children. So both things are true, and you choose the one you want.

CLW But the latter explanation would account for the existence of the story in several cultures.

MOMADAY Yes. Sure.

CLW You say that without irony?

MOMADAY No. I say nothing without irony. [Both laughing.]

CLW I know that. Which makes this process a little more difficult. [Both laughing.]

CLW What do you think of the human impulse to climb Devils Tower?

MOMADAY I don't know. That's a foreign impulse to me. I have no desire to climb it. A lot of people do, and I really wouldn't know how to account for that. It's a challenge, obviously, and it's satisfying to meet a challenge, but the things that challenge me are of a different order.

CLW Would you like to soar over that rock?

MOMADAY I would. I'd like to see it from as many angles as I can, and certainly I would like to see it from the air. I would like to know it in every way that it can be known, with the exception of climbing it. Maybe one of these days I'll have a chance to fly over it.

CLW The Kiowas, on their migration, would not have climbed it?

MOMADAY I don't think so. I cannot imagine that. I cannot imagine them finding a reason to. Its importance to the Kiowas is mythological, and climbing it doesn't satisfy the need to think of it in mythological terms. To go and see if the girls left anything behind on top, for example. That wouldn't be a reason in the mythological context.

CLW People who have climbed it say that there are creatures at the top. Snakes, for example. As well as birds. What do you think motivates those creatures to go there?

MOMADAY I have no idea. I didn't know that there were snakes on top. It doesn't come as a great surprise, but I must say it fascinates me that snakes would ascend all the way to the top of the rock. Snakes like rocks and fissures and they like to hide themselves, but that isn't the answer, is it? I don't know what the answer to that is.

CLW As the seven sisters run, are they leaderless and running in blind panic? Or is there an elder sister leading them or running behind urging them on?

MOMADAY [Long pause] In my mind's eye, they are leaderless. They are running in a state of panic. There is no organization, except that they keep together. I've never thought about that. They are little girls and enjoy playing games. But they are old enough to run fast. The youngest girl must be five or six years old.

CLW What sounds do you hear the bear making in pursuit?

MOMADAY I can't hear him. Of course, he crashes through the brush. But I don't hear roaring or growling. He's just coming. Maybe he stops. Maybe he pauses. But he comes. He's coming and he's irresistible and they know that he's coming.

CLW And the menace is greater, being soundless?

MOMADAY I think so.

CLW From what direction do they come running?

MOMADAY I think they're coming from the south and running in a northwesterly direction. Why? I cannot say. Maybe it has something to do with the terrain directly around the monument. I can see them more clearly running through that wooded area than I can on the other side where the ranger's station is.

CLW In what direction does the bear travel at the end of the story?

MOMADAY At the end he's at the tree. And that's where he is forever. There's nothing in the story after that. So I don't know. I would like to know.

CLW Do you wonder if the bear returns to the tree?

MOMADAY I'm quite sure that he does.

CLW In what attitude?

MOMADAY Reverence. When I say reverence, I do it without flinching. There's no question in my mind. My attitude is reverence and the bear's attitude is mine.

CLW Does he rise against the tree again?

MOMADAY Not in the same way. No. Well, I don't know. I have to think about that. Certainly not in the same way, though there may be a kind of symbolic reenactment of the story. When he comes, he does relive, in a sense, the first time—the original happening.

CLW Do you know anything of the parents of all of those children?

MOMADAY I know what I have written about them. That they did not grieve. And that they forgot the children's names. They remembered them collectively. And of course they experienced a great sense of wonder when they saw the stars emerge.

CLW How could they forget the names?

MOMADAY The girls in that strange ascendancy transcended names. They went out of the dimension in which names have the power to signify being. They're in another dimension.

CLW And the parents accepted that?

MOMADAY They had no choice.

CLW They recognized the inevitability of it? And were reconciled to it?

MOMADAY They probably found great solace in it.

CLW Were they thereafter childless? Do you think of them as childless in the absence of those children?

MOMADAY I do. I do.

CLW What of weather and seasons at the tree? How do those transformations affect you and your attitudes toward it? We went there in the snow, for instance, and you've been there in other seasons and at other times of day.

MOMADAY The power of the place remains constant. The spirituality of the place remains the same in all seasons and weathers and times of day. It's very striking in every season, but in a different way each time. It's different by day than it is by night. I have seen it under the full moon. Then it had a quality that it could not have had under any other conditions. But I've never failed to be greatly, greatly impressed by it. Night or day, summer, winter, whatever.

CLW Will the tree always be there?

MOMADAY Yes.

CLW What if those stars fell?

MOMADAY I don't know. I think it might be the end of the world.

CLW Is that inconceivable to you?

MOMADAY It is inconceivable. You know, I can say to myself, "Well, of course, it is possible that they should fall and that Devils Tower should not be there." But that possibility is so far from my idea of things that it matters not to me.

CLW Would you prefer to live in another time?

MOMADAY I don't think so. This is a very exciting time, and I wouldn't prefer to live in another one. Though certainly, I like to project myself in my imagination into other times. I often wonder about what it was like to be a Kiowa in the nineteenth century or in the eighteenth century—what it was like to experience that migration. For that matter, what it was like to migrate across the land bridge twenty thousand years ago.

CLW If you were required to live in another time, which time would you choose? Would you be, for instance, at the beginning at the migration? Or would you prefer to live during the flowering of the Kiowa culture?

MOMADAY Well, I think it would have been enormously exciting to have been in on the flowering of that culture. To have been alive on the southern plains in 1830. To have existed on that landscape—that must have been very exciting. A time full of adventure and fulfillment. I'm sure that the Kiowas had the sense that they were a lordly people at that time. It must have felt good.

CLW What do you imagine your role would have been?

MOMADAY Well, I would have been a member of the Rabbit Society first. Then I would have been a warrior. In my youth, I was healthy and vigorous, and I would have probably been a pretty good warrior. Then, of course, I would have become a storyteller. [Laughing.]

CLW If you'd lived through the warrior phase.

MOMADAY [Laughing.] That's right.

CLW That was not guaranteed, was it?

MOMADAY By no means. By no means.

CLW Especially among the Kiowa.

MOMADAY One took his chances. [Laughing.]

CLW Mildred Mayhall wrote that according to her research, old men in the traditional culture frequently committed suicide.[10] What do you know of that?

MOMADAY Very little. I think it is true of the early days—the prehistoric Indian times. And that's been true of many societies around the world. There was a time in the Kiowa world, for example, during the height of the plains culture, say, when it was possible for an old man to outlive his usefulness to the tribe. It was the understanding of the whole society that when that happened the man must go. He must go away. Old people in the Navajo society used to do that. Just wander off by themselves. And there were many instances of abandonment. The Kiowas had a term for it. Someone was "thrown away." I suppose that term had several meanings, but one of them is surely abandonment. When someone reached the point where he could not contribute or pull his own weight, as we say, then his expectation and the expectation of everyone was that he would go away. He would disappear from the society. Now, to what extent we're talking about actual suicide, someone willfully taking his own life, I don't know. I think that more often, probably, life was simply given up.

CLW That's an interesting distinction. Mayhall was defining that as suicide. Going off to die.

MOMADAY Apparently so.

CLW What do you think of that behavior, from your contemporary point of view?

MOMADAY I think there was no choice at the time. It was the society. It was in the interest of the culture. It was a sacrifice in the deepest interest of the society and the culture. It was how the culture survived. It was a fundamental necessity. I've spent some time in the Arctic in Eskimo villages and I've heard from a number of people that in former times when a female child was born, it was killed. It was put under the ice. Because the society was so dependent upon the hunting economy that what was really needed was someone who could bring food in rather than someone who would consume food, and the girls were not hunters. So they were not cherished in the same way that boys were. They were not depended upon for the sake of the culture. For the well-being of the culture. And they were frequently killed.

CLW Doesn't that seem terribly heartless to you?

MOMADAY Of course it does. But I can also imagine that there was no choice. That there were instances in which to have heart was to commit a kind of cultural suicide. Do you see what I mean?

CLW I suppose I understand the argument on some intellectual level. Can you imagine yourself old, going off voluntarily?

MOMADAY I've thought about that a lot. Yes, I can. Yes, I can imagine that. I have imagined it. I do imagine it. I'm coming fast to the point! [Both laughing.]

CLW And what goes through your mind as you imagine that?

MOMADAY I think it a very noble thing to bring oneself to the realization, to the affirmation, of one's time. That is a wonderful thing. In a poem called "Wreckage," I have written that had circumstances been different, "I should have come loudly, like a warrior, to my time."[11] When I have served my purpose and I have earned my death, then I want to accept it willingly. I want to accept it with good will. That seems to me a very positive and noble thing.

CLW What of the Dylan Thomas line "Do not go gentle into that good night"? Those people who wandered away went "gentle," didn't they?

MOMADAY I don't know if that's what Thomas was talking about. I see his statement as meaning do not give up if there is some chance of resisting. The Indian world that I'm thinking of was full of resistance because of the warrior ideal. There was the idea of pinning the sash to the ground and standing to the death. Perhaps that is what Thomas was speaking of. But this idea of taking one's leave when it is appropriate is another matter. And I think our society as a whole will come to deal with that matter very soon. Because we now can keep ourselves alive long after it is appropriate to do so, it seems to me, and there are moral questions involved with that which are very serious. I don't want to be kept alive on a machine. I hope that never happens, and I will certainly resist it if I can. But to reconcile oneself. To come to that great moral reconciliation with death. To have the sense that you have earned it. That is somewhere intrinsic in the Indian mind. And I think it's finally a very good thing—a good idea of oneself in one's society. One's life.

CLW And connected in certain ways, too, to the well-known statement "It is a good day to die."

MOMADAY Yes. The warrior ideal again. That statement was made in many different ways, but it comes down to the essential idea that such fortitude is the ultimate part of life. It is a good day to die.

CLW Do you think those old men going away would have preferred to die in battle?

MOMADAY I don't think so. Of course, it's certainly not a bad thing, in terms of that cultural ideal, to die in battle. But there's also, I think, the notion that you preserve your life as long as you must or as long as you should. As long as it is morally right. The trick seems to be in realizing when the moment comes. Such moments easily come in battle. But they may come at other times too. And there is a place for suicide in that scheme of things. There is the story of Sitting Bear of which I am so fond. Sitting Bear did effectively orchestrate his own demise.[12] He knew that he would die immediately as a consequence of his action and he took the action and he died. And he died well, I think. There is also the story of Satanta, who jumped out of a window to his death simply because he could not tolerate life under the conditions that had been imposed.[13] He had lost his freedom, and that meant more to him than life.

CLW In both cases they sang their death songs, didn't they?

MOMADAY Yes.

CLW Is any of this summarized by Shakespeare's "Ripeness is all"?[14]

MOMADAY Possibly. I hadn't thought of that. I need to think about it at greater length, but that seems to be what I'm trying to articulate. Yes. Shakespeare is always doing that to me. [Both laughing.]

CLW It seems to me that women are central to *The Way to Rainy Mountain* and to what I have seen of *Set*. The more I read *The Way to Rainy Mountain,* the more conscious I am that the energetic center of the book is female. Old women beginning and end. And old women energize the tellings. And again in *Set,* there is the mysterious, magical power of women. There is an intense relationship between a very old woman and a very young woman in that book. Their relationship seems mystical, and it is provocative and informative. What of the centrality of women in those books?

MOMADAY I think that's the way it is. In the culture that I'm dealing with, women were at the center. They were sometimes set aside, moved into the shadows, to make way for the warrior ideal, but generally they were indispensable. I mean indispensable in every way. Women are life bringers. They are sacred. Sacred in their identity as women.

CLW Do women have access to things men don't have access to?

MOMADAY Certainly. I wouldn't know how to enumerate the things they have

Anthracite, 1976, graphite and wash, 23 inches x 30 inches

access to. But certainly. They do in any society. They have access to spiritual recesses that men cannot reach. In Kiowa culture, I think of the old women particularly as being, even more than the old men, repositories of the cultural vitality. The men took the stage, but the women really were the center of things. It's a nice equation. It worked. The men were the hunters and they wore the feathers. And the women remained in the camps. But the culture couldn't do without them.

CLW So there is, in your view, a degree of misunderstanding, historically, in thinking of these plains societies as predominantly patriarchal? There were matriarchal elements?

MOMADAY Oh, yes.

CLW These women were culture carriers?

MOMADAY I suppose it is true, because of the stereotypes that have been created, that people really do think of the plains cultures as patriarchal. That's a false view. It is true that men were most visible in those societies. But that is not to say that the women were less important.

CLW I suppose the perceptions that women were less important arise out of things such as you refer to in *The Way to Rainy Mountain.* You write that the lives of women were hard and describe cruel treatment of them. For example, there is the story of leaving the woman to stand freezing in the snow.[15] There was physical dominance by men.

MOMADAY Yes. But I don't think it was manifested uniformly. Consider Big Bow, in the story to which you refer. I think that story says more about his character than it does about the culture. I don't think women were regularly mistreated in Kiowa culture. Their lives were hard. In some sense harder than the men's. The men were the warriors. They went on raiding parties, and those must have been gratifying and satisfying and exhilarating. The women did without that kind of intensity in their lives. And they were indeed less physical for that reason, but the most powerful things are usually less visible than are other things.

CLW But the men also tended to be the spiritual leaders, the medicine men.

MOMADAY Yes, you think of the medicine man as being the spiritual leader, and indeed he was. But in a different sense the women, too, were repositories of the spiritual world. Of the spiritual life. The men had the medicine. They were the keepers of the medicine. But I think the knowledge and the spirituality of the medicine was as much in the possession of the women. I cite my own example. I have learned much more of the world of the Kiowas from old women than I have from old men. I've talked to both, but it's the women who seem to me to hold the knowledge.

CLW Why couldn't the women, then, be the medicine beings?

MOMADAY I think there were more medicine beings among women than we realize.

CLW You say in *The Names* and elsewhere that events "take place." Could you tell me why that statement is so important to you?

MOMADAY Yes. I think that the sense of place is extremely important to most writers. Certainly it is to me. I identify very strongly with places where I have lived, where I have been, where I have invested some part of my being. That equation between man and nature or between writer and place—I don't think there is a relationship that is more important than that. I don't think one can write without a certain sense of space or place. But I sometimes think that it might be even more important to me than it is to other writers in general. I know that it means a great deal to me.

CLW Isn't there reciprocity there, too? Doesn't the event create the place as the place intensifies the event?

MOMADAY I don't see what you mean.

CLW Doesn't the writer create place as surely as place creates experience? Doesn't he create place by writing about an event in that place?

MOMADAY Well, yes, yes. You create an impression of place. It precedes the experience, whatever it may be. The earth was here before I was. When I came, I simply identified place by living in it or looking at it. One does create place in the same way that the storyteller creates himself, creates his listener. The writer creates a place. An excellent example of that is Isak Dinesen's *Out of Africa*, in which the sense of place is so important. I sometimes say to my students that I suspect that the Africa of *Out of Africa* never really existed outside of Isak Dinesen's mind. She went there and she invested herself in the actual African landscape, but when she wrote about it, she created a place that probably doesn't exist outside the pages of that book. And this may also be true of *The Way to Rainy Mountain*. One might argue that Scott Momaday has given us his *impression* of the place.

But it may not be as I have described it to someone who plants his feet on the mountain. So one of the writer's responsibilities is to create place.

CLW They are no less true, though—those landscapes you have created? The landscape Dinesen made out of whatever her experience was in Africa? Maybe you could even go so far as to say that her landscape is truer than the "reality"?

MOMADAY I could say that. I would say that. It's truer to me, and it's truer, obviously, to her, than would be the description of the same landscape by a geologist, for example.

CLW Hers is a mythic landscape, isn't it?

MOMADAY Yes. Very definitely.

CLW And it's also fair to say that of the landscape in *The Way to Rainy Mountain*?

MOMADAY Yes.

CLW Driving up to Rainy Mountain, and saying that it's not really a mountain, but a knoll or a hill, misses the point, doesn't it?

MOMADAY Exactly.

CLW The fact of it is not the truth of it.

MOMADAY That's exactly right. You have put your finger on it.

CLW What, do you imagine, is that "awful commotion beneath the surface" which you describe in *The Way to Rainy Mountain*?[16] What was it your grandfather Mammedaty saw?

MOMADAY I think it was a water beast. Something like an alligator. He saw young alligators on a log on Rainy Mountain Creek or in the Washita River once. Nobody else saw them, but I have no doubt that they were there. It's like the Loch Ness monster. There are always these unaccountable things beneath the surface of the water. I think he did encounter some strange creature there.

CLW Is that creature still there?

MOMADAY Well, I wouldn't be surprised. I don't know. There are a lot of creatures in the Washita River. I know that. [Laughing.]

CLW They are there as surely as we think of them there, aren't they?

MOMADAY Oh, yes.

CLW Your grandfather also saw four things which you call "truly remarkable" in *The Way to Rainy Mountain*.[17] One was the mole blowing the fine, powdery earth in a circle around his hole. Have you had such experiences?

MOMADAY I've never seen that. I've not seen the same things my grandfather saw, although I've seen things that are remarkable. But those were things that made such an impression upon my grandfather that he passed them on to my father, and my father passed them to me. I think those things defined my grandfather's power in some way. He thought of those things as gifts. He was privileged to see extraordinary things, and that privilege was translated into power. Because he saw those things, he was powerful.

CLW Those things really symbolize the earth, don't they? The earth's potential?

MOMADAY I think that's put well. Yes. Such things are revelations. When you have them, you perceive the earth's reality to a greater depth.

CLW A related matter is what you say in your poem "Headwaters."[18] I've always liked that as a summary of the earth's implications. Its potentiality. And more broadly, the energy in origins. In describing a seemingly stagnant pool, you say, "What moves on this archaic force / was wild and welling at the source." Meaning that there's something very powerful beneath contemporary surfaces. The tremendous energy of the Kiowa past. Of the American Indian past. Physical experience. History, culture, traditions. What was "wild and welling at the "source" still exists as potential. Cultural energy.

MOMADAY Yes. That's truly the commotion beneath the surface.

CLW In a 1972 article, you wrote, "We have failed in our time to articulate the beauty of the world, for we have failed to perceive that the world is beautiful."[19] Has anything changed since you wrote that? Or does that statement still apply?

MOMADAY I think it still applies. There is a growing concern for the preservation of wilderness, landscape, and natural resources. But I still believe that aesthetic principle holds: western man doesn't really perceive the world as beautiful. He perceives it, rather, as useful. And to be exploited for its economic value. And I think that's wrong. I believe that unless we change our view, we will simply destroy the earth. We will destroy its beauty, and that will be a very shameful thing.

CLW Do you think that what you say is true even, to some extent, among environmentalists? That there's not always an aesthetic intent in what they do?

MOMADAY Yes. I think so. To preserve the natural landscape is desirable what-

Mammedaty, 1976, graphite and wash, 23 inches x 30 inches

ever the motive, I suppose. But it would be better if the motive were aesthetic as well as whatever else, and I don't think that's always the case even among the environmentalists. At least, it isn't as widespread as I would like to see it. Even environmentalists can be too use-oriented, although their uses are not threatening to the earth. Use is not the first truth.

CLW Why do you like New Mexican weather?

MOMADAY Well, it's perfect, isn't it? I like it because it's clear and brisk. I like the light in northern New Mexico. On this November morning it feels good outside. The air is hard and cold and brilliant. Of course, I grew up in it, so it's mine. I think of this weather as the way weather ought to be.

CLW Tell me something about your "Landscape of American Literature" course at Stanford. What was the essence of that course, and what was your approach?

MOMADAY Well, it was a hodgepodge of things. I used a variety of books which dealt with the landscape in certain ways. Of course, I got into the subject of painting landscapes in America. But basically, the course was meant to investigate how Americans have traditionally thought of the landscape. And so we used all kinds of commentaries on the landscape. Including novels in which people comment one way or another upon the American landscape. There are all kinds of materials that you can apply to the subject, and I just got beneath the surface. But it was a very interesting course. I learned a great deal from it. And I want to know more.

CLW You've written movingly of the old man, Cheney, the arrowmaker who prayed at dawn.[20] The old man who prayed the sun out of the ground. What was the source of his power? What was his gift?

MOMADAY I think his gift was the perception of the earth as vital. Of the sun as a deity. It was the quality of his belief, his simple, absolute belief. He believed completely in what he was doing. This relationship he established between himself and the world was holy, real, elemental.

CLW Did he do that? Pray the sun out of the ground?

MOMADAY You mean did he think he did that?

CLW No. Did he?

MOMADAY Did he. Well, there is a sense in which he did. Yes. Had he not been there to pray, the sun would have come up, I think. But in another and very important sense, yes, he prayed the sun out of the ground. His affirmation of that principle, whatever it is, was creative.

CLW But would it have been that sun, if he hadn't prayed it out?

MOMADAY How could it have been?

CLW The sun would have come up. But not that sun.

MOMADAY Yes. That's what I'm saying. It's like telling a story. It's a unique act, and never happens the same way twice. If Cheney were not there, it would not be the same sun.

CLW That realization makes it a very beautiful moment, doesn't it?

MOMADAY Oh, yes. Yes. It is a very beautiful moment, and it's a particularly indigenous moment. The most important thing we talked about in my landscape course was the way people have perceived the American landscape. That is what I think finally makes American literature what it is, as opposed to all other literatures. It focuses upon a unique landscape, and that makes the difference. If there is anything American about American literature, it has to be that. The awareness of this landscape. The response to the shape of this continent. That's its uniqueness.

CLW Is there more focus on landscape in American literature than in most other literatures?

MOMADAY I think so. Yes. I'm particularly interested in American literature, and I don't know as much about other literature, but I would venture to guess that American literature is probably more closely focused upon the landscape than is British or French literature, for example.

CLW Will you imagine farther back than the stories in *The Way to Rainy Mountain*? Will you write about the Bering Strait migration?

MOMADAY I haven't thought about that in recent times, but I like the idea very much. I was at one time very much interested in early man and the crossing of the Bering bridge, and I did some research on it. I talked to knowledgeable people about that area and about its history and prehistory. But I'm not sure that I will get to it, as I once thought I would.

CLW At least it's not as immediate a possibility for you as it once was?

MOMADAY That's right.

CLW What changed?

MOMADAY Oh, I don't really know. I guess other things became more accessible to me. That's fairly inaccessible—that remote time and place. I've traveled in the Arctic, so I have a sense of that physical world. I've learned a lot about the migrations of early man. I wanted very much to go to Siberia at one time, and it very nearly happened. I came within two weeks of it, and then it was canceled by the Soviets. That was a disappointment, and I think I took it as a sign. It discouraged me from the writing. I thought, Well, I'll put this in abeyance.

CLW But until then you were prepared to try it?

MOMADAY Yes.

CLW You wanted to experience the landscape?

MOMADAY I had even signed a contract with a Russian publisher to write about it. Everything was planned. But two weeks before I was to leave—in 1979—I got a letter saying that it would not be possible.

CLW Did they say why not?

MOMADAY No. Of course not.

CLW Do you speculate?

MOMADAY I have, but you know, I really have no idea. They had asked me to specify where I wanted to go, and with the exception of Eskimo villages right on the peninsula, I didn't know. So I looked at the map and picked out what I thought must be native centers. Then I wrote back and identified those places, and I may have named five of the great military installations in the Soviet Union—I don't know.

CLW And they thought you might make another kind of map. [Both laughing.]

MOMADAY Anyway, I don't begin to understand the politics of all that. But it was a near miss, and I am sorry that I didn't get to go. It's the only part of the Eskimo world that I haven't seen. I've traveled all over the place in the Arctic, and it would have been especially nice to go to Siberia, because that's along the ancient route. I could have been in the landscape and imagined myself there thirty thousand years ago. It would have been very meaningful to me. It may still happen, but the chances are growing slimmer and slimmer.

CLW Wouldn't the task be doubly difficult because there are no longer even any physical remnants of the journey? In doing what you did with *The Way to Rainy Mountain*, you had cultural artifacts to write about and some sources to draw from. You had enough to enable you to re-create the spirit of the experience. Perhaps there's no substitute for those resources?

MOMADAY You may be right.

CLW Then it's impossible to go farther back?

MOMADAY I just don't know. You're right about the physical remnants. The hard evidence of migration up there is almost nonexistent. But I have an idea that in Siberia one might find cultures that are not definitively Eskimo cultures. Cultures that are native. And one could probably find traditional elements that would engender a fascinating imagining. One might still be able to imagine the Kiowas, the American Indian, back across thousands of years. Siberian traditions might reflect those thousands of years. It would be wonderful to get glimpses of such things. It might just generate all sorts of impulses and creative energies.

CLW And so you might yet make the journey?

MOMADAY Well, it's something that I hold out as a possibility, but I'm fifty-two now, and a trek into that country would be strenuous. So it's getting pretty close to the edge. I think I could do it now, but it would take some preparation to get myself in shape for it. In another ten years, it would be, I think, out of the question.

CLW Would you have to experience it firsthand?

MOMADAY That's the best way to do it, as far as I'm concerned. I suppose that one could write the sort of thing I had planned without going there, but somehow in my mind the journey was indispensable to the project. One must know the land. And one must move to understand movement.

Wordwalker

Evident in Momaday's poem "Plainview: 1" are many of his attitudes about language and literature:

There in the hollow of the hills I see,
Eleven magpies stand away from me.

Low light upon the rim; a wind informs
This distance with a gathering of storms

And drifts in silver crescents on the grass,
Configurations that appear, and pass.

There falls a final shadow on the glare,
A stillness on the dark, erratic air.

I do not hear the longer wind that lows
Among the magpies. Silences disclose,

Until no rhythms of unrest remain,
Eleven magpies standing in the plain.

They are illusion—wind and rain revolve—
And they recede in darkness, and dissolve.[1]

First, there is the storytelling voice. The teller is nameless, but strongly revealed through his sensitivity to his physical environment, and through his meditative attitude toward the birds he sees, and through his uses of sound and silence.

The teller is aware of the slightest implications of what he is experiencing—the quality of the light, the effects of the wind upon the grass, the "longer wind" beyond his hearing, and the uncertain quality of the air. He is a physical being, traditional in his close relationship with the things of the earth. He is literally reading the wind.

And as he reads he reflects. That is evident in his concentration upon the magpies, and in the measured pace of his description of them. He studies them patiently, and carefully recounts what he sees.

And he accentuates his voice. Word and sound repetitions and parallel structures intensify his statement at regular intervals, and silences punctuate it. These devices are essential elements of the Native American oral tradition. They are ways of sending a voice. One repeats sound and sense to dramatize one's story and to cast a storytelling spell. And one pauses for effect. As Momaday said in an early interview, storytelling is "the modulation of sound and silence, the conjugation of sound and silence."[2] In this poem, silences literally "disclose." They are creative pauses that reveal meaning. The dramatic reflective pauses between stanzas are intensified by periods, and the internal punctuations further dramatize the voice.

The storytelling poet is thus revealed through the manner of his telling. He achieves an identity through his voice. He is, to use Momaday's term, "the man made of words." So, too, is Momaday, as he tells and retells his ongoing "story" in his writings. That verbal identity is one kind of permanent existence, in Momaday's opinion. One's voice is individual, but as it communicates shared cultural experience, it is also ancestral and capable of transcending time. In words, there is eternity.

The poem also reveals the poet's delight in language—his sense of play. The subjects of the poem are, after all, magpies. *Magpies*. A word that has comic sound and sense connotations. Cantankerous, meddlesome creatures. Busy and often raucously noisy. Yet here they are, stilled, in a silent environment heavy with implications. Motionless in the long distance. Word and sound and being contrasts to the rest of the poem in which they exist. They are evidence of Momaday's increasing interest in such matters. They are evidence of the verbal playfulness that increasingly flavors his work, varies his texts, and dramatizes through contrast his serious intentions.

The poem is also beautifully imaged, and an example of Momaday's enthusiasm for descriptive writing. He is interested in the poetic surfaces of things, thinks of himself as primarily a poet, and writes prose poems and vividly poetic prose. This poem is intensely multisensory, an intricate intertwining of sights and sounds, and it is a descriptively detailed juxtaposition of distances and foreground particulars. The image of "silver crescents on the grass" dominates the description in its creative intensity and in the way its brightness contrasts with the gathering darkness of the rest of the scene. And it is vividly accurate—literally the shape of sporadic wind across grass that silvers as it turns in the last long light of day.

Also evident in the poem is Momaday's commitment to well-ordered language. He is a methodical stylist who slowly sculpts his prose until it is resonant and symmetrical, and who employs traditional versification methods in much of his poetry. In this case, the iambic pentameter line and the end rhyme give the poem an incantatory quality that reinforces its meditation. Those devices also demonstrate Momaday's commitment to precision and economy of expression, the concise and economical naming of the world. It is his belief, as he has Tosamah say in *House Made of Dawn*, that in the modern world we have "multiplied and diluted the Word" and in so doing have devalued language, the word, as "an instrument of creation."[3] In this poem, the surgically precise language is heightened by regular measure and by emphatically rhymed couplets.

Finally, as is the case with much of Momaday's writing, there are apparent surfaces and many implications in this poem. Here are simple ingredients, and complex meanings. "A word has power in and of itself," Momaday says in *The Way to Rainy Mountain*. "It comes from nothing into sound and meaning; it gives origin to all things."[4] In "Plainview: 1," the storyteller has spoken. We are informed by his sounds, transported by his images, and, finally, moved to contemplate the implications of what we have been told. His words are powerful and persuasive. They are creations that create listeners in the process of the telling. They are the carrying on of an ancient oral tradition in letters across the page.

CLW What are some of your favorite words?

MOMADAY Hmm. I like words that are concrete. The names of animals. The word *bear*. The word *eagle*. The word *hawk*. I also like words that center upon landscape. I like *mountain* and *prairie* and *sky*. When I write poetry, I use such words and I also use abstract words. But it is difficult to give you a list of favorite words because words become vital—they come alive—within a certain context. A given word is extremely important and vital in one context and not very interesting in another. It depends upon what's around the word. The environment. Although some words are naturally interesting, in my opinion. Like some creatures. The fox, I think, is a creature of almost immediate interest to most people. Other words are not as immediately interesting, or are even negatively received. Like some other creatures. The lizard, for example, is a creature most people wouldn't ordinarily care about. But in its natural habitat and in its dimension of wilderness, the lizard can be seen as a beautiful thing. Its movements are very wonderful to watch. Similarly, you can take almost any word and make it interesting by the way in which you use it.

CLW So it's a matter of finding the word's best environment?

MOMADAY Yes. That's a part of what writing is, you know. Showing words to their best advantage. And you can make words ugly by misusing them—by placing them in the wrong company.

CLW Don't you do that deliberately sometimes?

MOMADAY No. I don't think so. Not intentionally. It happens, you know. But I try to avoid that.

CLW What about the characters you want to present unfavorably? You sometimes do that with negative levels of language, don't you? Sometimes in very subtle ways?

MOMADAY I see what you're saying. Yes, certainly. If you want to expose the weaknesses of a character, as you often do. If you want to put someone in a very negative light, you might debase his language in certain ways. Not just what he says, but how he says it.

CLW The old priest at the beginning of *House Made of Dawn* comes to my mind as an example of a character's very negative language.

MOMADAY Yes. He was fascinating to do. I had a wonderful time working that part of the book out. I got Fray Nicholas in my mind and I was fascinated by him. But yes, as I think back on it now, my job was to reflect the distorted quality of that man's mind, and I wanted to do it out of his own mouth.

CLW His first offense is an offense against language. His perversion of a particular language, the language of exclusive and narrow religious belief, reflects his perverted values.

MOMADAY Yes. There are patterns of language, and we fit ourselves into them as it is convenient for us to do so. Fray Nicholas existed in the element of what might be called biblical language, and he perverted that language to his advantage. A good many people did that in his time and in his occupation, I think. And some still do.

CLW What are your least favorite words?

MOMADAY I don't know that I have least favorite words. I think all words have potential for the writer. Certainly, there are words that are not as pleasant in their sounds as other words, and I'm conscious of that. I hear what I write and read, and obviously there are words which are more fluent and soft to the ear than are other words. There are harsh-sounding words. But I think they all have a purpose and I don't exclude any words. Words are wonderful. Sometimes the mispronunciation of a word, or a word pronounced differently in certain situations, catches my attention. My wife is Bavarian, as you know, and she has intriguing inflections of English words sometimes. I'm always amazed by the way she pronounces the word *apparatus*, for example. Her pronunciation is much more pleasant, it seems to me. [Laughing.]

CLW On the subject of pronunciation: I've noticed that in some interview situations you sometimes change the pronunciations of words spoken by interviewers. Sometimes the interviewer's pronunciation is incorrect, but sometimes you simply give the word an alternative pronunciation after the interviewer has pronounced it. Why do you do that?

MOMADAY Yes. Why do I do that? I think it makes things more interesting. [Both laughing.] I get tired of pronouncing words in the same way all the time.

CLW It also disconcerts the interviewer, doesn't it? He's asking himself, "Did I screw up that pronunciation?" [Both laughing.]

MOMADAY I think it really does come down to the fact that it is more interesting to pronounce words in different ways, and so on the spur of the moment I do that sometimes.

CLW Because it's interesting. Maybe it's also a way of distinguishing your voice from that other voice?

MOMADAY Ahhh—that may also be a motive. Hmm.

CLW Back to the topic of favorite and least favorite words. It seems to me that you have a particular enthusiasm for words like *exactly, precisely, certainly, absolutely, altogether*, and *totally*.

MOMADAY [Laughing.] Really? I didn't know that.

CLW Yes. There's an interesting pattern of those words in your writing and in your speech. What do you think that means?

MOMADAY Well, it must mean that I have a very strong investment in totality and absolutism and precision. [Laughing.] Yes, I recognize some of those as words that I do use frequently. I find myself using the word *precisely* quite often. I suppose it is because I want to get as close to the reality as I can, and be as precise as I can be. I'm someone who appreciates precision—especially where words are concerned. That is the business of poetry, isn't it? Precise expression?

CLW Usually, I think. But I also get the impression that you use words like *precisely* to express the certainty of some of your beliefs. To identify those things which you believe absolutely.

MOMADAY Yes. I see what you're saying. And I recognize that as having some validity. Someone once told me that I use the expression "I believe" quite frequently, and that's true, now that I think about it. But maybe I'm also qualifying my statement when I use that construction? When you attach "I believe" to a statement, it does a couple of things, doesn't it? It indicates your conviction that the statement is true. But at the same time, it excludes everyone else from blame in the matter if it's not true.

CLW That depends on whether you emphasize *I* or *believe,* doesn't it?

MOMADAY Yes. [Both laughing.]

CLW I've been told that there are far fewer swear words in many Indian languages than there are in English. What do you make of that?

MOMADAY I don't believe it, first of all. I think there are swear words in Indian languages, but they're not at all like English swear words. When a Navajo gets angry and swears, his utterance is not very much like an English sailor's utterances, but his words are of the same emotional intensity and achieve the same purpose, in my opinion.

CLW What are the differences?

MOMADAY I don't know. I suppose there are a great many if you're talking about Indian languages as a whole. But every culture has its own notions of what is bad. When you curse, you're either insulting someone or you're articulating the wish that something bad would happen to that person. So it depends upon what the culture thinks of as bad. I have a wonderful book called *An Ethnologic Dictionary of the Navajo Language*, which was published years ago.[5] When I get into a particular state of mind, I go to the shelf and take that book out and thumb through it, because it's full of wonderful lore. There's a little section that deals with swearing in Navajo that is very funny. Funny because it's novel to me. I have heard a lot of swearing, as we all have, and I suppose it can be an art. I've heard people swear a blue streak, and sometimes you have to admire someone who can do it well. But the Navajo idea of swearing is not like that at all. It's simply the idea that I hope you don't have a good day at all. I hope this or that happens to you on your way to the corral, or whatever. But I'm sure that the feelings are probably very much the same as those behind English-language profanity.

CLW I encountered the kind of swearing you're talking about in the military, especially in training. Where sometimes the statement was so absolute and so complete that it was almost breathtaking.

MOMADAY I know exactly what you mean. [Both laughing.]

CLW One can have a grudging admiration for such language. Such a purple string of expletives so creatively arranged and so astonishingly cadenced and enunciated.

MOMADAY Yes. I remember once when I was walking down the street in San Francisco. Across the street from me, some men were making a delivery from a truck. Several men were in or around it, and one of them for some reason lost his temper. And he carried on for quite a while. Nonstop cursing that was truly creative—it was really impressive. [Laughing.]

CLW And you stood and listened?

MOMADAY I stood and listened. I think a lot of people did. It was loud, and in a crowded neighborhood. I'm sure that little old ladies kept at their windows just to hear this wonderful example of the English language in one of its more remote manifestations.

CLW Was there a temptation to provoke him further to hear more?

MOMADAY No one dared to do that, but we were all, I think, a little saddened when he stopped.

CLW Tell me about the evolution of your attitudes toward language. Have you become progressively more word-sensitive as you've grown from childhood, or have there been hitches in that? Regressions? Times when you haven't been so close to language?

MOMADAY Well, I had a very fortunate upbringing within the element of language. My parents, and maybe especially my mother, set an example for me that was very fortunate. I can remember when I was in an English class in military school and the teacher one day said something that took me by surprise, although I've since come to understand a little of what he was saying. He told me that I had the best preparation in the English language of anyone in the class. That was amazing to me, because much of my childhood was spent in situations in which English was not the only language, or even the first language. But there I was, having somehow had the benefit of this wonderful exposure to the English language. My parents were very knowledgeable about language, and they transmitted that to me. Then, I've had good experiences with speakers and writers and books along the way, so my interest in language is not hard to understand. There was oral tradition on my father's side and a great interest in literature on my mother's side. How could I not have become interested in language?

CLW What other language experiences did you have, growing up?

MOMADAY Well, I grew up on Indian reservations, and so I was hearing a lot of language that I didn't understand. English was spoken in my house, of course, and it was spoken by my teachers, but frequently I was the only person in my classroom whose native language was English. So maybe that had some effect on my use of the language. I don't know. It's an interesting thing to speculate about.

CLW In *The Way to Rainy Mountain*, you talk about your grandmother's regard for language. You say you didn't understand Kiowa but that there was a good deal being communicated to you by her manner as she prayed. Is that true of other non-English speakers in your experience? Were there particular attitudes toward language communicated to you by any of those people?

MOMADAY Yes. I think so. Probably in more ways than I know. Indian people have a very strong sense of language. You can perceive this even though you're not in their particular language element yourself. You're watching from the outside, but you can see the importance of the language—what it means to the people who are living in that language. My grandmother spoke with great emphasis much of the time, as the Kiowas do, in general. It's fun to listen to such people, especially the old people, who speak so dramatically and with so many gestures. It's enjoyable to hear old people speak Kiowa to each other because there is so much attention paid to emphasis and inflection, and you do not fail to understand that they are very much involved with language. And I think that's true of the Indian world in general. I happen to know a little bit about the Navajo language, because I studied it intensively for several months. I very much enjoy listening to native speakers of that language. They speak in a different way, it seems to me. They can be casual, but at the same time they invest a lot of themselves in their language, and you can perceive that, listening to them.

CLW Do you think that might be true, to some extent, of old people in general? That degree of investment?

MOMADAY Now that you mention it, yes. I think so.

CLW That's been my experience, anyway. I think there's certainly an increasing regard for stories and storytelling as people grow older. And for talk for talk's sake.

MOMADAY Yes. Language is what we have. The older we get, the more we become aware of that. And maybe as we grow older we come to understand more clearly that what we have to leave behind is in that element. That's an interesting idea. I haven't really thought about the age-interest equation much, but I think there's something to it.

CLW What do children teach us about language?

MOMADAY They're wonderful teachers. They make you aware of language, because they can use it in such an imaginative way and make it fresh for you. They see the world in an interesting way, without all the distortions that accumulate with age, and they can say things that astound you in their clarity and perception. And they develop interesting patterns of speech. They will get hold of a word or a phrase and try it out and use it in different ways. To see a child do this is wonderfully instructive, I think. A couple of years ago, my daughter Lore, who's just turned six, got hold of the word *actually*. I don't know where she heard it, but it was obvious that it intrigued her. So she went around saying that word for maybe a couple of months. And she would use it in ways that we adults would not think of. She would say things like, "Well, I have to go to the potty, actually." It was wonderful. I began to see that the word was much more alive

Mad Buffalo, 1985, watercolor, 11 inches x 14 inches

than I had realized. One could do much more with it than I ever realized. I don't know that anybody but a child could have made that so clear to me. And that's just one example out of many.

CLW When you said that, I thought of the repetitive request of one of my children when he wants a drink. He says, "I want some cold cold water and a lot." He always says that. That's his formulaic request. [Both laughing.]

MOMADAY It makes the point, doesn't it? Oh, yes. I still remember when my eldest daughter was Lore's age or even younger. She would come up to me and say, "Daddy, is it tomorrow yet?" And that staggers you. How do you deal with that? Is it tomorrow yet? And you know, I had to say, "No, it isn't." But I felt under some serious obligation to explain the matter of tomorrow, and I don't know that I could. Tomorrow never comes. You reduce it to that cliché, which certainly doesn't satisfy a four-year-old. Nor should it.

CLW Maybe what we've done in this discussion is summarize the regard for language on both ends of the age spectrum? I'm reminded of Tosamah's storytelling grandmother—your grandmother, actually—in *House Made of Dawn*. And the receptivity of the listening child.[6]

MOMADAY Yes. A reverence for the word. Those two people appreciated each other in those terms.

CLW Do you think your view of language is in contrast to the majority attitude?

MOMADAY Well, I think it is in the sense that I have made it my business to think about language, and it isn't the business of most people to think about language.

CLW Are any of your views different from the views of those who do think about language?

MOMADAY I suppose there are similarities and some differences. I don't know, because I don't keep up with people who think about language. I am aware of some theories concerning language, and I'm in agreement with some and in disagreement with others. It's such a large and complicated subject that it would be remarkable for two people to come to the same conclusions about language and its origins and nature. But those of us who are trying to understand language more completely stand on common ground here and there. There are certain common denominators, and people who think about language a lot know what those common denominators are and share a belief in them.

CLW What do you mean by the term "verbal equation"?

MOMADAY Any combination of words assembled for a particular effect.

CLW You also say that words are magic. Could you explain what you mean by that?

MOMADAY A word is intrinsically powerful. If you believe in the power of words, you can bring about physical change in the universe. That is a notion of language that is ancient and it is valid to me. For example, the words of a charm or a spell are formulaic. They are meant to bring about physical change. The person who utters such a formula believes beyond any shadow of doubt that his utterance is going to have this or that actual effect. Because he believes in it and because words are what they are, it is true. It is true. One can disarm an enemy by talking to him, as in the Kiowa story of the arrowmaker. One can even bring such an unaccountable presence as Devils Tower into one's own sphere of instinct and experience by means of language. What could be more magical? Every day we produce magical results with words. And there are people, like holy men and medicine men, who make occupations out of the magic of words. In some, there's a dark, sinister aspect to that. For example, the whole business of witchcraft is really centered upon the magic of words.

CLW What of the shaman? Is he more advanced than we are in the use of words?

MOMADAY Probably. At least in one type of language he is more highly evolved, and he probably understands more about the possibilities of that type of language than do the rest of us in general.

CLW Would you fear such a person if he allied himself against you?

MOMADAY Yes.

CLW Physically fear him?

MOMADAY Yes. There are people who dedicate themselves to doing mischief with words. They are people to be feared.

CLW What could such a person's words do to you?

MOMADAY Disarm me. Reduce me to a very vulnerable condition. The power of certain charms seems very obvious to me. Such charms are hypnotic. There is the Crow warrior who says, "At night when we lie down, listening to the wind rustling through the bleached trees, we

Shaman, 1978, graphite and wash, 23 inches x 30 inches

know not how we get to sleep but we fall asleep, don't we?"[7] That's almost irresistible, you know. The man to whom that is directed is disarmed. You can understand how it happens. You look at those words on the page, or you hear them, and you feel sleepy. You know that the speaker is very powerful.

CLW Could you use words that way?

MOMADAY I think so. I have come closer and closer to that sort of possession of language. It's not something that I have set out to do, but I have on occasion come to that understanding of language. I could utter a charm to effect, I think.

CLW Will you?

MOMADAY Any day now. [Both laughing.]

CLW I take you more seriously than my tone of voice implies.

MOMADAY These are serious matters.

CLW Why is your autobiographical book entitled *The Names*?

MOMADAY I meant to indicate how important names are to me. Because it's an autobiographical narrative, the great principle of selection in the book is the principle of naming. I wanted to tie all kinds of varied experiences together, and the common denominators of those experiences were the names of people who were important to me, growing up. And the names of places.

CLW Naming is really complicated, isn't it?

MOMADAY Oh, yes. Naming is very complicated, and a sacred business. I don't know where to begin with this. It's a large, large topic. I have the idea that names and being are indivisible. When you name something, you confer being upon it at the same time. That is what I believe language does. Language is essentially a process of naming. When you talk about a tree, you must use its name. If the object does not have the name "tree," its existence is brought into question. The same is true of people. I tell a little story in one of my prose poems about a boy who appears in camp one night and speaks a language nobody understands.[8] The next morning he's gone. Everybody has been enchanted by him. They have delighted in his presence and they have listened to his nonsense with pleasure. They're all disturbed that he's gone, until somebody points out that he never was. An old man says, "Well, you know, we can't believe in the child, because he spoke not a word of sense, and so what we saw, if we saw anything at all, must have been a dog or a bear come down from the high country." And I think that's true. If there is one unimaginable tragedy, it is to be without a name, because then your existence is entirely suspect. You may not exist at all without a name. That's a fascinating idea. So an awful lot is involved in this business of names, and I meant to indicate that in the title of my book. I don't see how you could find a more intrinsically powerful title than *The Names*.

CLW How do you name your characters?

MOMADAY That's a good question. I name my characters in a great many different ways. I hear a name that appeals to me, a name that sounds good to me, and sometimes I choose the name of a character on that basis. The sound suggests certain things. I have known people whose names suggest qualities in their personalities to me. Sometimes when I'm thinking of a character, I want to refer at least for my own use to those human qualities I have experienced, and so I give a character the name of someone I once knew or heard about or read about. I choose names which have meanings, of course. Especially in the Indian writings. Some of the names that I'm working with in writing *Set* were chosen because of what they mean. Literally. So there are several bases upon which I choose names.

CLW Of the names you've used in your writing so far, which are your favorites?

MOMADAY Well, of course I must mention a couple of the characters in *House Made of Dawn*. Tosamah comes first to mind. John Big Bluff Tosamah. I like that name. It has certain resonances for me. And meanings as well. I like Angela as a name. Angela Grace St. John is, to me, a beautiful name. Although somewhat ironic, I suppose, given the character. Then there are some of the real names in my nonfiction writings. I love my grandmother's name, Aho. And my grandfather's name, Mammedaty, and my great-grandmother's name, Keahdinekeah. And that of Kau-au-ointy, my great-great-grandmother. All of those names are very dear to me, so I would have to include them in the answer to this question. I am writing about a character now whose name is Grey. I love that name.

CLW Why?

MOMADAY I don't know if I can tell you. It just appeals to me. Grey. I like the color. It suggests to me a mystery of some kind. I think of grey and I think of smoke and a misty quality.

CLW What of the word *Tosamah?* Do you like first of all the sound?

MOMADAY Yes. I like the sound of words in general. *Tosamah* is a pleasant-sounding name. On second thought, I'm not sure that pleasant is exactly the right word. The sounds of that name duplicate sounds that come out of my experience. Tosamah happens to be a name that is both Kiowa and Jemez-sounding. For example, I know a Kiowa man whose name is Tonamah. There is at Jemez a family whose name is Tosa. There were perhaps many things in my mind when I made up that name. But it appeals to me. Maybe for those reasons among others.

CLW Is Tosamah's full name an ironic combination? Because John Big Bluff is talking about the Gospel of John in his sermon?

MOMADAY Yes. Certainly. Although not a particularly conscious one, I think. When I was working with it I wasn't thinking about that irony very much, but I think I must have been thinking of it to some extent, because there is an obvious irony involved. I'd hate to think that I missed that idea. [Both laughing.]

CLW Angela Grace is Mrs. Martin St. John, isn't she?

MOMADAY I don't know. That sort of rings a bell, but I'd forgotten Martin. I think you may be right.[9]

CLW At any rate, that's really an accumulation of Christian-religion names, isn't it?

MOMADAY Yes, and in the book as a whole. There is also Abel.

CLW Why do you suppose your father changed his name from Mammedaty to Momaday?

MOMADAY I really don't know. I've wondered about it. If I ever asked him about it, he just tossed it off or didn't come to grips with the question.

CLW Traditionally, it was tribal custom for men to have three names—given at birth, in adolescence, and in adulthood. Do you have multiple names?

MOMADAY I do. I think of Tsoai-talee as my Indian name, but I also have a name that was given to me by a Sioux elder when I was very young. And I have another Kiowa name, which is Tso-Toh-Haw, which means "red mountain" or "red bluff."

CLW Why were you given that name?

MOMADAY I don't know. I don't even know who gave it to me, offhand.

CLW When and where was it given?

MOMADAY It was given when I was very young, probably in the first year of my life. I was given both Kiowa names in Oklahoma.

CLW What is the Sioux name you were given?

MOMADAY It's Wanbli Wanjila, and it means "eagle alone."

CLW And how old were you when you were given that name?

MOMADAY Three or four, perhaps.

CLW Do you know the occasion?

MOMADAY I don't, offhand.

CLW Will there eventually be another book of names? A full autobiography?

MOMADAY I don't have any plans for extending that book now, but it certainly is not beyond the realm of possibility.

CLW You talked about that at one point before *The Names* was published, as I recall. In fact, you talked about extending *The Names* through your Stanford days.[10] Why did you change your mind?

MOMADAY Well, when I first thought of writing an autobiographical narrative, I meant to bring it up to a later time, but when I got into the writing, it became more and more the story of my growing up. And when I came to that point where I left home to go to military school, that seemed to be an appropriate place to end it. That was one story told. The whole story. And if I had taken up the Stanford days, it would have become another story. And I didn't want that.

CLW Is language really physical, do you think?

MOMADAY I think there are physical dimensions to language. People use language to achieve physical change. Language itself, of course, is not a tangible property, except as you see it on the printed page, and then it achieves a substantial character. But in its nature, language is an abstraction, and so it is symbolic, rather than real. But it is used as an instrument to determine or to change physical realities.

CLW Isn't there a big difference between your belief in the physical effects of language, even the magical effects of language, and the perspectives of people who view language as a more passive thing? To be used primarily for the exchange of information and for record keeping?

MOMADAY Yes. Some people seem to view language as lifeless. As mere currency. I consider myself fortunate because I believe in the energy and power of language. Language is provocative, and enormously creative. These beliefs about language are very good for my work and they are very good for me. They sustain me.

CLW You've suggested that the teller of the arrowmaker story achieves an enduring identity through the telling of that story.[11] Is that what you're doing consistently through your storytelling? Is your storytelling identity emerging?

MOMADAY I think that's a fair statement. I as the storyteller am not who I usually am. I'm not Scott Momaday the cook or the teacher or what-have-you. I become, in the process of the story, someone else. I create myself in another guise for the sake of the story. We know little about the man who told for the first time the story of the arrowmaker. But what we know about him on the basis of the story itself is sufficient.

CLW Is it exhausting to tell stories?

MOMADAY It can be. Yes. When I tell stories for an hour to an audience, I come away having spent a good deal. I'm weaker and tired, and I can feel the result of the energy that has been expended.

CLW So storytelling is a very physical event? An exertion?

MOMADAY Yes. It's like acting.

CLW And therefore quite a contrast to the passivity of some contemporary uses of language?

MOMADAY Yes. I think you can make of language many different things, but the storytelling situation is one in which language is a consuming of energy. Most storytellers I've known have given a great deal of themselves in the telling of their stories.

CLW Blood and bone and adrenalin are involved?

MOMADAY Absolutely.

CLW Is that also true in writing?

MOMADAY Yes. It's very much the same thing. Writing, to me, is very much like speaking aloud to an audience. The energy that's consumed is the same energy, and the exhaustion is the same.

CLW Isn't reading, too, a very physical experience if the writing is good enough? A muscular response to muscular writing? A physiological effect?

MOMADAY Oh, yes.

CLW Then why do you think that reading and writing are often viewed as almost completely cerebral activities?

MOMADAY I think because of the perceived distances involved. There is the human tendency to view those experiences as basically passive, as you say. But when you are in an audience listening to a storyteller, the kinetic interplay is immediate and obvious, so you expect a considerable amount of energy to be invested. Whereas with writing, there is not that immediacy of contact between the writer and the reader. You're not aware of the writer so much when you read a book. You're not aware of the writer as a presence. And the same is true of painting. It's not nearly so concentrated an experience. I don't expend the same kind of energy in painting, because there is not the immediate relationship between the viewer and the artist. There is a space there, and you don't have to be in contact. I think the same is true of reading and of writing. People can control the motions of those things to suit themselves. I can pick up a book and read two pages and then go put the stew on the stove. In a storytelling situation, that kind of intervention, or period of relief, or whatever you want to call it, isn't possible. So I think the tension—the stress factor—is much higher in storytelling. It is therefore much more demanding.

CLW How do you, as a writer, compensate for reader passivity?

MOMADAY I don't know that I do compensate for it.

CLW Don't you have in mind ways to overcome the prose-page mind-set? Ways to insinuate a voice? To emerge from the page?

MOMADAY I don't really think of the reader and his impression when I'm writing. I suppose in the back of my mind I understand that the reader is part of the process. That the reader is somehow indispensable to what I'm doing. But I don't think about him setting my book aside, and so on. I write out of the assumption that I'm telling a story and that he will listen. It's there to be received, if I'm consistent with it and make it something memorable. I guess if I thought enough about the reader looking at the pages of my book, it would be intimidating in certain respects. But that really doesn't enter my mind when I write.

CLW You assume good faith?

MOMADAY That's it. I think maybe that's what a writer does.

CLW But it seems to me that there are so many influences from the oral tradition in what you write. In your writing, in my opinion, those elements of the oral tradition confront reader passivity and overcome it. The structure of *The Way to Rainy Mountain* makes it more declarative in many ways. More strongly voiced. And there are also contrasting voices in the book.

MOMADAY Well, yes. The voices in that book are very important. And I see what you mean about compensation. I hope I write as I speak when I am telling stories most effectively.

CLW What are some of the most powerful statements you know?

MOMADAY Many things in Shakespeare and in the Bible and in great orations by Indian chiefs. One of the greatest orations ever was delivered by the Kiowa chief Satanta. He says, "I have heard that you intend to settle us on a reservation near the mountains."[12] That oration is very powerful. It would be hard to find language more direct or simple than the language in that statement. Satanta says: "I love to roam over the prairies. There I feel free and happy, but when we settle down we grow pale and die." Just words that a child would use—nothing complicated or mischievous about his language, and it turns out to be a very powerful statement. Thank goodness there are quite a few such things around. When I read those things, I am always struck by the intensity of feeling behind them.

CLW The simple accuracy of them?

MOMADAY Yes. And the absolute conviction. The feeling comes directly from the heart. Most people use language in a careless way most of the time, and they're self-conscious about what they say. The result is that the language itself becomes self-conscious, and so it doesn't get at the truth directly. It wants always to approach the truth from a distance or at an angle. So when you see something like Satanta's speech—and of course there are many other examples—you see the value of the plain style. The importance of speaking directly and simply.

CLW You said a speaker can be at once careless and self-conscious? How is that possible?

MOMADAY Well, careless in the sense that we put words together without really thinking about what we're doing. We form careless habits of speech. And self-conscious because there is the tendency to resist saying something directly and simply. Some of the statements in the Satanta speech and in some of the very simple songs in the Indian tradition, for example, are much closer to the truth than is most language. Those traditional statements and songs contain language which is much more responsible, it seems to me. Consider, for example, the Lakota song which goes, "Soldiers / You fled. / Even the eagle dies."[13] I don't know that you can reduce an idea to something more precise or simple than that.

CLW What of Emily Dickinson's "Tell all the Truth but tell it slant"?[14]

MOMADAY Well, now we're talking about something else. I think she's quite right. What she has in mind is that the truth as most people perceive it is rather boring much of the time. In order to get at it in an interesting way, you have to apply the imagination. So telling the truth "slant" is really the business of a storyteller. What we were talking about a moment ago—the oration and the song and the prayer—in those voices there is usually a real need for telling the truth directly. But in storytelling, you approach the truth in a more intricate way.

CLW Isn't it also sometimes a matter of not being able to name what you are moved to say? So you approach it through indirection? I think you do that in your poem "Angle of Geese."

MOMADAY Yes. Absolutely I do. [Both laughing.]

CLW The first half of the poem is a definition of sorts. But the last half comes nearer, in terms of feeling, to what you want to express.

MOMADAY Well, it is sometimes advisable, even necessary, depending on what your subject is and how you want to deal with it, to construct a metaphor. Language itself is metaphorical. Words are not real. Words are reflections of reality. So one primary purpose of language is this construction of metaphors. You say something in terms of something else, and by doing that you actually approach your subject more closely than you could otherwise. "Angle of Geese" may be a case in point. You want to get at something, but you don't run head-on into it. You skirt it a bit and construct something that can be digested more easily.

CLW And made more memorable? Through metaphor?

MOMADAY Absolutely. More memorable. That's a large part of it. You want to construct something that will not only create the meaning that you're after but will also reveal some kind of aesthetic reality in the process.

CLW Speaking of Emily Dickinson, what has she taught you about language?

MOMADAY I couldn't begin to tell you. She teaches all who read her a lot about economy and precision. She can present a great idea in a very few words. When you see that happen, it fills you with wonder. You don't quite know how to account for it. She can say in two or three lines what it takes other people many more words to say. That is, as I see it, her greatest gift. She teaches you how to be spare and lean in your language.

CLW Who are the most articulate people you've known?

MOMADAY Hmm. I've known people here and there whose minds worked in a very efficient way, and they could say things that they meant to say quite easily. Then there are people who are just the other way around. I'm more often in the latter group. I find that I'm not articulate sometimes, and I wonder why. I've spent my life in the presence of words. I've made them my business. And yet I'm often wanting to say something that I can't say well, and it bothers me. But at the same time, I suspect that a good many people in the world are inarticulate, at least in a large part of their lives. I've known very few exceptions to that. But those I have known are very impressive.

CLW You really place yourself in the less articulate group?

MOMADAY I don't think that I'm less articulate than are most people, but I am inarticulate on many occasions, and I get tongue-tied sometimes. They say that a person who writes is often not able to speak easily, and I think there's some truth to that. There may be some sort of rational correlation there. When you write, you have time to work out what it is that you want to say and to put it in the language you want. Maybe the more often you do that, the less attention you give to speaking articulately. Nabokov, for example, did not give interviews. At last he gave a few, and they turned out to be so disappointing to him that he finally insisted upon writing out the answers to questions. He was, in his own mind at least, one of those people who could write extremely well but who spoke very poorly. He once declared that he thought like a genius, wrote like a professional, and talked like a baby. And I'm aware of those distinctions. If given enough time, I can write what I want to write, but in conversation, I sometimes grope for words.

CLW You don't seem to me to be uncomfortable with interviewing or speaking. You seem very comfortable with words—almost always.

MOMADAY I am usually fairly comfortable. I've spoken on lots of occasions, and when I stand before an audience now, I'm pretty much at ease. I used to get butterflies and be very nervous about it, and that still happens on rare occasions. But most often I'm comfortable. It's the same way with interviews. I've given lots of them and I know more or less what to expect, so I'm not ill at ease.

CLW Couldn't you also say that whatever apprehension you feel might be an advantage? Perhaps you might be less articulate if you were fully confident that you were going to be absolutely articulate?

MOMADAY It may work that way. Yes. It could be a good thing that one has a certain apprehension about these things. The saddest thing is someone who supposes he's articulate and really happens to be a blithering idiot. There are such people.

CLW There are several of those. [Both laughing.]

MOMADAY I have an aunt who writes poetry, or did. I've always remembered these lines of hers: "I think there can be no sadder state / than a poet inarticulate." I agree with that.

CLW What puts you most at ease in a conversation?

MOMADAY I'm at ease if I have rapport with the person with whom I'm conversing, and if we're talking about a subject that interests me. Of course, the physical setting has something to do with it too. This is a comfortable place to sit and talk. I'm much more at ease here than I would be in more businesslike places.

CLW Do you detect attitudes in some conversations which increase your interest? Or conversely, can you think of any attitudes or demeanors which diminish your interest?

MOMADAY Well, I'm put off by people who seem to be dishonest in one way or another. People who are looking not so much for an exchange of ideas as for an opportunity to dictate their own ideas. I don't like people who are presumptuous in conversation. I've had the uncomfortable experience of talking with people, from time to time, who I thought were showing off. People who were not interested really in conversing, but who had some special interests to declare. That's a good question. I really haven't thought about that. I find it easier to talk to beautiful women than to less-than-beautiful men.

CLW Why?

MOMADAY I don't know.

CLW I'm not going to take that personally, by the way.

MOMADAY Okay. [Laughing.] I wasn't intending it personally. I was being funny to an extent, but not entirely. I have always found myself more comfortable in the presence of women. I find that I can talk to them more freely. I don't know why that is. I find that they are generally more articulate than the men I know. And I can give you lots of examples of that. Among the people with whom I like to converse, probably seven out of ten are women. Once in a while I can fall easily into conversation with a man. I'm now talking about my adulthood. When I was a teenager and palling around with buddies, it was very easy to talk to them. But past that stage, I have found it more difficult to talk to men than to women. This is going to be a psychological exposé of some kind.

CLW [Laughing.] Not at all. I think there's something to what you say in my experience, and I can't fully explain it either. Maybe it has something to do with the greater hesitancy of men to exist in language, to use your term. Women tend to be more comfortable in the medium of words. At least, that's true of most of the men and women I've known.

MOMADAY I wouldn't be surprised if that's the case.

CLW We're shaping some great sociological statement about America here.

MOMADAY We're breaking ground. [Laughing.]

CLW Is conversation an art form?

MOMADAY Oh yes. Certainly. And I have delighted in overhearing conversations that were artistic. I like to listen to people talk. I enjoyed the Dick Cavett show, because Cavett is so articulate and apparently at ease, and his guests on that show were by and large people who were very interesting to listen to, and Cavett had the knack of bringing them out. So when I watched that show, I had the sense that it was an art form. Cavett was making it artistic.

CLW Was he creating himself as well as creating language?

MOMADAY Absolutely.

CLW And there were different Cavetts? There were different selves in different circumstances?

MOMADAY I think he was a different man depending upon who he talked to. He was a different man every time. And of course that happens outside the realm of television. I have overheard conversations at dinner parties, for example, which delighted me because they seemed to be so well formulated and so well performed. I wish that I could just at random go to dinner with someone and produce wonderful conversation. There are people who can do that, and I admire that very much.

CLW Do you create yourself in conversation the way you create yourself in writing?

MOMADAY I think everybody does. I think that's one of the functions of speech. Every time you open your mouth, you create yourself. I think we all do that without necessarily being aware of it.

CLW It's obviously important for you to become more articulate in conversation?

MOMADAY Yes. I would certainly like to be a better conversationalist than I am. I admire the way my colleagues make their points in departmental meetings. They speak up, and they do it wonderfully well. I sit there planning something to say and phrasing it, and generally, by the time I've worked it out, everybody's gone on to another subject. [Laughing.] So I have a keen sense of that, and I sometimes think that means that I'm less articulate than they are.

CLW I know what you mean. One of my colleagues always numbers his points. And the numbering is symmetrical and logical, and quite persuasive. He'll wait a moment or two after a declaration is made, and then he'll say that he has three points to make in response, and then he numbers them as he's making them. That's the kind of thing you're talking about, isn't it?

MOMADAY Yes. It's a matter of thinking on the spot and articulating what you think easily and quickly and well. And I simply cannot do that. If I could write it out, I would feel very sure about it.

CLW They could delay the meeting and then you could deliver a prepared statement. And it would be definitive.

MOMADAY Exactly. [Both laughing.]

CLW What are some of our word-power losses these days? And are there any gains?

MOMADAY I believe there are both losses and gains. The losses are rather easy to get at. For some time, we have suffered from "word inflation," as Margot Astrov once put it. In *The Winged Serpent*, in a wonderful essay on language, she talks about that.[15] The losses are obvious to us, and we can see how we have taken words for granted. We've been encouraged to do that by junk mail and by the proliferation of language in the various media. So word inflation is easy to understand and to account for. The benefits are harder to imagine. Because I don't think we're so much aware of them. But I think there has been some great good in the development of television. Through it, we are exposed to language and information across such a much wider spectrum. We can be in distant parts of the world instantly. There are both good and bad things about that, of course, as far as language is concerned. Maybe it does tend to make us take language even more for granted, but at the same time, we are moving into possibilities of language that we didn't even know about fifty years ago. My words can reach you now virtually wherever you are, so that extends the influence of my words beyond what I could have imagined yesterday or the day before, and I think there must be some real good in that. We need to understand what the responsibilities of that may be, but if we do understand them and we meet those responsibilities, then I think we've opened up a whole new world of language. And that world is rich. There's a great deal of good in it.

CLW What responsibilities are there?

MOMADAY Well, there are the responsibilities that were attendant upon the nineteenth-century man in an oral tradition. He knew quite well that when he opened his mouth he bore risks and responsibilities. He had to deal with words in a simple and direct and honest way. Words were powerful. They were not to be abused or misused. He spoke the truth not only because it was in his personal interest, but because it was in the interest of the whole language community that he speak the truth. He did not deceive with words. That was bad—there were consequences involved. When he spoke, he expected others to listen. He was making a claim upon their time, and that's a serious matter. He could not afford to waste that time. So there were all kinds of responsibilities then which we can see clearly enough. What we have a harder time seeing is that the same thing applies to us in our very different language era. The need to speak clearly and truthfully, the need to understand that when you speak you are calling upon others to commit time and attention. Those are serious matters, so you use language in a serious way. You don't take language for granted and you don't play with it. You don't throw words away. That is one of the greatest problems in our time, in my opinion. We have been encouraged to throw words away, and that's a dangerous thing. We have to relearn the lesson that words are not cheap. They are important. They matter. They are worth something. You do not throw them away.

CLW Do you then take a dim view of what we call small talk?

MOMADAY Hmm. I do unless you fully understand that you are engaged in small talk. The real danger is to make small talk and not be aware of it. That's the problem. But certainly there is a place for small talk among people who understand what they are doing. I can make small talk with my daughter and it can become a wonderfully interesting game, but we must understand what we are doing. We must be sure that we're not violating the rules that pertain where language is concerned.

CLW What are some of the problems caused by small talk?

MOMADAY Well, by making small talk you can fall into a trap. Small talk can become your mode. Patterns within language are infectious. You can get into poor habits, and those can become very serious and present great problems. People at summit meetings should not make much small talk. But it's easy for small talk and habits of small talk to creep into even the more serious conversations. Talking to a child, for example, can be wonderfully creative and entertaining, but sometimes it can also undermine habits of speech.

CLW Can't small talk also be used to create a receptive attitude toward larger talk?

MOMADAY Oh yes. There is a real art to that. People write books on how to make small talk at parties, which is the natural environment for small talk. Certainly one can make small talk in an inventive and artful way and that talk can easily be used to lead into something that is more serious. I don't want to create the impression that I think language must always be serious. What I want to say is that language must be taken seriously, but there's lots of room for playfulness in language—jokes, trivia, and verbal repertoire. Language is wonderfully various, and so there's plenty of opportunity for the nonserious. But at the same time, one must not lose sight of the fact that language is essentially a serious matter. It is to be controlled, because it is very powerful. Language can be destructive, I believe.

CLW You sometimes start classes with trivia questions. There's playfulness there, but also a more serious progression, isn't there?

MOMADAY Oh, I hope so. Yes. I don't know how I got started with the trivia game, but it's become something that happens regularly now in my classes. And I think there's some value to it, in that it gets us off on the right foot. We begin by having a bit of fun, and we establish a mood in which discussion can more easily take place.

CLW Words are exchanged before you begin to speak? After we're comfortable with each other in language?

MOMADAY That's right.

CLW Do you like gossip?

MOMADAY Not much. I don't seem to have that fault. That vice.

CLW Is it a fault?

MOMADAY Well, I object when people want to give me information about other people that I'm not interested in having. And I don't get the same satisfaction that some other people seem to get in talking about matters that are, to me, rather trivial. I know gossip is great fun for many people.

CLW Isn't there also a considerable amount of narrative interest in it sometimes?

MOMADAY What do you mean?

CLW Well, I would think that gossip—juicy gossip—would appeal especially to writers because of their curiosity about human experience and human behavior.

MOMADAY Well, I suppose so. Yes. In fact, I know a playwright who tells me that he has at times simply gone out and positioned himself on a bar stool in order to hear how people talk. That's very valuable to him and to what he does. I don't think of that as being particularly useful to what I do. Maybe because I'm less interested in dialogue, or depend less upon it, than he does. But actually it seems to me that you're asking another question now. Yes, if you're interested in how people talk, then you listen. But I was thinking of gossip in another sense.

CLW But that was my question. I was asking about content and curiosity about human behavior.

MOMADAY I do like to hear people talk. I find that interesting. In fact, one of my bad habits is listening to talk programs in the night. I'm addicted to radio talk. I usually have an earplug when I go to bed and I listen for a while to conversations and to newscasts and things like that. So I'm not sure what the answer to your original question is. Gossip for its own sake doesn't interest me. But if it's a matter of listening to understand something about language and the way in which people use it, then I'd have to answer it another way. Yes, I'm interested in that.

CLW Why do you call addiction to talk shows a bad habit?

MOMADAY Well, I think that it might be possible to clog the mind with trivial information if you listen to many of those shows. I think of such talk as an intrusion upon the mind, but it's one that you can become addicted to.

CLW It's also a kind of gossip, isn't it?

MOMADAY Yes. Certainly. Much of what's on the radio is.

CLW But because it's public you don't feel guilty about listening in on it?

MOMADAY Well. [Laughing.]

CLW Your hesitancy otherwise has to do with privacy, doesn't it?

MOMADAY I think so. That's probably getting down to it. You're right. Although I'm sometimes embarrassed by what I hear on the radio. [Both laughing.]

CLW So the answer to my original question is that you're energized by gossip as long as it's permissible gossip. These people have agreed to go public, and you're curious about what they have to say. You simply don't want to intrude on someone's privacy by listening to private statements.

MOMADAY Yes. I think there is a connotation to the word *gossip* that I tripped over the first time around. I think of gossip as being trivial and I think there are better things to do. But there are, as you say, other ways to think of it.

CLW About that nineteenth-century speaker you mentioned: Wasn't much of what he did dependent upon his physical circumstance? Isn't there these days a great risk in sending words flying so far? How do we send context with them? Isn't disembodiment part of the danger of electronic transmission?

MOMADAY Yes. That's a real risk, of course. Sending language out of your own situation into something that isn't your situation. Something happens, and you're not sure what. At the least there can be a misunderstanding, and at the worst, I suppose, the misunderstanding can be so grave as to be destructive.

CLW How do you feel about talking on the telephone?

MOMADAY I guess I have mixed feelings. I resent the phone at times when it intrudes upon my work, and I'm careful to see that I don't have a phone in the room where I'm working. There are times when I unplug the phones in the house. But I enjoy talking to people. And I use the telephone a lot when I'm not working. I frequently call friends across the country and chat. I find that satisfying. Telephones seem to have become almost indispensable to us as a society. Certainly they are convenient. I would not want to be without one. But I had an interesting experience this past winter. I spent about two months in a place without a telephone. And it was inconvenient for me to go to the phone. I had to drive a distance in order to make a call. And I found that peculiarly satisfying. I liked being without a phone. I found that I was more productive. The telephone can be a distraction.

CLW Why don't you like the word *communication*?

MOMADAY It's overused in our society. Too much emphasis is placed upon it. We are confusing our students. We are misrepresenting literature to them by telling them that it is a means of communication. They write papers now in which they say, "The object of literature is to communicate ideas." That's the wrong way to look at it. Expression is closer to the truth of literature than is communication.

CLW What's the difference?

MOMADAY Well, communication is designed to reach someone else at a rhetorical level or to inform, and that's really not, as I see it, the function of literature. Literature functions to express the perceptions that are in me. Secondary is the idea that I'm communicating something. Expression is the basic idea.

CLW But isn't expression by definition communication?

MOMADAY No. You can express your spirit in a meaningless way. I can paint a picture which you will recognize as beautiful, but you will not necessarily understand what it means, if anything. And a poem the same way. Now of course a poem ought to mean, and generally does, but what I'm suggesting is that its meaning is not necessarily the ultimate objective. Expression is probably more important, in the final analysis. Using the language to its full potential does not necessarily mean that you are communicating something, as we understand that term. We do not ordinarily use the word *communicate* when we talk about music. But language is very much like music, isn't it?

CLW To use your example of painting: You paint the picture and I derive something from it which you do not necessarily derive from it. You're still communicating something to me by having an effect on me, aren't you?

MOMADAY Well, I don't think of that as communication. When I think of communication I'm thinking of the communication of one meaning.

CLW You mean singular intent and singular effect?

MOMADAY Yes. What I'm saying is that we attach far too much importance to meaning and the conveyance of meaning, whereas art is really concerned with other things as well.

CLW Is language limited?

MOMADAY Language is limited. We know that because we know there are things that we can perceive but not express. There are certain ineffables in the world. Language cannot express what is inexpressible, and yet we live with the inexpressible all the time. So language is limited, and that's a wonderful thing to contemplate, because we don't know what the limits are. It's like saying that there is only so much oxygen in the universe. Yet we cannot conceive of exhausting the supply, and the same thing is true of language, I think. It is limited, but that's not really something that we need to worry about, because we're not about to reach the limits. We have not exhausted the possibilities of language, nor will we.

CLW You don't think that it's conceivable that eventually the inexpressible can be expressed?

MOMADAY In language? No. Well, I don't think so. I cannot conceive of language growing to that extent. It is an artificial invention, after all. It's a wonderful invention, but it's man-made, and nothing man-made can comprehend the universe in its entirety. We're good, but we're not that good, and I doubt that we ever will be. But who knows? We're playing with things that were far beyond our imagining not long ago—things like computers—and we have seen farther into the universe than our forefathers could have imagined, so who knows?

CLW How effective is language, apart from meaning?

MOMADAY Very effective. Especially in poetry, where the emotional content is so important. Meaning is not incidental, but it is only one of the objectives of language. Expression is, as I see it, the paramount objective of literature, and expression, as I've said, is or can be apart from meaning. You and I have encountered literature which did not mean to us. Perhaps the meaning was beyond us. But we have responded to it nonetheless. Sometimes in unforgettable ways.

CLW Can you give me an example or two of that in your life?

MOMADAY Well, let's go back to something we were talking about a little earlier: my grandmother and her regard for language. I remember very vividly the number of occasions when I heard my grandmother pray in Kiowa. We would be the only two in the room, and she would be preparing me for bed and preparing herself for the night. She never neglected to pray just before going to bed. She would pray aloud in Kiowa, and I didn't understand what she was saying. But the quality of that language and the force that lay behind it, the great conviction and the profound belief in what she was doing, the belief in the efficacy of language implicit in her prayer, could not be doubted. I could not even as a child fail to understand that something important was happening. I couldn't say what it was in terms of meaning, but it was not lost upon me.

CLW Do you think of an example of that from literature?

MOMADAY Yes. I have heard things read in languages that I don't understand which have been profoundly moving to me. This happened frequently when I was in Russia. The Russians have such a great love of poetry, and when a poet gives a reading, it's always very well attended. I happened to hear a number of poets read when I was in Russia, and they read so movingly. I would listen and not begin to understand what was being read at the level of meaning, and yet I would be greatly moved because the reading was done with such feeling and such obvious meaning. And I have certainly read moving things in the English language that I could not comprehend completely.

CLW You were moved mainly by the expression?

MOMADAY Yes. That happens all the time. That is a great positive value in literature. That happens to me time and time again in reading the poems of Emily Dickinson. She wrote poems which are impenetrable to me. And yet I believe that we have not begun to exhaust the possibilities of meaning in Emily Dickinson. Take a poem like "The Moon upon Her Fluent Root." That appears to me to be a great poem. There is a profundity to it that is unmistakable, and yet I could not tell you what the poem means. That's just one of many examples in Emily Dickinson alone. And of course one can find such poems by other poets, too. Poetry is not necessarily easy to understand, and it is not particularly necessary to understand it. Isak Dinesen said something about that in one of her stories, I believe. She said that it is not necessarily a bad thing that only half the story is understood.[16] I believe that's true. What this boils down to is that meaning is just one of the benefits of literature. If you don't grasp the whole meaning of something, that does not mean that the literary experience has been frustrated. There are other things to find in literature.

CLW We talk too much these days, don't we?

MOMADAY Yes. I think we do go too far in language. We don't always understand that we can use language moderately, and judiciously, and achieve great results. I think it is human nature to believe that we have not made our point, have not said enough, and so we go too far.

CLW Isn't there also a human compulsion to fill the silences?

MOMADAY Absolutely.

CLW Why is that?

MOMADAY We are afraid to be alone. Silence reminds us of our isolation. So we fill it because it creates the illusion that we are among friends and in the midst of lots of activities. We can lose ourselves in activity and destroy our loneliness in the process. But the great value of silence, it seems to me, is loneliness. It gives us to know that we are alone in the universe.

CLW Where's the comfort in that?

MOMADAY There is comfort in the knowledge that we are an infinitesimal part of something very grand. Most of us live in cities and communities, and very few of us get out into the wide-open night and see the stars. But to be alone at night in a place like Lukachukai, Arizona, and to look at the stars, is a humbling experience. I suppose one can react to an experience like that with fear and loathing. But I think it is good to be in such a place at such a time. There we see that we take ourselves too seriously. There it is hard to take oneself seriously. The self becomes incidental, as it were; one achieves a state of selflessness.

CLW Why did you think of that place?

MOMADAY Because that is the last place where I saw the night as it can be seen. I went up there a little over a year ago, and the stars were out and the air was very clear, and there was absolutely no light pollution where I was. One just does not see the night like that very often, but it's there. And there's great consolation in knowing that it's there.

CLW So solitude is an affirmation in certain ways? And a consolation?

MOMADAY I see it that way.

CLW But harder and harder to find?

MOMADAY Yes. Maybe our attitudes towards it are changing, too. We're not understanding that it is positive.

CLW Isn't it also true that people tend to be uncomfortable being silent together?

MOMADAY Yes.

CLW How do you account for that?

MOMADAY Silence has become an embarrassment. I suppose we don't know

Star Shield, 1987, graphite and wash, 11 inches x 14 inches

how to live with silence very well because we don't have much of an opportunity now. We're not used to being silent. A quiet situation is disquieting to us. I know that because I have experimented with it a bit. I teach a course in oral traditions, as you know. I remember once at Stanford when I was teaching a very large class. I went in and I said, "Let me tell you a story." And I didn't say anything for the next two minutes. And two minutes is a long time. You cannot imagine the agony in that room. People became extremely uncomfortable, and then they began to shuffle, shift, move their books and papers, anything to make noise. And the coughing. You would have thought that there had come a great epidemic of something, listening to the coughing. And by the end of two minutes it was clear that everybody was ready to run. They wanted sounds. They wanted me to talk, shout, sing. They wanted an airplane to go over. Anything to break the silence. That is interesting to me, and sad, too, because it means, I think, that not enough of us really appreciate silence for what it is. It is a great restorative, and a very good and creative condition. The great poets in the world know that. And they write their poems out of that context of silence, and they don't escape it or destroy it. They make use of it. They incorporate the silence into their words, or they couch their words in the context of silence. The relationship between sound and silence is always very much in their minds, and that's good.

CLW Can you think of any particularly striking examples of dramatic silence in literature?

MOMADAY Oh, there are a great many. You can take almost any good poem and find the silences that inform it. And you are amazed at how effective those silences are. If you listen to a good reader of poetry, somebody like Charles Laughton or Dylan Thomas, you know how important silences are. You can't mistake the importance of them.

CLW What are your attitudes about theater? Is it one of your enthusiasms?

MOMADAY Yes. I don't attend much, but I like the form. I've always said that I would like to write a play. I have had some experience writing screenplays. Bad experiences, for the most part. Well, not bad, but negligible. But I like theater. I have a close friend who is a playwright, and I enjoy learning certain things about theater from him. He introduces me to actors, and I find them to be fascinating people. I admire what they do. I love to watch actors work.

CLW You've mentioned that you may write a play. Do you have a subject in mind?

MOMADAY Before Isak Dinesen became a household word, I thought of writing a play based upon her relationship with her lover. I was going to have a cast of two characters, and focus largely upon the storytelling situation on her farm in Africa. I still think that's an imaginative possibility, but it has been diminished by the recent notoriety of her existence.

CLW What's your favorite of the Shakespeare plays?

MOMADAY *King Lear*.

CLW Why?

MOMADAY Because the character of Lear is one of the great realizations of the human imagination in literature. I can't imagine a writer looking at that character and not having wished he had created it. It's a thing much larger than life and full of life in such a wonderfully lyrical way. It astonishes me, as of course it astonishes a great many people.

CLW What has been the effect of the cinema on American culture?

MOMADAY It's been profound. Who hasn't been profoundly affected by cinema?

CLW You have, certainly. You talk about films quite often.

MOMADAY Yes. I think one has to be affected. Films have become so much a part of our lives, such a part of our imaginations.

CLW Does the cinema have any effect on your art? Are there cinematic effects in your writing?

MOMADAY I think that my descriptions of certain actions and certain landscapes must have been influenced by what I have seen on the screen. But I can't give you examples of that.

CLW How are you able to make people listen when you lecture or tell stories? Are you conscious of what you do to create an audience?

MOMADAY I'm conscious of what I do, but I don't know that I think about how to make people listen. I expect them to listen. That just seems automatic to me.

CLW Are you aware of your uses of silence?

MOMADAY Yes. Yes. I think I'm more and more aware of the importance of using silences. I seem to be more conscious now of pauses and silences.

CLW There are comparatively few good listeners.

MOMADAY Yes. I would think so. Comparatively few. Thirty-nine. [Both laughing].

CLW How would you describe the quality of your voice?

MOMADAY My voice. Well, I have a pretty good "vocal mechanism," as one of my instructors once told me. I'm pleased with my voice. It changes from time to time. It's exhaustible, but in general I think it's strong enough.

CLW How does it sound to you when you're hitting your stride?

MOMADAY Wonderful! [Both laughing.] I'm aware of how I sound. In the course of my speaking career, I've become aware of how I can use my voice. A microphone makes a great difference, and if you understand what the difference is, you can do things with a microphone that enhance the quality of the presentation. You can speak very low and softly and yet project a great deal, and there are many benefits to that.

CLW It's clear to me that it's a very pleasurable experience for you when your voice is coming forth the way you want it to.

MOMADAY It is. There's a great satisfaction in that. You understand that you have learned how to do something that is influential. You can move people, or you can make an impression that is creative. That's satisfying.

CLW Is it simultaneously moving you when it's working that well for you?

MOMADAY Yes, it can. Now that I think about it, yes, it does. The right words have a very energizing effect.

CLW How would you characterize your written voice? How does it compare to your speaking voice?

MOMADAY I think that the two are closely related. My physical voice is something that bears upon my writing in an important way. I listen to what I write. I work with it until it is what I want it to be in my hearing. I think that the voice of my writing is very much like the voice of my speaking. And I think in both cases it's distinctive. At least, I mean for it to be. I think that most good writers have individual voices, and that the best writers are those whose voices are most distinctive—most recognizably individual. I hope that my writing is not quite like anybody else's, and you can say that, of course, about a great many writers. The individual voice is very important.

CLW Faulkner comes immediately to mind.

MOMADAY Faulkner—sure.

CLW The poet Donald Hall says that poetry "happens mostly in the mouth."[17] That's really the same thing, isn't it? Sound first?

MOMADAY Yes. Sound contributes to one's verbal identity.

CLW So your writing must first pass the sound test? The right sounds don't routinely occur in the course of your writings?

MOMADAY No. I have to work for them. Writing is work. And the right sounds don't come about without a lot of conscious effort. Well, let me revise that to say that a large part of writing is unconscious, so the vocal qualities in my writing are perhaps to some extent beyond my comprehension. Things are going on in my writing of which I am not aware at the conscious level. But I also understand when something is pleasant or satisfactory to my hearing, and I work to create good sounds.

CLW Do you imagine that you're carrying forth a voice? Is there something of your ancestry in your voice? Do you imagine that your voice is the voice or voices of the past?

MOMADAY Oh, yes, absolutely. I don't doubt that for a minute.

CLW You imagine yourself speaking as your ancestors spoke?

MOMADAY I sometimes imagine that I am my ancestors. That as I write I am speaking what my ancestors spoke or would speak through me.

CLW Is it a transformation, or are we talking about an intellectual choice?

MOMADAY It's not something of which I am intellectually aware. That's not the best of it. It is something of which I'm instinctively aware, I think. But I am aware of it. It is a kind of transformation. It occurs when I think of such things as the story of Devils Tower. I think of the word *reincarnation*, and I think sometimes that my voice is the reincarnation of a voice from my ancestral past. Not only when I write but when I lecture, and even when I speak on a one-to-one basis, I sometimes have that feeling, and I think, Yes, this voice of mine is proceeding from a great distance in the past.

CLW That must be a very energizing feeling.

MOMADAY Yes, but it's not something that excites me or gets my adrenalin going. It is something that brings about a great serenity. I think of it as being irresistible. It is the way the universe is ordered. When I have this awareness that I am speaking from an ancestral point back in time, I feel very peaceful. I have the feeling that I have entered into the flow of things.

CLW Which of your father's physical gestures do you remember most?

MOMADAY My father had a very well-developed sense of humor. And he loved to "kid," to use his term. When he was in such a mood, and that was very often, he would smile in a particular way. He would break into a smile and sort of squint his eyes. That's the first gesture that I remember.

CLW It was a foreshadowing of things to come, wasn't it? [Both laughing.]

MOMADAY And just after he had said something funny or made a joke he would sort of toss his head and smile.

CLW What do you remember about his movements? His walk or his manner of moving?

MOMADAY Everything. I remember it all. He was a tall man—taller than I—about six feet four inches. And straight. He walked well, and used his hands to good effect when he was talking. He was gregarious. He liked people, and he liked to be in their company. He enjoyed conversation.

CLW What kind of a storyteller was he?

MOMADAY Easy. Natural. I'm sure that he had heard many stories from his father. So he just continued the process by telling me stories. He was not a professional storyteller. I don't think he spoke to audiences very often. But he had an intrinsic and natural ability to tell stories, and he did. I think he was born with that ability. It was in his blood.

CLW Do you use any of his postures or gestures or attitudes as you tell stories?

MOMADAY Not consciously. I think it's a genetic thing. I resemble him physically in certain ways, and I'm sure that I have some of the same gestures and some of the same intonations. I've been told that.

CLW Can you picture him telling stories?

MOMADAY I remember. I remember him telling stories. And one of the things that we delighted in, he and I, was storytelling. I would visit my parents, and one of the best things that happened during such visits was that he and I would talk about the Kiowas. I would always ask him to tell me things about his childhood, and about my grandfather, a man I never knew, and about things that happened before I was born. He delighted in those tellings. He was always very glad to tell me about those things, and we had wonderful exchanges.

CLW Do you recall his attitude toward you as he told his story? Was he centering on you as he told it?

MOMADAY He was absolutely focused on me. He was creating his listener.

CLW Did your father write?

MOMADAY No. He was not interested in writing. His expression of those things, outside of the storytelling framework, was painting. He got a lot of storytelling into his paintings—the mythical elements of Kiowa history and tradition. Painting was the principal expression of his spirit. But he was a good storyteller, too. Although quite a private storyteller.

CLW How did he react to your writing?

MOMADAY Oh, quite well. I think he was very proud of the things that I wrote.

CLW Did he recognize something of his voice in the way you re-created those stories? Did he remark on that?

MOMADAY No, but I'm sure that he must have noticed, because it's there. His voice comes through in my writing, and I'm sure that he recognized it.

CLW Did you tell him stories eventually?

MOMADAY Yes. But of course, I was in no position to tell him many stories in that tradition, because he knew so much more than I did. But sometimes I would hear something about the Kiowa history from another kinsman, and I would tell it to him, and he was always very interested.

CLW Did he ever question those other tellings? Or authenticate them in any way?

MOMADAY No. He simply accepted them for what they were. When I was putting *The Way to Rainy Mountain* together, I came across variants. I would mention those to him, and he would be very interested. He might say, "Oh yes, that's right, I remember hearing that version of it once." Or he would say, "Ah—I never heard that version, but that's interesting too."

CLW Which is an important point with you, isn't it? Taking the story for what it is?

MOMADAY That is very important to me.

CLW Can you say anything more specific about your feelings about your father's power? Can you characterize his power in any way?

MOMADAY I don't think so. It's not something that he and I ever talked about. But when we were spending time together years ago, I began to suspect that he had some sort of power, and I still do. And other people tell me that my father was some kind of medicine man. That he had powers that he didn't reveal. What kind? I can't say. His father was a peyote priest, and he certainly had power, and so it would follow that my father, too, had an investment in that dimension. But I don't know what it was or how it worked.

CLW But there were observable effects? You apparently felt affected by whatever it was? You sensed something extraordinary?

MOMADAY Yes, there was a feeling—a sense. I can't define it more closely than that. But I remember him pretty well. And I think about him frequently. He was a good man to have as a father.

CLW You are fairly quick to tell audiences in question-and-answer situations that you do not speak Kiowa, and you say it in a way which implies that you've not thought it a matter of much consequence. You obviously could learn to speak Kiowa. Why haven't you?

MOMADAY It would take a great effort. And though I would like to be able to speak Kiowa, it isn't something that I think I have to do. I couldn't write better than I do if I spoke Kiowa. I'm firmly convinced of that. There is no point in trying to write in Kiowa, because I wouldn't be understood. But I've run across that question so many times in so many places. "Wouldn't it be wonderful if you could write in your native language?" The answer is clearly no, it wouldn't be wonderful at all. It would be a great mistake. What if I had written *The Way to Rainy Mountain* in Kiowa?

CLW A small but appreciative audience?

MOMADAY There are maybe two people in the world who can read Kiowa, and one is a Swedish linguist and one is a Norwegian. [Both laughing.]

CLW Is the story of the arrowmaker the story you are most interested in?

MOMADAY That and the story of Devils Tower. They are the two most important stories that I know. Important to me, I mean.

CLW Why is the story of the arrowmaker more important to you than, for example, the story of the buffalo with horns of steel?[18] Don't they have very similar implications? Aren't they both about language—the risks and the gains?

MOMADAY Hmm. The arrowmaker story is much more complex than is the story of the buffalo with horns of steel. You're right that the implications are the same in some respects. But the arrowmaker story has a far greater number of consequences. I have lived with that story virtually all of my life, and I have thought about it in various ways, sometimes with great intensity. But I still don't understand that story in all its dimensions. I believe that it is so rich that it becomes like Borges's *Book of Sand*.[20] It is an infinite kind of story, it seems to me. I haven't come to the end of it, and I don't know that I ever will. I like it for that reason. To me it exemplifies the real magic of story-

THE ARROWMAKER

If an arrow is well made, it will have tooth marks upon it. That is how you know. The Kiowas made fine arrows and straightened them in their teeth. Then they drew them to the bow to see if they were straight. Once there was a man and his wife. They were alone at night in their tipi. By the light of the fire the man was making arrows. After a while he caught sight of something. There was a small opening in the tipi where two hides were sewn together. Someone was there on the outside, looking in. The man went on with his work, but he said to his wife: "Someone is standing outside. Do not be afraid. Let us talk easily, as of ordinary things." He took up an arrow and straightened it in his teeth; then, as it was right for him to do, he drew it to the bow and took aim, first in this direction and then in that. And all the while he was talking, as if to his wife. But this is how he spoke: "I know that you are there on the outside, for I can feel your eyes upon me. If you are a Kiowa, you will understand what I am saying, and you will speak your name." But there was no answer, and the man went on in the same way, pointing the arrow all around. At last his aim fell upon the place where his enemy stood, and he let go of the string. The arrow went straight to the enemy's heart.[19]

telling. It has everything. Great suspense, and mystery. Maybe mystery more than anything else. I think it has meanings and implications of which I'm not yet aware. Maybe I'll never be aware of them.

CLW What is it you do not understand in that story? Which elements mystify you?

MOMADAY Well, one of the things that interests me about the story is the presence outside the tipi. I know what the storyteller says about that presence. I take the story as I heard it from my father, who told it to me many times. I have what a scholar might call a reliable text. It's the oldest story in my experience, maybe the first story that I ever heard, and it has never become less than wonderful to me. But what the presence outside the tipi is . . . we're not told. Except we are told that it is an enemy, and we understand that the enemy is vanquished. He is vanquished at the level of language. He is done in by words, and the arrows are metaphors, I suppose. But I have a lot of questions about that presence outside. I imagine the situation. I see it in my mind's eye, and I try to approach that figure outside and I can't. I can get only so close, but not close enough to see who it is or to read anything in his expression. But I'm very curious about it. And the same thing, of course, applies to the boy who turns into a bear. I want to know much more about him. And I feel quite free to imagine that boy, and in writing *Set,* that's what I'm doing. But it's good that there is much that's not explained in the arrowmaker story. That's as it should be. That gives me a certain latitude to imagine, and a story must do that.

CLW Are you confident that the enemy in darkness is in fact a person?

MOMADAY Well. That's the way I see it. The storyteller says someone is standing outside, and so I imagine that it is a man who's standing there. It is an enemy. There's no way to get around that—the storyteller tells us that. But even so, the figure is infinitely mysterious. What's he doing there? Where did he come from? What does he intend? How would it work out otherwise? And those things are wonderful to contemplate.

CLW Do you intend to understand the story better? Or do you have the feeling that you've reached the limits of your understanding?

MOMADAY I can't say. I think it's likely that I will see more.

CLW What would you say to the person who says that you're making too much of a simple story? You've had that reaction, haven't you? It's a fairly typical reaction, historically, to Indian stories and legends. What would you say to that person?

MOMADAY Well, I would say, "You may be right, but I doubt it. It depends upon what you expect from a story. I can tell you this: I have looked into that story as deeply as I can and I have not done it harm. It's still there, and still alive, and I find some point in looking further."

CLW But acknowledgment of the possible complexity of such stories is a comparatively recent development in much of academe, isn't it? Against the historical tendency to see those stories as simple things, with few, if any, implications?

MOMADAY Perhaps. But I think it's up to every individual who reads or hears the story of the arrowmaker to take away what he can, and I certainly don't want to insist that he take the story as seriously as I do. I have a personal investment in it, I suppose. It's enough for me that you hear it, and if it brings you wonder and delight, that's fine. If it doesn't, that's okay too.

CLW Another example of what I'm saying, though, is some of the initial response to *The Way to Rainy Mountain*. In my opinion, there was a tendency in some of the reactions to the book to undervalue the stories in it. To condescend to them, even. I think attitudes about such stories have changed dramatically, even in the short time since *The Way to Rainy Mountain* was published.

MOMADAY Yes. And that's very gratifying to me. I know exactly what you're saying, and it's good that people are now taking those stories more seriously. There has been a tendency to regard the whole oral tradition of the Indian as a big collection of fairy tales. It's much more than that, and now we're beginning to understand that fact.

CLW To what do you attribute that attitude historically?

MOMADAY To bias. The Indian oral tradition twenty years ago, or even at the time that *The Way to Rainy Mountain* was published, was virtually unknown. No matter what reading public you're talking about, there is a tendency to regard anything outside your own literature as inferior, or as something less immediate and less important than what your own traditions give you. There is a tendency to look with suspicion upon outside things. "Oh yes, here are some stories that the American Indians told. Probably a lot of interesting things about animals and trees here. Kid stuff." There's that tendency, unfortunately, which is natural enough. But the material is much more than that. It's a very serious body of literature and very rich.

CLW There is also, in my opinion, the tendency to celebrate obscurity in modern American literature. Out of the idea that a work is not profound unless it is stylistically and structurally complex. In some quarters, unless it employs convoluted and even tortured language. I recall the dramatic contrast in my graduate school experience between, for example, what I was reading in a modern novel course and the clarity and accessibility of those stories in *The Way to Rainy Mountain*. Yet those stories are really, as you say, profound. Their vividly descriptive language heightens their intrigue.

MOMADAY I hope they are surfaces with many implications.

CLW Just a few more questions about the arrowmaker. You call your version of that story "a reliable text." And you once told me that the story is "timeless." Does that mean that storytellers cannot hereafter alter the story? That it must be recited rather than told from now on, lest it become a different thing? Changes would date the original, wouldn't they? And then the story would no longer be timeless?

MOMADAY You've lost me.

CLW Well, I've heard you differentiate between recitation and spontaneous storytelling. You've said that sometimes recitation is important and at other times total spontaneity—literally telling the story new each time—is appropriate.

MOMADAY So?

CLW So what of the story of the arrowmaker? Is it now pretty much what it must remain? Or is it organic? It can't exist outside of time unless it has pretty much acquired its permanent form, can it?

MOMADAY I still don't follow that. The arrowmaker is what it needs to be. Yes. Because it is valuable for its own sake. It's an admirable thing and it ought to remain that, and I'm sure it will. Then I don't follow.

CLW Well, it is timeless only as long as we do not change the story. As long as we do not alter the telling, even in subtle ways. Wouldn't it be a different story, and therefore dated, if we did?

MOMADAY Well, I'm not sure that I understand or accept that theory of language and the temporal dimension. You're saying that if you changed the arrowmaker's story, you would create another story. But you can't change it, because it's there. I'm talking about the story as it exists, and I'm saying that it has existence in a timeless dimension.

CLW But isn't that so only as long as it's retold in its current form? Will this story of the arrowmaker exist a thousand years from now? And if so, how?

MOMADAY I'm sure that this story will exist a thousand years from now. We may not recognize that it exists, but it'll be there in the air. It'll be out there in the timeless wastes. [Laughing.]

CLW It'll be hovering wordlessly forever? [Both laughing.]

MOMADAY Sure. A story does not have to be told to exist. Though now we're getting into metaphysical areas, and I'm not sure of my ground. I think that the story of the arrowmaker exists, and that nothing can change its existence. Even if all the storytellers in the world or all the people in the world were to cease to exist, that particular story would remain. Of what practical value it might be, I don't know. [Laughing.] But there it is.

CLW It's difficult for me to imagine its existence if it had no realization in words.

MOMADAY Well, you've heard the idea that all the words that were ever spoken in the world exist in aerial dimensions, and that we may by the miracle of technology someday retrieve them all. And I don't know that we want to do that, but I do believe that every word that we speak passes not into death but into some other dimension of existence. I think that every story that was ever told might be right out there above the mountains. Sort of floating around in space. [Laughing.]

CLW Can you imagine the effect of being able to retrieve all of that language?

MOMADAY I think it would be disastrous.

CLW Talk about words closing in on us.

MOMADAY I don't want everything I say to be retrieved, God knows. Some of it, maybe. But certainly not all of it. [Both laughing.]

CLW What does the oral tradition teach us about language?

MOMADAY The oral tradition helps us to understand that words are more valuable than we have been led to believe. It demonstrates the importance of memory and the importance of listening carefully. There's always the very tenuous link between being and nonbeing in the oral tradition. If the word is lost, it is lost forever. Lost to us, I mean.

CLW At what point do writing and the oral tradition merge?

MOMADAY Well, there is a tendency when you're talking about oral tradition to want to distinguish it as much as you can from written tradition, and of course the distinctions are real, but I think that at some point the two traditions come very close together, and perhaps merge. As in *Moby-Dick*, for example, when you have such wonderfully brilliant imagistic description as in the "Spirit-Spout" chapter.[21] The things which inform that writing and make it great literature are the very things that inform oral tradition at its best and distinguish a great storyteller. There the two traditions merge, and they are more apparently different than really different.

CLW What is the function of the writer?

MOMADAY Well, I guess the function of the writer is to reduce experience to verbal expression. And if he's really serious about it, it is well done. There ought to be a great precision and a great accuracy and a perception that goes deeper into experience than other kinds of expression. So the function of the writer is to reflect the real world.

CLW You said "reduce experience." The writer's role is to reduce?

MOMADAY Yes. Writing is in some sense reductive. You put experience into a rubric of some kind, and you extract the essence of reality. Poetry is especially that way, it seems to me. Poetry is more essentially expression than are other kinds of writing. That's the soul of poetry. Precision, condensation, concentration. This reduction we're talking about.

CLW Is painting similarly reductive?

MOMADAY Yes, it is. Of all the things that one might paint or see, the painter's job is to choose the essential part which reflects the whole. And to do justice to that concentrated element of the whole.

CLW Could you say something about the process of Abel's loss of language in *House Made of Dawn*?

MOMADAY Well, I believe that as soon as Abel leaves his traditional ground, his language begins to deteriorate. He is bombarded and threatened by the language around him. He is threatened by the currency of the English language, and so he is isolated in his own language, and finds that it does not operate for him outside its context. And so little by little, as this is driven home to him, he falls silent. In the court scene, where everybody is not only talking in something other than his language but talking in a language that is even more highly artificial than languages in general—legalese—at that point he's just done in. Language becomes his enemy. It has turned on him, and he understands that there's nothing he can do about that. So he turns

Squaw Dance, 1978, graphite and wash, 14 inches x 12 inches

his back and remains silent. And that's the loss of his language—the loss of his voice. What could be more devastating? In the scene where Abel wants to say something and can't, he is reduced to something almost subhuman. He's very nearly lost his life at that point.

CLW What does the experience of war have to do with his loss of voice?

MOMADAY That's a very interesting question, and the answer is large. But for Abel it's the chaos, the great activity of war. War is a concentrated kind of experience. It's overwhelming in itself, quite apart from language. And in a situation of that kind when you do have language—when you have people barking orders at you—that simply intensifies the chaotic aspect. Not only is there all of this intense activity, but it is accented by a language that is not mine. This chaos has its own language, and that's devastating to someone in Abel's position.

CLW Those Abels you knew who returned from the war—do you think they had a sense of the futility of language? The impossibility of expressing what they'd experienced?

MOMADAY I think certainly some of them did. People don't go around thinking about language. Even when they're being victimized by it, they are not aware of it, necessarily. It takes a very reflective sort of person to really question the intent and effect of words. A lot of the men I knew who had come back probably at some level knew something about the loss of language—the necessity to fall silent in certain circumstances—but I don't think that they thought about it much.

CLW Yet on the most basic level, didn't many of them have the attitude that talk was pointless?

MOMADAY Yes. Many fell silent. You would have a better physical understanding of why than I do.

CLW *House Made of Dawn* contains that understanding. I was struck by it when I first read the book, shortly after my war experience.

MOMADAY I appreciate that verification. I meant to demonstrate some of the natural consequences of war in that book.

CLW But then, there are also larger implications, aren't there? Implications beyond the immediate context of war? Can't any chaotic experience be reductive and overwhelming and make the present "immediate and confused," as you say in *House Made of Dawn*?[22]

MOMADAY Yes. Our society can be very confusing. I sometimes have the experience of going into a crowded room and simply being overwhelmed by the activity in that room. There's no center to it. You're not sure where you're going. You're simply caught up in confusion. You're not sure where you are in relation to your surroundings. And I have the kind of hearing which increases my confusion in such circumstances.

CLW What do you mean?

MOMADAY I'm attending to too much. It's all pouring in on me too quickly, and I don't have enough aural discrimination. I have to concentrate hard in order to hear what is being said directly to me. I think war must be like that in some respects. In many contemporary situations, there's just too much to take in, and you don't know what part to try to take in, and the result is a terrible confusion.

CLW Sensory overload?

MOMADAY Yes. Sometimes it is so terrible that you know that it can be destructive. You can lose your sanity in situations like that.

CLW Is Abel's voicelessness part of his distance from Tosamah? Does Tosamah measure him in terms of his inability to speak? Because Tosamah is so articulate?

MOMADAY Yes. Because Tosamah is so glib, he tends to take advantage of people who are not as articulate as he is. And certainly Abel is a prime target for Tosamah. Tosamah is not a nice guy, when you come right down to it. He can be sensitive, certainly, and he is intelligent, and above all articulate, but he will take advantage. He will exploit.

CLW Weren't you in some respects risking yourself by giving Tosamah, who has those negative qualities, so much of your background, your past, your experience? Don't you risk having people wonder if there's an equation there? If you are Tosamah, in some respects?

MOMADAY I guess I really haven't thought of it so much in terms of risk, but yes. Tosamah is my mouthpiece in a certain way. I use him to present some of my views concerning language. That's the basic thing. And I've been asked if Tosamah is a reflection of me. The answer is yes and no. I'm not a relocated Indian in Los Angeles, which, after all, is a very important part of Tosamah. His situation determines him to a great extent. But I suppose the answer is yes, there is a certain risk. Just between you and me and several million readers, I think Tosamah is perhaps the most interesting character in the novel. He certainly was an interesting character to develop. He fascinates me. I like him and dislike him deeply. [Both laughing.]

CLW Will you return to him?

MOMADAY I don't know. I like him as he is, and I would almost be afraid to tinker with him. And I now have another character who interests me in somewhat the same way.

CLW What about Tosamah's sermon on Logos, "the Word"?[23] Where's the wisdom in that?

MOMADAY It says to me that words are original and originative. The word is original in the sense that it antedates everything. Everything proceeds from the word. That's what the Gospel of St. John says, and I think that is a good way in which to look at language. Words are creative—they are instruments of creation.

CLW And Tosamah also makes the point that John goes on too long.

MOMADAY Yes. John should have stopped while he was ahead, Tosamah says in effect.

CLW You told me once that there are a number of questions in *House Made of Dawn* for which you have no answers. Do you still feel that way?

MOMADAY Well, yes. Yes. But I think that's true of all writing. Writers are very frequently astounded by their work, and they often have many questions about it. They have perceptions and intuitions in the writing that they don't understand. A lot of things happen in *House Made of Dawn* that I can't explain in a logical way. They are based upon insights which I think are valid, but those insights are not fully conscious. That is, they weren't consciously developed. They exist beneath the level of everyday consciousness, but they are nonetheless real.

CLW Can you give me an example or two?

MOMADAY Well, what comes to my mind is the journal of Fray Nicholas. I don't know where that idea of a journal came from, but it was the right thing to put into the narrative, and I like the way that it functions there. It was not something that I set out to do. It was an intuitive inclusion. And fortunate, I think. And there are other instances of that kind of thing.

CLW And you were fascinated by the character of Nicholas?

MOMADAY Yes. You know, he exists almost as a shadow in the novel. He's a very disturbed man and fascinating to me, and I can imagine going on with that character and building a whole book around him. He's got great potential, although discovering that potential was not my purpose. But I was fascinated by him. I could say the same thing of other characters. Angela is also a very interesting character.

CLW Dominant in your characterization of Nicholas is his self-pity. He seems consumed by it.

MOMADAY I think he is consumed, and I feel that he's a desperate man. His circumstances are such that he is holding on by his fingernails, and I feel strongly about him. That is, I appreciate his desperation.

CLW He's almost absolutely insensitive to his circumstance, isn't he?

MOMADAY That's his defense, I think. He's in a position where he has no advantage. All of his strengths, which are predicated upon Christian faith, are futile. And so he's under the weight of all that, and I think he's close to madness.

CLW Or mad.

MOMADAY Or mad. Yes.

CLW He is apparently representative of white insensitivity to traditional Indian culture.

MOMADAY Yes. Yes. I suspect that there have been lots of people like him in his situation. Priests on the reservation. Missionaries. I'm sure that life must have been terribly hard for those people. It probably still is, but at one time it must have been even more difficult. The isolation must have been almost unbearable.

CLW So you are, to some extent, sympathetic with his circumstances?

MOMADAY Hmm. Sure.

CLW Although he's self-consumed and really makes no attempt to accommodate himself to his surroundings?

MOMADAY Well, the question may be, Can he? Is it a matter of his refusal, or is he simply determined by his situation?

CLW Father Olguin makes some accommodation.

MOMADAY Yes.

CLW I can't imagine not trying to make some accommodation, but then, maybe I can't imagine the context out of which those men came—their conditioning. I certainly have the advantage of hindsight, but going into the intensely spiritual cultural circumstances of Indian people, why wouldn't you naturally want to make some accommodation? I'm confused by the absolute quality of withdrawal in Nicholas.

MOMADAY I think there is a fanaticism which remarks a lot of religious experience. Think of the Puritans, who came into New England and simply made no concession whatsoever. I suppose they believed that as Puritans, as Christians, as enlightened, chosen people of God, they could not compromise their faith at all. And so it became almost purely destructive. It destroyed people. How do you account for that? I think something of that same thing is true of Fray Nicholas. He's a Franciscan. He's on God's side, and he's in a pagan world, and compromise is dangerous. Adaptation. Concession. Any accommodation would be an admission of failure, and a repudiation of one's ideals. So he's blind. And I'm sure that was probably truer of his generation than of Olguin's.

CLW It also seems to me that there's much more violence in *House Made of Dawn* than in anything you've done since then. Violence is relatively minor or nonexistent in your writings since that book. Why?

MOMADAY I don't know. There is a lot of violence in *House Made of Dawn*. In the novel I'm writing now, there's a lot of violence. Violence seemed appropriate to *House Made of Dawn*. It was not appropriate to *The Names* or to *The Way to Rainy Mountain*. It's a valid dimension of that novel, I think.

CLW The violence is situational, then? It's because of your subject matter?

MOMADAY Much of it depends upon the people you're dealing with in your writing. The characters in *The Names* are not passive, but for the most part they're not violent. In *House Made of Dawn*, Abel is intentionally opposed by me the writer to a violent world, a world of witchcraft, a world by which he is threatened. Threatened not only psychologically, but physically as well. That seems important. And as you know, I based some of the episodes in *House Made of Dawn* upon actual events that took place at Jemez. The killing of the albino is based upon something that really happened. That murder did happen, though not to an albino, and I was close enough to it so that I knew things about it and could write about it with accuracy.[24] In *Set*, I'm writing about Billy the Kid and the killing of the guards at the Lincoln County Courthouse, and so there's a lot of violence in that too. And there will probably be violence in the protagonist and the bear. Because bears are so violent.

CLW Why the great distance in time between *House Made of Dawn* and *Set*, your two novels? Especially considering the enormous success of *House Made of Dawn*?

MOMADAY I don't really know how to answer that. One part of the answer is that I don't often think of myself as a novelist. I started out writing poetry, and I identified with poetry and the poet when I was earning my wings, and I still think of myself as a poet. I haven't had, until *Set*, a strong desire to write a novel. I was more interested in writing other things, and I did write other things. But then this idea of the novel came upon me again, and so I'm trying to turn it out. But I'm slow. Just very slow as a writer and a reader. If you count everything, including my dissertation, which was published, and all the books that I've done, there's something like seven over a course of twenty to thirty years. That's about my rate, I think. [Laughing.] I would be surprised if I turned out more than that.

CLW Did anything specific precipitate *Set*? Or has the book simply evolved as a possibility you've been thinking about for a long time?

MOMADAY I think it's been more of an evolution. It's just an idea that grew up in the end. It took a long time for the seed to germinate. It came about quite naturally, I think. I think of all of my work as being one story, so there are obvious connections between *House Made of Dawn* and *The Way to Rainy Mountain* and *The Names* and *The Gourd Dancer*, and I think *Set* is another chapter in that long story. It proceeds out of the same prehistoric legendary experience, and it comes about quite naturally. But it took a long time for me to work it out. For it to come to the surface of my mind.

CLW It seems to me that the humor in your writing is underexamined critically. For example, I think *The Names* is very funny. It is in many instances explicitly funny. The way you label those photographs, for instance. And the textual voice is frequently comic. But I find that most of the discussion of *The Names*, and even of those Billy the Kid poems which people have seen, is very serious. Do you think that's a fair assessment?

MOMADAY Yes. I agree with it. I think it may be difficult to perceive some of my humor because it is understated, and it doesn't always come off as humor. A good many writers are like that. I think of Nabokov, for example, as being extremely funny, and yet you have to look very carefully into the text to really catch the joke. It can pass over you very easily. But I like it for that reason. I like to see Nabokov playing jokes in his writing, because his is a wonderfully subtle kind of humor.

CLW I think that your sense of humor is revealing itself more and more in what you do. You've pointed out those humorous things in *House Made of Dawn*, but overall, that book and *The Way to Rainy Mountain* are pretty serious. *The Names*, on the other hand, is a very interesting mixture of the comic and the serious. It's akin in some ways to what you did at the beginning of a recent reading, when you started with that comic preparatory description of an urban buffalo drive and then turned it to something very serious, the death of a culture, as you read the poem about the buffalo drive.[25] You calculated that effect, didn't you?

MOMADAY [Laughing.] Yes.

CLW And it was interesting to watch. People were embarrassed to finish the laughs they had started, because the turn was so sudden. You were creating a very dramatic contrast.

MOMADAY That's exactly right. And I enjoy that. Making that switch. I've done it several times at readings, and it's always interesting to see how the audience members take it. In a sense I'm playing a joke on them. Maybe a trick. Maybe a malicious trick. [Laughing.] But it's fun.

CLW Some of those Billy the Kid poems which were originally intended for *The Gourd Dancer* contain the comic element that we're talking about. Why did you decide not to include them in that volume?

MOMADAY Because they seemed to represent too much of a departure from the rest of the collection. The three sections I do have in *The Gourd Dancer* seem to me to go together pretty well, but the Billy the Kid sequence would have been too different from the other sections.

CLW You've subsequently published several of them in *American West* magazine.

MOMADAY Virtually the whole collection. I knew that I wanted to publish them somewhere, and I kept thinking about maybe including them in a book of poems, maybe extending the sequence. There are now twenty-one pieces, one for each year of Billy's life. Then I painted a suite of portraits of Billy and his contemporaries, and they made a nice accompaniment to the piece.

CLW So is it fair to say that you're exploring more and more the possibilities of humor in what you do?

MOMADAY I think that's a fair statement. There is more humor in my recent work than there is in my earlier work.

L. G. Murphy, from *The Billy the Kid Suite*, 1984, ink and watercolor on Arches paper, 23 inches x 30 inches

CLW Why do you suppose that is?

MOMADAY I'm getting old and mellow, and I'm seeing more humor in things. [Both laughing.]

CLW It's as simple as that?

MOMADAY I think so. Young men, and maybe particularly young writers, tend to take things very seriously. If they stick around long enough, they outgrow that.

CLW Is there much humor in your current book?

MOMADAY There is a great deal of humor in one of my characters in *Set*. The character of Grey. She's nineteen, and she's half Kiowa and half Navajo. She's like Tosamah in the sense that she's very bright and articulate, but she finds great satisfaction in assuming the dimensions of the stereotype. So she goes around affecting western dialect. She fantasizes about Billy the Kid and talks about him a lot—you see, I get him into almost everything now—and she mouths almost verbatim the style of the dime novel. There's one passage, for example, in which she describes herself in those stereotypical dime novel terms. She says, "My eyes are the blue of cornflowers, my throat is long and unblemished, my mouth is like a Cupid's bow, and so it's no wonder that I inspire love from Master Billy, because here I am this lithe and beautiful young woman." And that's terribly funny, I think. To read that, and then to read the narrator's version of what she looks like. And to see her affect her dime novel attitude. That kind of humor excites me because it is very American, essentially. I'm sure you don't find it elsewhere. It's very indigenous, and it's rich.

CLW How is it American?

MOMADAY Well, the language of the dime novel, for example, probably doesn't exist anywhere else. You might find something reasonably close to it in the eighteenth-century English novel, but not quite the same thing. Because it is centered in the American wilderness, you get that whole Daniel Boone type of extravagance. I'm sure it's unique. So I like it for that reason. I'm playing a lot with that kind of humor in this novel.

CLW Do you think that the lack of significant reaction to the humor in your other works has anything to do with what readers expect because of the subject matter? That historical tendency to see Indian peoples as solemn? And a related tendency to view you as a solemn spokesman?

MOMADAY I suppose you're right. The voice of authority. But my inclination is to think of exceptions. Voices of authority which have been primarily not serious. I think there are quite a few.

CLW For example?

MOMADAY Huck Finn. Holden Caufield in *Catcher in the Rye*. I should think there are quite a number of others.

CLW I guess my point was that readers might be more conditioned to think that those voices, the voices of mischievous white boys, are comic.

MOMADAY Yes. You're right about that, I think.

CLW But maybe part of all this has literally to do with your voice? Your speaking voice as well as your writing voice? I think there's a certain solemnity of tone to much of what you've done and much of what you say. And so maybe that overpowers the humorous elements?

MOMADAY Yes. Although solemnity can also be funny, sometimes.

CLW How difficult is it to be original?

MOMADAY Pretty difficult, I should say. You have to find a voice, and its originality has to be cultivated.

CLW Has there been any lessening of the difficulty over time? Is it easier now than it used to be?

MOMADAY No, I think it's probably harder to be original as time goes on. People keep presenting new voices, and sometimes they're highly original, even unique, and the more of those there are around, the harder it is to be original. It's harder and harder to find a sentence that hasn't already been articulated.

CLW And because so much more has been written about your subject matter than when you started writing about it?

MOMADAY That's certainly a reason, too. Another is that when writing about the Indian world, you have to overcome stereotypes. We were talking about the dime novel. I imagine that it was very difficult for people who had read those novels to write in other terms in those days. You have an established kind of dialect in the dime novel, and people who came along later and wanted to write about the same thing probably assumed the same voice.

CLW Why are there repetitions of stories and themes in your work? Why is part of *The Way to Rainy Mountain* in *House Made of Dawn*, and why are you carrying the Devils Tower story forward into *Set*?

MOMADAY I don't know what to say about that. It's simply the way I work. I like to build upon things and carry them on. Because I'm writing basically one story, I carry it on from book to book. There's a continuum. That continuity seems very valuable to me.

CLW Why do you suppose some critics view repetition as inappropriate? There is, I think, a contemporary idea that one shouldn't repeat oneself.

MOMADAY I think you're right. I think there's that idea. That you should come up consistently with new and different subject matter. But I think that's invalid. And I certainly don't think of myself as having failed to come up with new material. That's simply not a question in my mind.

CLW Is your material new in the sense that you mean newness?

MOMADAY Hmm. I think so.

CLW I'm reminded of something Eudora Welty said which I jotted down the other day. She said: "Fiction accomplishes its ends by using the oblique. Anything lighted up from the side shows things in a relief that you can't get with the direct beam of the sun. And the imagination works all around the subject to light it up and reveal it in all of its complications."[27] You're taking a subject and working all around it, aren't you?

MOMADAY Yes. Hers is a beautiful idea, and I think it is exactly right. My exploration of my story is an ongoing process.

CLW What do you think you share with Faulkner on the level of storytelling?

MOMADAY Faulkner is, to me, a legitimate genius. In some of his work he simply excels. He's one of the really accomplished writers of modern American literature. He can also be so exasperating and transparent that I sometimes wonder how he can be tolerated. So I have very mixed feelings about him, and I really can't speculate as to how the two of us might be compared.

CLW Can you say something about that transparency? Give me some "for instances"?

MOMADAY I think he often states the obvious. He becomes drunk with words. He frequently loses sight of his objective and becomes so deeply engrossed in his language that he becomes trapped in his own devices. Where he is best is in his mythic imagining. When he begins talking about the South and its romantic ideals, and when he writes about the bear, which is a mythic evocation of the South and the southern

THE FIRST WORD

The first word gives origin to the second, the first and second to the third, and third to the fourth, and so on. You cannot begin with the second word and read the poem, for the poem is itself a cumulative process, a chain of being. There is a poem in me; I have been writing it for a long time, truly, as I have heard it in my heart. It matters that, having heard it, I should write it down.[26]

landscape, that's great. But when he writes those interminable sentences which one has to go through with a comb in order to glean meanings, I become exasperated. I have a complicated idea of Faulkner, and I think of him as being very complicated in his own expression. It's hard to formulate a statement about him. I teach him, and I greatly admire some of his work. I think *The Sound and the Fury* is truly a classic. *As I Lay Dying* is a superlative novel, and so highly concentrated in its several voices that one can only stand back in awe of such an accomplishment. But I don't think Faulkner is a man to emulate. I wouldn't want to try and write like Faulkner, though maybe I do in small ways because I have read him. His voice, no matter how complicated it might be, is very much a part of my hearing. My experience. But I hope that my writing is less convoluted than his.

CLW More controlled?

MOMADAY Much more controlled. I hope.

CLW Do you have problems with what is referred to as writer's block?

MOMADAY Yes, I do. There are times when I can't get past a certain word on the page and times when I can't even seem to get started. But it's not something that I think of as a major problem in my work.

CLW Do you have techniques for overcoming the problem when it occurs, or do you just go away from the work when you feel blocked?

MOMADAY I usually just go away from it. I wait for another moment when the juices are flowing more easily. I've tried to counteract the block by moving to another section of the work, but I haven't had much success doing that. It's better for me to simply wait for a better flow.

CLW Do you ever have impulses so strong that you stop the everyday thing you're doing and sit down to write?

MOMADAY Occasionally. But not often enough. I sometimes get an idea and I think, Oh, this is very nice, I need to follow through with it. Then I jot it down. But more often when those moments come I say, Well, yes, I'll tuck this away in my mind and I'll come back to it later. Then I probably lose it altogether. [Laughing.]

CLW How have you chosen your landscapes as a writer?

MOMADAY Well, I wouldn't consider writing about a landscape that I didn't know intimately. I do know intimately the landscapes of the Great Plains and the Southwest. I would be foolish to write about any other landscapes. Somebody once said that the writer is the intelligence of his soil, and that only by being supremely regional can one be truly universal.[28] And I think there's something to that. So to be called a western writer is not a bad thing. The landscape of the West is vast, and as important as any landscape in the world. To identify the writer with such a landscape is to pay a compliment to the writer. But I don't care much for labels, and I don't take them very seriously. I have been called an Indian writer. But I don't know what that means, beyond the fact that I'm an Indian and that much of what I have written has grown out of my experience in the Indian world. It's my subject, or one of my subjects. But the designation doesn't say much, as far as I'm concerned.

CLW What of the ongoing contention that there is an eastern prejudice against the western region?

MOMADAY Oh, I think that's true. If we're talking about the economics of publishing, I think that's quite so. Western writers have always been given short shrift by the eastern publishing establishment. I think that's changing, but slowly. There is still a bias against writers west of the Mississippi, in my opinion.

CLW Is there any legitimacy to that?

MOMADAY None whatsoever, as far as I can see. You can understand how it came about. In the nineteenth century, there was really no literature of the West. Everything was in New England or along the eastern seaboard. Those conditionings die very hard.

CLW What is the critic's role? You're a creative writer who has written some criticism, so how do you think the critic should function?

MOMADAY Well, I don't think that I have been a critic to speak of. I think there is a critical role. The critic can serve a legitimate purpose. But it's not a part of literature that interests me greatly. I don't find myself going to books about books very often. I suppose the critic ought to be a reliable witness to the value of something. An interpreter, perhaps. Someone who can lead us more deeply into a book or movie, for example, than we could go ourselves. Many critics seem to me very superficial, and I don't read criticism very much.

CLW You did some criticism early on, didn't you?

MOMADAY I wrote reviews and things like that on occasion.

CLW And you also considered doing a book of criticism?

MOMADAY Well, I was thinking of that, but I didn't do it. I considered the work because I got very much interested in Emily Dickinson and Frederick W. Tuckerman and other people of their time and place. In western Massachusetts in the nineteenth century there was a stronghold of conservative attitudes and there was a marriage of science and literature which interested me. And it still does. But what I had proposed to do was to write an account of that relationship between science and literature as I found it in certain figures, including Emily Dickinson.[29] I wasn't thinking of that as a work in criticism so much as an exposition of historical conjunctions that seem to me to be very interesting. It's not that I've lost interest in that idea, but I have turned to things which interest me more immediately. I don't know if I'll ever get back to it. But somebody ought to do it, because it is a valid thing.

CLW How have you been treated critically?

MOMADAY Very well. I have no complaints.

CLW Are there trends in criticism of which you disapprove?

MOMADAY I don't know enough about the whole school of criticism to answer that intelligently. I know that new things keep coming up, and recently a lot of people have been talking about deconstruction. I must confess that I haven't the foggiest notion of what that is, and it's not something that I intend to investigate. [Both laughing.]

CLW You know enough about it to have some general sense of what is meant by the word.

MOMADAY I certainly do not. I have no idea. [Laughing.] Deconstruction. That sounds very negative to me.

CLW I think it can be fairly negative.

MOMADAY Well, you'll have to instruct me as to what it is.

CLW It would take the rest of the afternoon to talk about it, if either one of us knew. [Both laughing.] From what I know about it, it seems antithetical to what you think and write.

MOMADAY Perhaps I'd better learn something about it in self-defense?

CLW I don't know. [Both laughing.] Perhaps your work is defense enough. On the subject of criticism, it seems to me sometimes that when critics write about your works, they press the matter of influences when it would be more appropriate to suggest similarities.

MOMADAY Yes. I would agree.

CLW There's a tendency to say, "Here's Faulkner and here's D. H. Lawrence and whoever. There must be a cause and effect." My opinion is that more often the word *recognition* is more appropriate. That is, there are other writings which reflect how you feel, but those writings did not necessarily create your feeling.

MOMADAY Your word *recognition* is important. One finds resonances of one's thoughts and themes in the works of others. In the works of those with whom one has a natural affinity.

CLW And those discoveries are confirmations, but not necessarily influences.

MOMADAY I agree completely. As to influences, I make that shift in gears every time I'm asked who influences my writing. I say truthfully that I don't know, but I can tell you who I like and admire. And it's not the same thing. There's a distinction to be made, as you say, between an influence and the sharing of an impulse.

CLW But in criticism there's usually a desire to establish cause-and-effect relationships.

MOMADAY Yes. A number of times, people have pointed to passages in my work and then to passages by other writers and remarked at the similarity. For example, a friend of mine in Italy who has just translated *The Way to Rainy Mountain* to Italian wrote a wonderful essay in which he speculated that my image of the cricket in the moon was remarkably like Willa Cather's plow on the horizon.[30] And I was struck by that, because it was a very well-made point and I've since read Cather's passage several times with great admiration. But the fact is, I did not know of it when I wrote *The Way to Rainy Mountain*. And there are other instances like that in my writing experience.

CLW The kind of essay you're talking about might motivate some other critics to try to find out how old you were when you read Cather, right?

MOMADAY Exactly. [Both laughing.]

CLW But I think criticism can perform a very important service. Because I believe that art ought to begin a sequence and doesn't do so often enough. I tell my students that I think it's common for people to experience something good, and appreciate it, and then fail to articulate that experience. I have the impression sometimes that our so-called culture is a small, sheltered thing, because it's not transmitted as it should be, and that frustrates me. Do you ever feel that frustration? I think a chain reaction ought to occur, and doesn't often enough.

MOMADAY A chain reaction?

CLW Yes. If someone sees a movie, for example, and believes it to be excellent—artful, even—that person is likely to say, if anything at all, that the movie was "good." If pressed, he's likely to say that it was "really good." In other words, there's not enough specific sharing of enthusiasms, in my opinion. And therefore very little contagion. I would like to see works of art have more ongoing effects.

MOMADAY Well, that's not my experience. I think that art is contagious. I saw a very great movie lately, and I went around telling people about it. And I think I aroused the interest of those people. I think that routinely happens. It must happen with my art too. I think that people have seen paintings of mine that they admired and they have told other people about them. Then those people have been moved to come and have a look for themselves.

CLW But how representative are you in that regard? And isn't your sphere of influence comparatively limited?

MOMADAY I resent your saying that my sphere of influence is limited. [Both laughing.]

CLW "Comparatively," I said. Much larger than most, I might add. [Both laughing.]

MOMADAY But isn't some response by those people who truly care about the work really all one can hope for?

CLW I don't think so. I think there have been times when societies were more broadly cultural. When there was more transmission of interest in the arts.

MOMADAY When? In the 1920s? During the Renaissance? When do you mean?

CLW Yes, during the Renaissance, for instance. My impression of the Renaissance is that there was then a broader-based appreciation for what was going on in the arts than we find in contemporary society.

MOMADAY Well, yes. I think that's probably true, but for good reason. What was the alternative to art in the Renaissance? That was one of the principal diversions for people across the board—the aristocracy in particular—but also others. Now there are many more diversions. Even at the level of real art, there are many more paintings available to us in the United States now then there were available to the citizens of Florence or of Italy in the time of the Renaissance. Plus the fact that we have so many thousands of books published every year, so many movies made, and so much going on in television. I see what you're saying, but I wonder if there has been any real change across time. I'll concede that in Russia there seems to be a diminishing appreciation of the arts. People seem to be losing their once very great interest in poetry, to a measurable extent. Perhaps that's because television has begun to seduce the Russian people, as it has been seducing us.

CLW That's certainly what goes on here, isn't it? The primary audience for poetry in this country is poets. Other people are watching TV. Even poets are watching TV.

MOMADAY Yes. But I don't think we have ever had in this country that same situation for poets as the Russians have had, and there is still a tremendous interest in books of poetry and in the readings given by poets in Russia. It's a wonderful thing to see. But there is also sad evidence that it is diminishing.

CLW How do you feel about teaching creative writing?

MOMADAY I'm not comfortable with it. I have a hard time instructing people in the ins and outs of writing. I appear at some workshops, and I think that students get help at such places, but probably more from each other than from me. I suspect that's how it works at most workshops. Students share their concerns and interests and trade ideas. Those are very good things. But it's difficult for me to conduct a workshop. It takes a lot out of me.

CLW Does it bother you to be judgmental? Is that why you're not comfortable with teaching creative writing?

MOMADAY It does bother me to some extent to be judgmental concerning somebody else's writing. Writing, to me, is such a private business, and I know that it requires a great sensitivity and writers tend to be sensitive, and I don't like being placed in the situation where what I might say to someone will discourage him or offend him in some way. Or belittle him. I suppose that's what I really worry about.

CLW And about unrealistically raising his expectations?

MOMADAY Exactly. But I tend, in my comments, to try to be positive. I want to give some encouragement, even when there's very little reason that I can see to offer it.

CLW In writing about *The Names*, Edward Abbey says that your prose is "formal, symbolic and precise. Like so much of the pictorial art of American Indians."[31] What's your reaction to that?

MOMADAY Oh, I think that's a wonderful statement. I would be pleased to live up to it.

CLW Why do you like it so much?

MOMADAY Well, in the first place it's highly complimentary, and I'm honored to have my work spoken of in such a way. Beyond that, though, I also believe that he's making a real equation. There is a relationship between verbal expression and graphic expression which seems to be a very precise equation. And I would like to believe that he is correct about my writing being equivalent with Indian art. That's something that seems to me to be worth striving for and if I do achieve that, then it's to the good.

CLW I've heard you speak admiringly of a statement Irvin Howe made about dealing with the surfaces of literature.

MOMADAY I think that Howe's statement is quite perceptive. He said, "Any graduate student can deal with symbols, but it takes a first-rate intelligence to deal with the surfaces of literature."[32] And I think he's right. Literature is a superficial thing, finally, but that doesn't mean it is not important. It means that it is a reflection. Language is symbolic. It is superficial in the sense that words are reflections of reality rather than realities in themselves. And I think the writer has to understand that. That there is the reality, and then around that there is a circumference of appearances, and literature has more to do with the appearances than with the reality. Literature *is* the appearance rather than reality. That's what I think Howe meant, and I agree with him entirely.

CLW And that's why you like to think of your writing as mainly descriptive? That same philosophy?

MOMADAY Yes. I'm fond of describing things I like. The great value of descriptive writing is essentially its visible dimension. Somebody once said that the very best writing is that which enables you to see, and I believe that. So I try to write descriptively and I try to paint pictures in words. I want people to formulate a very clear image of what it is that I'm writing about.

CLW What is the intent and effect of repetition in Native American songs and chants? That repetitive use of language?

MOMADAY It creates rhythms and it establishes a norm. You're saying the same thing over and over again. You can inflect and create great ranges of sounds. You can be various more easily if you're repeating. You can

The Horned Horse Shield, 1976, etching, 23 inches x 30 inches

say the same thing, but you can say it differently. There is the idea that if something is repeated, its power is more greatly realized. And language is powerful. Most of the prayers and charms and spells in Native American literature and in other traditions make use of a great deal of repetition. And in that there is the irresistible accumulation of power.

CLW — And you do that in a number of your poems, don't you?

MOMADAY — I have, yes. Especially in poems like "The Delight Song of Tsoai-talee" and "Plainview: 2," with its "remember my horse" repetition.[33] There's also the hypnotic effect of repetition. You can bring about a certain condition if you repeat something.

CLW — Is there a fundamental difference between poetry and prose?

MOMADAY — Absolutely.

CLW — What is it?

MOMADAY — Poetry is composed in verse.

CLW — Yet you write prose poems.

MOMADAY — Yes. I don't call them that, because they're not poems, but there is such a thing as a very lyrical short prose piece. I think that's a very legitimate form, and I like to do it. But to answer your question: the only practical distinction you can make between prose and poetry is that poetry is composed in verse. That is, it is measured. And it is very precisely measured, at least in traditional English poetry, and that makes all the difference. It is a crucial difference.

CLW — So those pieces in some of your collections of poetry are really lyrical prose?

MOMADAY — Yes. And in "The Colors of Night," for example. That's not poetry, technically speaking. Those pieces are what one critic called "quintessential novels."[34]

CLW — Would you say, then, that the words *free verse* are usually misapplied? That most of what people call free verse is lyrical prose?

MOMADAY — Certainly. Free verse is a contradiction in terms. As is prose poem. There are no such beasts.

CLW — Do you ever debate those points with students?

MOMADAY — Oh, yes. I get into wonderful discussions sometimes. I had an interesting experience in meeting with a creative writing class in poetry at a large university last week. I came on pretty strong with the idea that poetry is bound by rules and regulations. That greatly alarmed some of the people in the class, and so I was challenged. And I was uncompromising. But several people in the class were wanting to prove me wrong. I do encounter people, and particularly students, who mean well, who really want to enter up to their armpits in literature, but who don't quite know how to go about it, and some of them have formulated false theories. It's very hard to deal with that. You want to say, "No, you got off the track back here somewhere. This is the way you ought to look at it." But they have become entrenched, and are sometimes so defensive that it's hard to talk to them.

CLW Where does that come from?

MOMADAY A part of it comes from impatience. There are many people who think they're writing poetry but who are not, because they don't understand what a poem is. Some of them are doing good work, and some of them are getting recognition for their work, but they don't really understand what poetry is. They don't have possession of the historical and traditional development of the poem. You tell them that a poem is a statement concerning the human condition composed in verse and they don't know what verse is. I want to say, "Look," and this is what I did say in the class I just mentioned: "Look, you can't really ignore this great body of traditional matter. You can't write poetry without steeping yourself in these traditions—without understanding what great poets of the past were up to." But a lot of people want to argue with me about that. They want to say, "Well, that's irrelevant, really. I'm writing poetry for the here and now. And it doesn't matter to me that iambic pentameter happens to be the norm of English poetry. It doesn't matter to me that people like Shakespeare were developing sonnet forms. That's all a waste of time to me. I want to sit down on the basis of my eighteen years in the world and write what I'm calling poetry." And I say, "Well, that's fine with me, but I happen to believe that it isn't poetry you're writing—it's something else. And you have every right to do that. But let's not create a lot of misnomers in the process. What you're writing is not really poetry as I understand that term, and believe me, *I* understand that term. I've paid my dues. There was a time when I didn't. I was like you, the eighteen-year-old to whom I'm talking. I thought I knew what a poem was, and I discovered rather painfully that I didn't. But it turned out all to the good. It was worth learning. And my advice to you is to find out what poetry is in

English. Where it begins. How it develops. Make sure that you master the forms before you say that you're writing poetry. If you do that, then you can legitimately lay claim to being a poet." I'm sometimes very hard on such people. But I believe that many people who are writing "poems" that are not in recognizably traditional forms are doing good things, and God knows that even some of the poets who do know what iambic pentameter is chose not to write it. That's fine. But my argument is that you ought to know a little bit. In fact, you ought to know a lot about the development of poetry in English. Because I think it will improve your poetry a good deal. It's a practical thing to me.

CLW How do you differentiate between some quite well-known poets who don't have the background of which you speak and those students? Are they the same?

MOMADAY I think so, and that's why I would go on to say that I think poetry is in a pretty sad state in America. I think we have lost the kind of discipline that poetry necessitates. Most of the people who are publishing now are not poets in my sense of the word. They are something else, and they are perpetuating this failure to understand what the poem is and to work according to rules that were established hundreds of years ago. I think that the discipline of poetry is being dissipated. Traditionalists, and there are still a few, are very much in the minority now, and I think at times that the battle may be lost. I think now that maybe one day nobody will pay much attention to that long evolution of the poem in English. And I think it's a sad thing, because our literature will be the worse for it. We may eventually come to the place where nobody understands what has been lost.

CLW I've noticed that you sometimes use questions in your poems.

MOMADAY Yes? I'm trying to think of an example, so I'm probably not conscious of it.

CLW "Simile," for example, is a question. "Walk on the Moon" ends with one. And there are questions in "Angle of Geese" and "The Bear" and "Buteo Regalis."[35] In some of your main poems.

MOMADAY Well, now that you mention it, yes. I'm not sure why those questions are there. Maybe because I have a sense of wonder. And the belief that there are elemental questions to be addressed.

CLW There are also motionless moments in your poems. In "The Bear," for example. And at the end of "Angle of Geese" and "North Dakota,

North Light" and "Long Shadows at Dulce." And in "Headwaters" and "Before an Old Painting of the Crucifixion" there are dominant stillnesses.[36] What attracts you to those moments?

MOMADAY One of the most exciting things in life is to fix time. Bring it to a stop. That is one of the great illusions in literature, I think. It's powerful and provocative. Emily Dickinson does that often. There are many poems in which she deals with motionless essences. I think my favorite of her poems is "Further in Summer Than the Birds." In that poem she does exactly that. She stops the moment and there it is. And then it passes. Even as she expresses the wish that it remain there forever, the scene has changed. The passage of time has changed it. I think that's probably my subconscious motive. That is one way in which you can control the power of language. It's a good thing to do in a poem.

CLW Conversely, what of your emphasis upon symmetrical motion in some other poems? "So much symmetry!" is an exclamation at the end of "Angle of Geese." And symmetrical motion is apparent in poems like "Buteo Regalis" and "Simile" and "The Story of a Well-Made Shield."[37]

MOMADAY Symmetry is very important to me. Design in one's writings is important. I like to see the shape of what I write, and I like things to come full circle so that the relationship between the beginning and the end is readily evident to the reader. There are constructions of that kind—symmetrical constructions—throughout my writing, as you say. Those are things for which I strive.

CLW Speaking of symmetry, there is your growing enthusiasm for epitaphs.

MOMADAY [Laughing] Writing them is habitual. Writing epitaphs is a fine exercise for a poet, first of all. It's like eating peanuts. It's hard to stop once you get started. They become very appealing. And writing good epitaphs is not easy to do, as J. V. Cunningham once said. "Verse is not easy," he said.[38] But it's gratifying. Cunningham taught me how much you can get into a couplet. Couplets can be profound, and many of his were. So I respect those very short verses. Epitaphs somehow appeal to me especially. Writing something which you might find on a gravestone. They can be humorous, and they can be profound. They can also be utterly ironic. So I have grown to like them. I like writing them and I like reading them. And I have no doubt that I will write more of them.

CLW There are degrees of seriousness in yours. Some are very playful, even comic. And then others are extremely serious, and philosophical. The form suits all of those attitudes?

MOMADAY Yes. The variety is unending. And I think that they are closely related—maybe closer than other kinds of poetry in English—to Indian oral tradition. Think of the equation we've talked about: "Soldiers / You fled. / Even the eagle dies." That could be an epitaph. The epitaphs that Cunningham wrote are not far removed from the verbal expression of the Indian. The epitaph—the epigram—is close to that traditional formula.

CLW Are your poems ever completed?

MOMADAY I don't know that I understand the question. Completed?

CLW Do you usually have a sense of closure with the poems you write?

MOMADAY Yes. Certainly. There are certain poems that I think of as being fully there. They have the whole content, the beginning and the end, and they're finished and complete.

CLW You say certain poems. Are there other published poems that you feel are not complete?

MOMADAY Some, I think. There are degrees of that, somehow. I sometimes have the experience of going back to a poem and thinking that I could do otherwise with it. That I could rewrite, for example, the last line. The sense of completeness is not as striking as it is in other instances.

CLW Do you sometimes rewrite that poem?

MOMADAY Oh yes. It's not a good thing to do long after the fact, in my opinion, but if I think that there is some real point in rewriting a part of a poem, I'll do it. Hmm. I was about to say that I don't think I've ever taken a published poem and reworked it, but I may have done so once or twice.

CLW You would do that if you felt so inclined?

MOMADAY Yes. If I felt that it was a serious matter and well worth doing, I would not hesitate to do it.

CLW Are you writing poetry these days?

MOMADAY Yes. At my usual rate. Very slowly.

CLW What are its forms and content?

MOMADAY The last poem I wrote was imagistically stark, and very serious. And I've recently published three poems in the *Paris Review*.[39] One is in free verse. . . .

CLW You mean "lyrical prose"? [Both laughing.]

MOMADAY Yes. And the other two are in verse. So its hard to classify what I'm doing these days. I'm doing a variety of things.

CLW For whom do you write?

MOMADAY Well, I think I would answer that with the old cliché that I write for myself. I think that's basically true. What I write finally has to satisfy me in one way or another. And if it does that, then I let it stand. If it doesn't, I destroy it.

CLW Have you destroyed much writing?

MOMADAY Yes. I've thrown away a lot of things.

CLW Why not just put them away rather than throw them away?

MOMADAY Because I think if you look at something long enough you really do understand whether it's worth preserving, worth salvaging and changing. And there have been things I've written and looked at later and found not worthy of revision. So I've thrown them away. Probably some immortal things. [Both laughing.]

CLW Deathless prose. And you killed it.

MOMADAY Yes. [Laughing.]

CLW Do you have any apprehension when you destroy something? Because of the possibility that it might prove to be useful later in some other context?

MOMADAY Well, I grant that you might make such a mistake. That's not something that bothers me, though. If you asked me if I ever have made such a mistake, I'd say probably not. I don't think of it as being likely.

CLW Do you think your writing will change people?

MOMADAY Yes. I suppose I do. Because that's in the nature of writing. I think people are changed by writing. We can't help reacting to it in one way or another and I suppose that reaction represents change. But I don't know to what extent or how. I think I have been changed by things that I have read and so I wouldn't be surprised if people are changed in some way by what I write.

CLW Can you think of writings which might have changed you the most?

MOMADAY Well, I've read things which have given me deep insights into life. Helped me to understand certain things better than I had before. I would say that the writings of Shakespeare and Emily Dickinson,

Herman Melville, and Isak Dinesen have affected me that way. My thinking has been changed by what they have written. That seems to me to be the way it works.

CLW Black Elk called John Neihardt a "word sender," and Kenneth Lincoln has applied that term to you.[40] Do you like it?

MOMADAY Word sender. How did Black Elk think of the term? What did he mean by it?

CLW I think he meant that Neihardt's words flew forth and had impact. I think the term also suggests one whose words transcend distances. And time. The ancestral voice.

MOMADAY I'm pleased with that nomination. Word sender. "Wordwalker" is a term that I used to describe myself in a lecture that I gave a couple of years ago. That's a very interesting idea to me.

CLW Why "wordwalker"?

MOMADAY That term seems to me to suggest someone who makes his way on the basis of words, and it also has the connotation of the migrant and migration, which is an important part of the Kiowa tradition. Wordwalker.

The Vision Plane

In the spring of 1976, Scott Momaday wrote to me about an exciting recent experience. Riding in a light plane flying low along the Missouri River above Fort Pierre, South Dakota, he had seen a large buffalo herd explode into a stampede. The experience was "unforgettable," he said, after a factual explanation of what had happened. It was, he concluded, "like watching a Wild West show from a roller coaster." His description of the experience ends a third of the way down the second page of the letter, and then his complimentary close and signature, "Best Yours Scott," plunges vertically downward along the left margin, one word per line. The line crossing the *t*'s in his name sweeps right, across the page, and becomes the top of the airplane in which he had flown. The plane is swooping, dropping down through the text, one wing drawn over the closing words, to loom disproportionately large over the herd, which is rushing left in terror, against the flow of the handwriting at the top of the page. The buffalo are drawn impressionistically, in tightly bunched, jagged lines, and the backs of the animals look very much like handwriting. The effect is one of almost continuous expression, across and down the page.

N. Scott Momaday has always been interested in the correspondences between words and pictures, those two ways of seeing. In an early essay entitled "A Garment of Brightness," he implies those correspondences, and describes them as traditionally Indian:

There is a remarkable aesthetic perception in the Indian world, I believe, a sense of beauty, of proportion and design. Perhaps this

> *quality is most apparent in children, where it seems especially precocious. An Indian child, by virtue of his whole experience, hereditary as well as environmental, sees the world in terms of this aesthetic sense. His view of the landscape is sure to be incisive and precisely composed; he is sure to perceive an order in the objects he beholds, an arrangement that his native intelligence superimposes upon the world—as in astronomy we superimpose line drawings upon the stars. He sees with both his physical eye and the eye of his mind; he sees what is really there to be seen, including the aesthetic effect of his own observation upon the scene, the shadow of his own observation upon the scene, the shadow of his own imagination. It is the kind of vision that is cultivated in poets and painters and photographers.*
>
> *The practical result of this vision one finds in the extraordinary variety and achievement of Indian art. At its best, it is an expression that is at once universal and unique, the essence of abstraction and the abstraction of essences.*
>
> *Perhaps this quality of abstraction, this understanding of order and spatial relationships, proportion and design, is most fully realized in language. The oral tradition of the Indian—his songs and stories, legends and lore—is perhaps even more than his plastic arts vast and various.*[1]

That dual vision of which Momaday speaks, that seeing both physically and with the mind's eye, has always been dominant in his writings. Through the years, as his interest in painting has increased, that dual vision has begun to connect his two mediums of expression in interesting ways. In his letter, he sees and describes the buffalo herd and the airplane literally in words and pictures, and he sees them through "the eye of his mind" in both mediums, too: the literal language of his first description leads to a vision of a Wild West show, and the jagged, impressionistic lines and close proximity of images in his drawing imply the modern menace of the machine coming down on the cultural symbol that is the running herd. Most interestingly, in this description, his letters and lines seem to merge to "superimpose line drawings" upon distant visions.

In his writing, Momaday has long been concerned with what he refers to as "angle of vision," a phrase that is clearly among his favorites. One of his early poems is "Angle of Geese," in which he examines ways of seeing:

How shall we adorn
Recognition with our speech?—
Now the dead firstborn
Will lag in the wake of words.

Custom intervenes;
We are civil, something more:
More than language means,
The mute presence mulls and marks.

Almost of a mind,
We take measure of the loss;
I am slow to find
The mere margin of repose.

And one November
It was longer in the watch,
As if forever,
Of the huge ancestral goose.

So much symmetry!
Like the pale angle of time
And eternity.
The great shape labored and fell.

Quit of hope and hurt,
It held a motionless gaze,
Wide of time, alert,
On the dark distant flurry.[2]

From the title to the end, this poem presents vivid physical images. There is the literal "angle of geese," and the angle from which they are seen by the wounded bird, and the angle from which the reader sees the juxtaposition of the abandoned one against the departing flock. Then there are philosophical "angles" on what the scene implies. The remaining bird is "ancestral," a representation of the past as well as the present. There are many implications for human experience in that suggestion, and in the concluding vision of the hopeless creature, "wide of time," fixing its gaze on the departing flock, which is "the pale angle of time/And eternity." Finally, there are the larger implications of the poem's dominant images. The poem is, after all, about grief, and feelings that are beyond words, feelings that are "more than language means." Through metaphor, in the last half of the poem, Momaday implies what cannot be fully expressed in the first three stanzas. Through vivid visual images, he suggests inexpressible distance and loss.

There are other significant uses of the phrase "angle of vision" in Momaday's writings. For example, in another essay he has this to say about a small glass whale paperweight:

The amber whale gathers light unto itself, and from every angle of vision the light strikes a different pattern in, on, and around the little glass beast. It is intricately illuminated. It occurs to me that if this little whale were the only object within the reach of my senses, that if I were to perceive it in a vacuum, it should suffice; it should sustain me in my imagination as long as I lived.[3]

Again, the angles, the ways of seeing to understand, are represented by memorable visual images. That which is literally seen will be transformed in the mind's eye.

In an essay entitled "I Am Alive," Momaday describes the giveaway ceremony at which his grandfather Mammedaty, who died before Momaday was born, received a beautiful black horse. In concluding the essay, Momaday shifts to the present tense to dramatically re-create the giveaway moment:

The light is flat and white on the hard ground, which reverberates with the music and motion of the dance. Suddenly there is a breaking apart of the whole scene, a splintering of colors and planes. The black horse enters into the circle and wheels, its great body bunched, tense and taut as the head of a drum. It is a vision, a vision of great moment and beauty; it has certainly to be believed in order to be seen.[4]

Earlier, he summarizes his reaction to his vision:

This blood recollection, which is an intricate image indeed, composed of innumerable details, is especially vivid and immediate to me, a whole and irrevocable act of the imagination. I have the sense always that the event, the dramatic action, is just now, in a moment, taking place in the real world. I have held on to this vision for many years, keeping it within my reach, bringing it into focus in moments of peace and quiet. I have walked about in this vision, taken it into account from many different angles, across many distances, in many different lights. And I have thought about it; I have tried to understand it in its own terms; I have tried to perceive myself in it.[5]

Clearly, Momaday's pictorial prose is a consequence of his exceptional ability to visualize images that inform him. Through his painter's eye, his vision has become so intense that he can live within it, experiencing it "from many different angles."

In a 1974 interview, I asked him why he used the phrase "angle of vision" so often. His response further suggests the broader implications of those words:

It seems to me that people, and perhaps most particularly writers, or artists, need to understand something about various kinds of vision. They have to deal in kinds of vision. Writing, I think, requires one to see things in a particular way, and so "angle of vision" suggests a process of selection, and perhaps elimination. You arrive at a slant of some kind—you see things in a way that enables you to express them.[6]

At about that time, Momaday's writing, which had always been dramatically pictorial, began to contain more explicit verbal connections between painting and prose. He was beginning to integrate the mediums through which he could create angles of vision. He was beginning to talk about vision "planes." For example, in *Angle of Geese and Other Poems*, published in 1974, under the title of "The Horse That Died of Shame," he repeats the story of the fearful man and brave horse that first appeared in *The Way To Rainy Mountain*, and then he says:

In the one color of the horse there were many colors.
And that evening it wheeled, riderless, and broke away
into the long distance, running at full speed. And so it
does again and again in my dreaming. It seems to con-

centrate all color and light into the final moment of its life, until it streaks the vision plane and is indefinite, and shines vaguely like the gathering of March light to a storm.[7]

There are even more dramatic planes in "The Burning," a poem first published in 1975:

In the numb, numberless days
There were disasters in the distance,
Strange upheavals. No one understood them.
At night the sky was scored with light,
For the far planes of the planet buckled and burned.
In the dawns were intervals of darkness
On the scorched sky, clusters of clouds and eclipse,
And cinders descending.
Nearer in the noons
The air lay low and ominous and inert.
And eventually at evening, or morning, or midday,
At the sheer wall of the wood,
Were shapes in the shadows approaching,
Always, and always alien and alike.
And in the foreground the fields were fixed in fire,
And the flames flowered in our flesh.[8]

In this apocalyptic vision, the intense visualizations of events on distant planes are juxtaposed against images "in the foreground," a reference obviously intended to reinforce the idea of a poem that is also very literally a word painting.

In Momaday's second collection of poems, *The Gourd Dancer*, "The Burning" reappears, along with a number of other poems with foreground-and-distance contrasts in them, and references to "planes."

In these lines from "New World," for example, there are both great distances and objects seen at close range:

Bees hold
the swarm.
Meadows
recede

through planes
of heat
and pure
distance.[9]

In "Winter Holding off the Coast of North America," Momaday speaks of another detail in the foreground, and another distant plane:

This dread is like a calm,
And colorless. Nothing
Lies in the stricken palm
But the dead cold coming.

Out there, beyond the floes,
On the thin, pewter plane,
The polar currents close,
And stiffen, and remain.[10]

A number of other poems in the collection contain similar pictorial juxtapositions of backgrounds and foregrounds.

The same volume includes "Before an Old Painting of the Crucifixion," a poem originally published in 1965, very early in Momaday's writing career, and reprinted in *Angle of Geese and Other Poems*. The poem consists of statements about what does and does not appear on the canvas of another artist, and the viewer's reactions to the experience of the painting and to the experience it represents. The poem is quite abstract, and philosophical, but there are also some descriptive particulars in it, and some long distances, as in these lines from the middle stanzas:

Old, the mural fades . . .
Reminded of the fainter sea I scanned,
I recollect: How mute in constancy!
I could not leave the wall of palisades
Till cormorants returned my eyes on land.
The mural but implies eternity:

Not death, but silence after death is change.
Judean hills, the endless afternoon,
The farther groves and arbors seasonless

But fix the mind within the moment's range.
Where evening would obscure our sorrow soon,
There shines too much a sterile loveliness.[11]

However, the poem is most interesting as a contrast to the new word paintings that also appear in this volume. Whereas "Before an Old Painting of the Crucifixion" is analytical and contemplative, and removed from the process of the painting it examines, a poem like "North Dakota, North Light" is born of that process:

The cold comes about
among the sheer, lucent planes.

Rabbits rest in the foreground;
the sky is clenched upon them.

A glassy wind glances
from the ball of bone in my wrist
even as I brace myself,
and I cannot conceive
of summer;

and another man in me
stands for it,
wills even to remain,

figurative, fixed,

among the hard, hunchbacked rabbits,
among the sheer, shining planes.[12]

Gone are the longer, conversational lines of "Before an Old Painting of the Crucifixion," and much of the abstract statement. Instead, there are images on a picture plane that imply complicated meanings, and a poet-painter imagining himself a part of the scene.

A similar word painting in *The Gourd Dancer* is "For the Old Man Mad for Drawing, Dead at Eighty-nine":

This late drawing:
in these deft lines
a corpulent merchant reclines
against a pillow.

Here is a fragile equation
for which there is an Asian origin.
In this and that and another stroke
there is something like possibility
succeeding to infinity.
In another year there might have been here
not apparently
a corpulent merchant and his pillow
but really
three long winds converging on the dawn.[13]

As in "North Dakota, North Light," there is a dominant visual image concisely presented and repeated beginning and end. But in this case, that image, the "corpulent merchant" on his pillow, is less fixed on the literal level. The few "deft lines" of the drawing, re-created with three emphatic word thrusts in the middle of the poem, are visual suggestions, philosophical implications, "possibility / succeeding to infinity." They "might have been" something far beyond them. They might have been, in the impressionistic sweep of their lines, "three long winds converging on the dawn." They might have been connections to fathomless things. In this piece, Momaday is clearly exploring the possibilities of painting in the medium of words; he is blending the two modes of seeing, in intricate ways, to discover implications beyond images.

The next "poem" in the volume, "Abstract: Old Woman in a Room," is perhaps Momaday's most comprehensive combination of his two creative enthusiasms. It is also one of his most dramatic demonstrations of how words and lines on canvas deliver abstractions:

Here is no place of easy consequence
But where you come to reckon recompense;

And here the vacancy in which are met
The vague contingencies of your regret.

Here is the will's disease. And otherwise
Here is no reparation in surmise.

Here the white light that touches your white hair
Replaces you in darkness and despair.

And here where age constricts you, death is dear,
And essences of anguish stay you here.[14]

In this work, the artist seems to be drawing as he speaks, and speaking as he draws. "Here" is both a word and a brush stroke, and implications unfold across the canvas and down the page. The result is a word painting that merges creative sensibilities to communicate artistic vision.

In the same year, Momaday published another such poem in *Carriers of the Dream Wheel*, an anthology of contemporary Native American poetry. The poem is significantly entitled "Wide Empty Landscape with a Death in the Foreground." Its subject is the quintessentially mysterious man of legend, Billy the Kid:

Here are weeds about his mouth;
His teeth are ashes.

It is this which succeeds him:
This huge, barren plain.

For him there is no question
Of elsewhere. His place

Is just this reality,
This deep element.

Now that he is dead he bears
Upon the vision

Merely, without resistance.
Death displaces him

No more than life displaced him;
He was always here.[15]

Since 1976, Momaday has published only a few poems. His presentation of the "essences" he focuses upon at the end of "Abstract: Old Woman in a Room," his expression of "the essence of abstraction and the abstraction of essences," has been mostly through his painting and drawing. And he has become more and more committed to presenting the essences of essential objects—sacred dolls, traditional Indian shields, and images of mysterious beings. His paintings are increasingly evocative, visions of wildness and mystery. In an essay entitled "Unholy Sights," Momaday describes an old Jemez Pueblo villager who was thought to be "crazy in the head." He describes him as having "a strong, heroic face, dark and expressive." After more discussion of the mystery of the man, the essay closes with this anecdote:

One morning I stepped out into the raw, January weather on my way to school. A truck was speeding by on the dirt road in front of me, and in the bed of the truck were several young men jeering, laughing, taunting. And in the dust of their wake rode the old man on a paint horse. He was standing in the stirrups and holding out both his arms like Christ on the cross, his long gray hair lying out flat on the wind, and the horse was running at full speed, bolting wildly after the truck. It was a splendid, breathtaking sight, something on which to build the most incredible faith, a faith in the real, often beautiful aberrations of this world.[16]

Here is "breathtaking sight," the "angle of vision" that provides glimpses of the world beyond the world. Here is imaginative visual experience that increasingly moves the artist to paint as well as write.

CLW Do you paint out of necessity or by choice?

MOMADAY I think that I need to paint. I certainly need to write, and painting seems to come from the same impulse. But I went years without painting, so I'm not quite as sure of my need for it. If I didn't write, I would cease to be. Writing is necessary to my being. I think most writers would answer in the same way. Painting, now that I have discovered it, is becoming a necessary activity for me—a necessary expression of my spirit.

CLW Do you ever paint out of frustration with your writing?

MOMADAY I suppose I do. I find it rejuvenating to go from writing to painting, but not necessarily the other way. Writing is such a concentrated activity that there is some relief in going from it to painting, which seems to me to be a much more spontaneous and easygoing process. It doesn't require nearly the concentration required for writing. Or perhaps I haven't yet discovered that it does. For example, I can listen to music and paint, and that's not possible with writing. Painting can be exciting, but it is also a form of relaxation for me.

CLW Is your painting sometimes a consequence of your writing? A concentration or compression of the images and ideas you're writing about?

MOMADAY It can work that way. And sometimes it does. But I also think that there is risk involved when that happens too much. I mean, the more you concentrate your images and ideas, the narrower you become, and the fewer your possibilities of expression. You work to achieve greater clarity and precision and concision, but you can work yourself into a corner doing that, too. So part of what I'm also doing now in my painting is expanding—moving in an opposite direction from my writing. For example, the watercolor is wonderfully free. The spontaneity of it is its life, finally. Not a concentration, but an expansion. And the watercolors that I've done recently are very free. When I sit down now and paint something, I'm apt to do it very freely and quickly. The element of freedom is very important in the process. But if I'm writing a poem, that kind of freedom can result in carelessness. In writing, you concentrate, and you dare not be careless. Everything must be definitive.

CLW That seems somewhat contradictory. I would think that you would need spontaneity and control in both writing and painting. Is there a conflict in your mind between those two means of expression?

MOMADAY I suppose there is. Though it's not a conflict that bothers me. Because we are, after all, talking about two very different creative activities. For me, writing a poem is a highly concentrated activity, while painting a picture is often not. Especially the kinds of paintings that I've been doing lately. They are not concentrated in the way that a poem is concentrated. They are much freer and more spontaneous.

CLW So you see painting and writing as being mostly different creative gestures?

MOMADAY Yes. As I think of them. However, they're not antipodal—they're not mutually exclusive. There are overlapping areas. Yet they're essentially different activities.

CLW But you've said in other contexts that writing and painting are in some ways strikingly similar.

MOMADAY Well, there are also some apparent similarities which fascinate me. I like the idea that literature may have proceeded from cave painting. I think that is a very valid notion. That's something that I came upon not too long ago, and I think it's true. Painting and drawing and writing are in some respects the same thing—at least in the sense that writing is incising. And cave paintings, like literature, are expressions of perceptions of the world. In those respects, the two things are the same.

CLW Writing and painting. But from what you've said about your spontaneous painting process, your paintings must be quite different from incisions. You don't incise your perceptions the way those cave painters did, do you?

MOMADAY For the most part I do not. But perhaps I do at times. And perhaps my painting is a progression from those origins. In general, I think that writing and painting are probably almost the same thing in some respects, or they are closer together than we are willing to admit. They merge like railroad tracks in the distance.

CLW In *Forms of Discovery*, Yvor Winters makes the following statement about the rodent of your poem "Buteo Regalis": "His frailty is discrete; that is, considered separately in the defensive turn. It is the abstract movement of the abstract rodent which we might get in a line drawing of two or three strokes."[17] I was struck by that statement about the abstract quality of the poem. Is there a quality of abstraction in some of your poetry which is also present in some of your drawings and paintings?

MOMADAY Absolutely. Yes. I just did a painting of a coyote which is abstract in the way that Winters says the rodent in the poem is abstract. Just a few strokes, but the coyote is there. The essential coyote and his essential motion.[18] I like Winters's statement very much. I think it's very perceptive. That's what I try to get into a good many of my poems—that abstract yet essential quality—and it certainly is something I try to get into my paintings as well.

CLW Winters uses the word "essential," too. He also says that in your poem "The Bear," you present "the essential wilderness."[19] Is that what you're doing in your paintings? Presenting essences?

MOMADAY That is something I would certainly like to do. I may not have accomplished that as yet, but it is certainly an ambition of mine. I want the things themselves to emerge. I want to paint those things, and I want to name them in my writing.

CLW Calligraphy is increasingly important to you. Why?

N. Scott Momaday hand coloring his etching *1849* (Courtesy of the Sun Valley Center for the Arts and Humanities, Sun Valley, Idaho)

MOMADAY Well, writing is also a kind of drawing, as I've suggested. So I like the idea of words on the picture plane. I have to do more about that. Sometimes I like to write the title of the picture so that it becomes a part of the picture. When I did those etchings of shields with calligraphy over them, that seemed to me a wonderful merger of two drawing techniques, and very valid. I think that combination is exciting.

CLW What is the effect of words on the picture plane?

MOMADAY I don't know clearly what the effect is. I wonder sometimes how other people think of it. To me, the writing on the picture is another dimension of drawing, and I don't care about the words as words. That is, you could write nonsense on the plane and it would be a good effect, I think. I'm not looking at the calligraphy as meaning in the sense that we write to construct meanings. I think of it, rather, as some aspect of the overall drawing. But an interesting departure from the ordinary image.

CLW What about process in your painting? Do you ever plan the process and calculate the effect? Do you picture the images you want to create before you begin to paint, and then plan the creation of those images?

MOMADAY I have not determined what a painting will be when I begin. It becomes in the process. It is not the photograph of something. It's a process of building and creation.

CLW So in that respect, too, it's different from how you write?

MOMADAY I don't know if it's so different. The writing, too, seems to happen in the process. It is more apparently planned, but its vital particulars, especially its images, evolve from within. You start with something and it grows, and you don't always know how it grows or how it's going to turn out.

CLW Kenneth Lincoln suggests that your art is at times based on what he calls "an organic premise." The premise, he says, is "that art, less than made, is revealed in things."[20]

MOMADAY Sounds good, but what does "organic premise" mean?

CLW Well, I suppose it means that the art grows from the inside out. That it's not a construction so much as an emergence. That's what you're saying about it?

MOMADAY Yes. I very much like the idea of emergence. The idea that the work becomes itself naturally as the process unfolds.

CLW Is that true of your painting even when you paint such things as

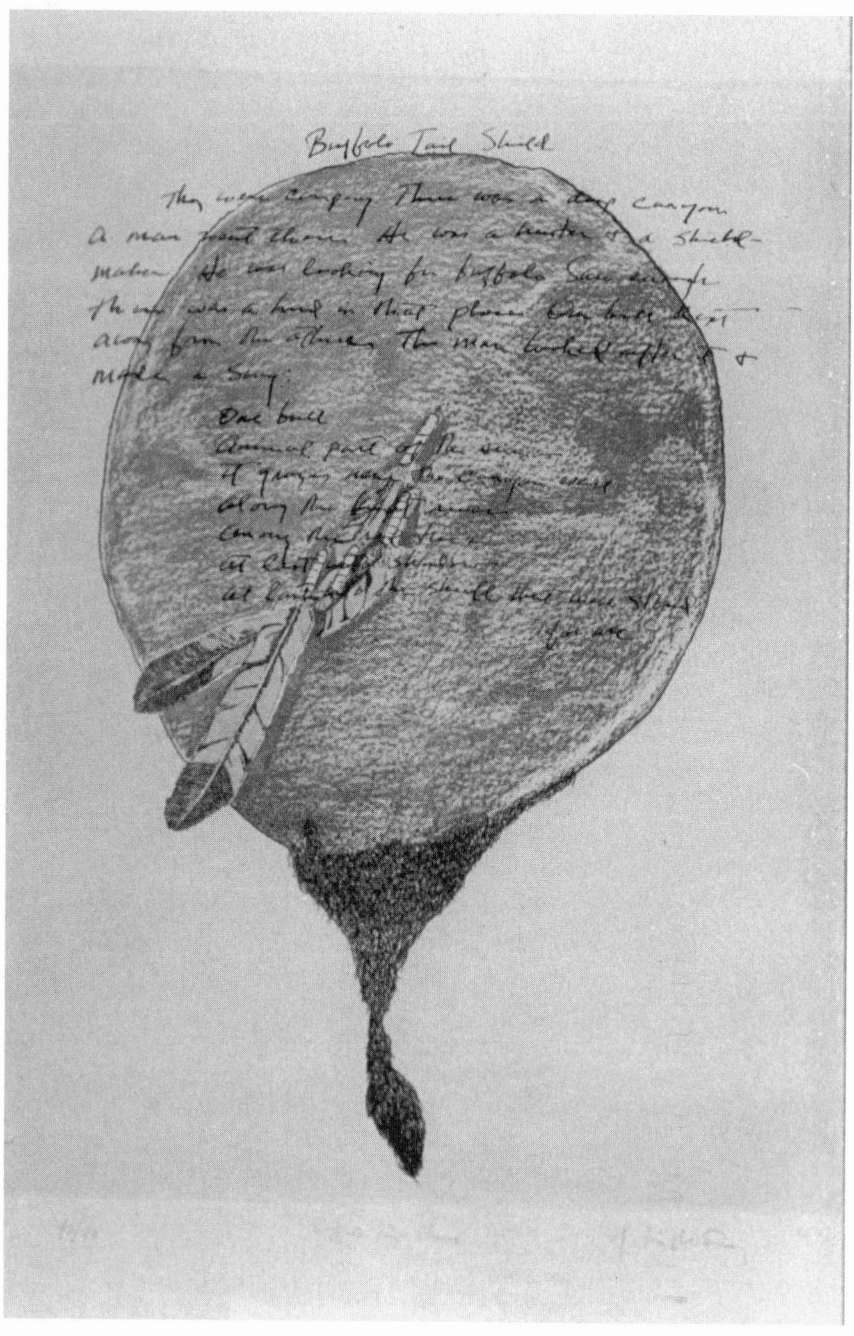

Buffalo Tail Shield, 1978, etching, 23 inches x 30 inches

shields or dolls? Works for which you have visual models? Even then, the painting takes its own shape as the process unfolds?

MOMADAY Both writing and painting work that way. You can look at something and paint it. There are, of course, painters who depict things precisely. Realistically. You look at their paintings and you look at the objects from which they were painted and there appears to be little difference. Sometimes those paintings and their objects are almost identical. But that's not the way I paint. I look at an object and start describing it in an image, and the painting and the object are at last not necessarily very close together. What happens is that in the painting, you develop an idea of the object. That idea is very real. Perhaps it's not the reality that one perceives by looking at the object. But nonetheless, it is an interpretation—a representation of the object that has its own reality. That's the kind of painting that I do most often.

CLW Are you ever surprised by what you write?

MOMADAY Surprised? Yes, I'm sometimes surprised by what I write. I think that most everyone is. Often, when you write something down, you express a part of your intelligence that you're not aware of, and sometimes perhaps you don't recognize what you've written at once. When you come back to something that you've written after a while, it may appear to you in a way that you could not have imagined, and you are surprised by it. Yes. That happens to me a lot.

CLW Are you also surprised by what you paint?

MOMADAY Yes. Oh, yes. In the same way.

CLW Are there more surprises in painting than in writing?

MOMADAY Probably not. Not that I'm aware of. They seem to be equal in that regard. But I can look at a painting as I can look at a page of writing and be completely surprised by what I see there. Sometimes time creates that effect. Recently I looked at a painting which I hadn't seen for a while, and it was not what I remembered it as being. It exceeded my memory in certain respects. I saw something in it that surprised me. Something that would be difficult to describe.

CLW You work in a variety of ways—with watercolors, acrylics, oils, pen and ink. Why such diversity?

MOMADAY Well, I want to learn how to handle various media. I'm interested in many kinds of painting. When I started out, I drew. I think maybe I have always been in love with drawing. From childhood, I scribbled and played with pencils, but about twelve years ago I got very much interested in learning more about drawing, and so I began working with pen and ink. Then I worked with graphite. I've always liked black on white. I prefer black-and-white photography to color photography. And I still like to draw with ink, and brush it around on the paper. I love to make lines with pencil or graphite sticks and then dip a brush in turpentine and move the graphite around. You get wonderful effects that way. So, I've kept that up, but from there I went to acrylic paint. And that's a very different medium. It's opaque, for one thing. I had never worked with paint, really, and I experimented a lot with acrylics on canvas and on paper. I don't know to what extent I've really become comfortable with acrylic paint, but I like it. I like it for its water base—it dries quickly, and you can work quickly. The opacity of it is also interesting. You can get very nearly the same effects you can get with oil.

CLW How about oils and watercolors?

MOMADAY I haven't really done much work with oils. But about two or three years ago, I started working with watercolors. I must say that I had a great bias against watercolors. My father was a watercolorist, and his technique was very precise. There was a great deal of draftsmanship in his work. And he was very good at what he did. But I don't have that same dedication to exactitude and precision in my drawing, and so I was very wary of watercolor painting. Then I started working with it, and got hooked on it. It is far and away at this stage my favorite medium. I just love working with watercolors. I like their transparency and spontaneity. I like to do things quickly, and it seems to me that my sense of spontaneity is just right for watercolor painting.

CLW Which colors do you favor?

MOMADAY I like blues a great deal. I think if I had to pick one color, I would pick blue. But I also like earth colors—yellows and ochers and dark greens. Oh, I think in my paintings one is apt to find almost any color. Maybe blue above the others, but otherwise pretty much a full range.

CLW Are there dominant Kiowa colors?

MOMADAY In certain motifs there are dominant colors. The sun dance colors, for example. One thinks of black and red and yellow, especially.

CLW You also mentioned an enthusiasm for black and white. Why do you like that combination?

Buffalo with Magpie, 1987, ink, 11 inches x 14 inches

MOMADAY There's a stark quality to black and white. If you want to make a more nearly absolute comment, black and white is better. Black and white creates a more fundamental image.

CLW What are the connections between what you're doing and traditional Indian painting? You're using traditional materials like shields and dolls as subject matter. But are there also stylistic affinities?

MOMADAY Well, my work probably fits into a continuum of American Indian expression which begins with ledger-book drawings and hide paintings and comes up through a traceable line to the present. I think I can be fitted into that evolution, although I don't believe that such placement says what my art is, particularly. But yes, I see similarities. My father was a traditional Indian artist, and his themes were Indian. He drew and painted peyote figures and buffalo hunters and did various kinds of mystical paintings. I think he comes directly out of the Kiowa artistic traditions which preceded him, and in some ways, especially with regard to subject matter, I follow in his tracks. So there's a continuum.

CLW You've said that he was more precise in his work than you are in yours. Are there other differences between what he did and what you're doing?

MOMADAY Well, although he used watercolors a great deal, his paintings were opaque. He wasn't concerned with watercolor transparency, as I am. That's a principal difference. And his subject matter was almost exclusively Indian. Whereas I've been going all over the place. A lot of my stuff is Indian, but a lot of it isn't.

CLW Are there Indian painters other than your father whose work you greatly admire?

MOMADAY There are many. I most admire those whose primary concerns are proportion, design, and symmetry. When I lived at Jemez Pueblo, for example, I came to understand that the people of the pueblo determined the motion of their lives with a solar calendar. I mentioned that in *House Made of Dawn*.[21] They understood the intricate patterns of the universe. In the Indian world, an understanding of order is paramount, and that understanding is reflected in the proportion and symmetry of the works of many Indian painters whose work I admire.

CLW What part does motion play in your painting? Is there movement in the things you do?

Momaday : culture offers
survival
↓
Anaya : culture offers
existence

CIS : culture offers
epiphany
(assimilation + ?
identity ?)

see 51

MOMADAY Motion is not one of the principles of my paintings, although there are several exceptions. The leaping coyote figure that I just mentioned is absolutely full of motion. But the shields have no motion. And the portraits have no motion. My father did many paintings of dance figures full of motion, and buffalo hunt paintings that were full of motion. But I haven't done much of that yet.

CLW Will you?

MOMADAY I really don't know. I'm not interested in painting buffalo-hunt scenes, although that is, of course, a traditional Indian motif. I like painting buffalo with magpies on their humps, but there's no motion involved, and I don't feel any desire to paint the kind of motion that informs traditional plains Indian art. The motion found in the hunting scenes, for example.

CLW Why not?

MOMADAY Those scenes have become clichés in my mind. If I were to do a buffalo-hunt picture, I think I would have a hard time convincing myself that it was not a cliché. It's probably possible to paint such a scene without creating a cliché, but I would have a hard time convincing myself.

CLW How did you conceive of your Indian-angel series?

MOMADAY I think the series probably began while I was painting a series of dolls. Something came into my mind that my father had told me about his going to a Christmas celebration at Rainy Mountain Church when he was a little boy. And I tried to imagine the setting. I suppose there was a Christmas tree. There was the giving of gifts. There must have been Christian pictures and representations around, and very likely an angel at the top of a tree, and I started thinking about what these things might have signified to him when he was eight years old. Then the idea of an Indian angel came to my mind, and I thought of the very great irony in that figure of an Indian angel. It is an irony that encompasses many things in the whole history of Indian cultures. White and native spirituality, Christianity and Indian traditions, those confrontations. So I started painting Indian angels. I've done several of them now. They're figures, images, that appeal to me.

CLW You value silences in your writings. You talk about the creative juxtapositions of sound and silence. Do you employ equivalents of those as you paint?

MOMADAY I don't think I have yet come to that in a painting. If I were doing

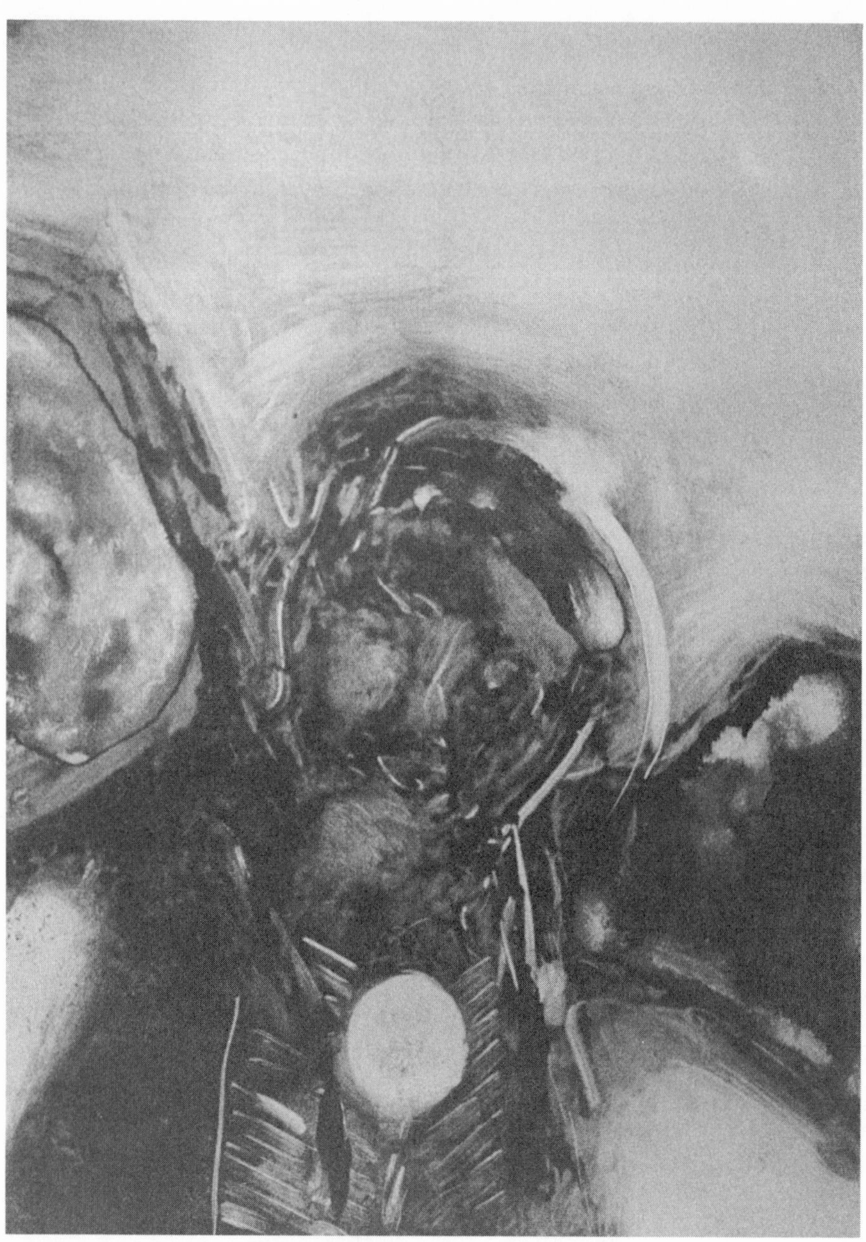

Indian Angel, 1987, monoprint, black and white with a trace of red, 23 inches x 30 inches

landscapes, there would be a greater possibility for it, in my opinion. A greater necessity for it. But in painting immediate objects, as I have most of the time so far, I have not yet begun to incorporate the kind of space, the kind of isolation, the kind of silence, which can be found in my writing. But I believe that I will at some point.

CLW Why?

MOMADAY Because I think it is so important. The idea of isolation and silence and space is very important to me, and I think that it will show up in my paintings sooner or later.

CLW Kenneth Lincoln also says this: "Momaday's position in *The Gourd Dancer*, as poet and sketch artist, seems one of waiting at the windows of reality. His own fine line drawings agitate the margins of tangible images, tentatively approaching objects, burying the outlines of things, hesitant of their thingness."[22]

MOMADAY Well, those drawings in *The Gourd Dancer* are certainly tentative—they're line drawings. They're very fast. In the case of the horse's head, for example, the pen did not come off the page until I had finished. I like to draw that way. I like to be very tentative and spontaneous in some of my drawing. In such work, I make no attempt to reflect an object in all of its dimensions. Rather, I attempt to express the essence of the dancer or the horse's head or whatever.

CLW Lincoln seems also to be saying that you're blurring the edges of things in such drawings. "Burying the outlines," he says.

MOMADAY I would agree, if that's what he's saying. I don't want to enclose the thing I'm drawing in a precise outline. Giving a thing such definition sometimes reduces it.

CLW You've frequently used the terms "integrity of vision" and "wholeness of vision" in your writing and speaking. Do either or both of those terms apply to your painting?

MOMADAY I think so. I think so. When you paint, as when you write, you want to have the whole thing in view in your mind's eye, and I suppose painting is a matter of transferring the image in the mind's eye to the picture plane. And I think of that as requiring a whole vision or an integrity of vision, just as writing something is often a matter of getting the image in the mind's eye onto the page. If you don't have the integrated image in the mind's eye, there's no possibility of getting an integrated image on the page. Either in writing or in painting.

CLW What would you say are some of your dominant "angles of vision" as a painter—to use the words you sometimes apply to your writing?

MOMADAY Well, it's most important to be involved in the sacred aspect of things. So that is one angle of vision—to see what is sacred in an object—whether it's an object that I'm describing in words on a page or one that I'm placing in paint on paper or canvas. I also like wilderness aspects, because I like wild things. I like wild country and wild women and wild dogs and wild horses. So wildness is another angle of vision. I like to perceive, if I can, what is primitive or fundamental or wild in, for example, the Kiowa leader Sitting Bear. There is in his photograph an obvious wildness in that man. To paint portraits of him without that wildness would be failure. I want to see such wildness in my painting. I want to create it. Well, I could construct a long catalog of what I think are different angles of vision, but you see what I mean.

CLW Tell me about the wild women you envision.

MOMADAY Just to give you an example, in the novel I'm writing now, the girl named Grey is very beautiful. She's an Indian girl, nineteen years old, and there is an aspect of the wilderness in her. She's a wild, wild young woman, and it is her wildness that is so irresistibly attractive. In the old woman Ko-sahn, about whom I have written several times, there is another kind of wildness.[23] It is something primitive that lies very deep in the blood. It suggests a continuum that goes back in time a long way. Her wildness proceeds from the real wilderness. I write about old women a lot. Ko-sahn is very important to me. My grandmother was important to me. But this young girl in *Set* is also important to me. The wildness I see in some people is reflected in many of my paintings.

CLW In *The Way to Rainy Mountain*, the cricket against the moon is a unique angle of vision.[24] Are you looking for such perspectives when you paint? Angles from which sudden realizations occur? Small against large? Near against far? Visual epiphanies?

MOMADAY I think so. When I paint I don't have such notions immediate in my mind, but those are things that I am looking for.

CLW Can you think of an example?

MOMADAY Well, I just did a painting of a doll's head, which is called *Rainy Mountain Christmas Doll*. It is a rather vague image, but perceptively the head of a doll or a child. The face is very white. The eyes are round, and the mouth is a little round hole. And it is decorated with ribbons and a headband, and there is color about the face. It represents to me a white child or a white man's idea of a doll, and I see it embraced by the Indian child who receives it as a gift at the Rainy Mountain Christmas giveaway. The image does not exist for its own sake. It is because of the ironic possibilities it represents that I like it. When I look at the picture, I see things that are not necessarily on the picture plane. There are meanings which are consequent to the piece. Yes, I try to get at things in that way through my paintings. The shields I paint are more examples. They are objects which are enclosed within the limits of the paper. But the meanings of the shields extend far beyond the objects which are in view. One of my deepest concerns in painting is to represent or to suggest or to embody by means of ironic relationships things that extend beyond the picture plane.

CLW Your shield painting is closely related to your writing, isn't it?

MOMADAY Very closely. I've been thinking for some years about drawing shields or painting shields to illustrate a collection of what we might call prose poems, for lack of a better term. Each a small story about a shield, and the shield itself in a painting or a drawing. I think that will be easy to do. I can compose texts of that kind fairly quickly and I can draw or paint fairly quickly, so now is the time to stop thinking about it and do it.[25]

CLW Why shields and prose poems?

MOMADAY I do both things well. Shields are fascinating to me. They are flags. Personal flags. My first show in 1979 was a collection of shield paintings. I had simply become fascinated with shields. I've seen many plains Indian shields and I've photographed them. And I've imagined a lot of them. To me they are wonderful personal expressions. They're like coats of arms, but they're more personal. They're individual and they're magic. They stand. The shield stands for its owner and he has to live up to it. It's a wonderful symbolic representation of the ideal of the self. So I want to make a book of shields. And this will be, as I say, a collection of very short stories—quintessential stories, each about a paragraph in length, each describing a particular shield and its meaning or telling its story. With each of these verbal equations, I want to draw a shield—the shield that goes with the story.

CLW Each shield will represent a different individual?

MOMADAY Yes. Each a personal story.

Rainy Mountain Christmas Doll, 1986, watercolor, 9 inches x 12 inches
(Courtesy of Karen Chamberlain, director, Aspen Writers' Conference)

CLW How are you proceeding? Are you imagining individuals in order to do that?

MOMADAY Yes. There may be two or three cases in which there is an actual man and an actual shield, but I foresee most of the shields as being mainly the products of my imagination.

CLW You create a being and then you create the shield which represents him?

MOMADAY Or vice versa. And I think of the book as being a fine-press production—brought out perhaps in a limited edition. It should be beautiful. I'm thinking of it as physically attractive.

CLW Something like *The Journey of Tai-me*, your first book?[26]

MOMADAY That's right. It's time that I did something like that again, given my interest in painting as well as writing. That is an ideal way, it seems to me, to put the two things together.

CLW You believe that words are powerful. Even magical. You believe that creative language can bring about enormous physical change. Can paintings be used in that way? Are they equally powerful?

MOMADAY I don't know that many painters work from that point of view—with that kind of power in mind. But I do. Because I do see a clear relationship between painting and writing, between painting and language. Because I see that writing is a kind of drawing, and drawing is an older and more primitive and more fundamental expression upon which writing is based somehow, and the two things are therefore very closely related. Consequently, I do believe that paintings—drawings—can be very powerful and can draw upon some sort of universal power in the way that language does. And when I think of the cave paintings, those oldest of all extant drawings, I think of them as being holy, sacred activity and full of power. I'm also very much interested in rock paintings. They are moving expressions of human concern.

CLW I've heard that Australian aborigines believe that paintings can have terrible power. That one can create and destroy with them. Some of their paintings are thought to have shamanistic power.

MOMADAY I think that power very definitely exists in some art. It's pretty obvious in certain things. Consider masks, the Eskimo masks and the northeast masks—false faces, as they're called—those things are extremely powerful and people believe in that power. They are afraid of those things. And so am I. The shamanistic element in art is very real.

CLW Are there shamanistic elements in things you've done?

MOMADAY Absolutely. In the dolls that I'm doing now, for example, those elements are very strong.

CLW What do you mean?

MOMADAY Well, some of the dolls that I have seen are intrinsically powerful. You look at them and you know that they are not playthings in the ordinary sense. They are to be respected. They are worthy of your regard, and some of them are frightening to behold. And some of them are beautiful. The frightening ones interest me most. I don't want to paint Raggedy Ann. I want to paint something that is full of power. So the images that come across in my paintings are shamanistic. Doll power.

CLW Like shields?

MOMADAY Yes. When I paint shields, I'm interested in indicating, if I can, not only the physical dimensions of the shield itself and the shield as a work of art, but also the shield as a source and repository of supernatural power. That is perhaps why I paint. Getting down such images is very inspiring.

CLW These dolls that you're painting are versions of dolls that you've seen?

MOMADAY Some of them are, and others I've just made up. Even to call them dolls is perhaps misleading.

CLW What do you call them?

MOMADAY Dolls. [Laughing.] But one might call them shamanistic images, or something like that.

CLW In dealing with such images, are there any taboos? Or any restrictions?

MOMADAY I don't know. I'm sure there must be. Well of course, of course, what am I thinking of? The *Tai-me*, the sacred totem of Kiowa culture, is a doll, and there are a great many taboos attached to that. And there must be many other such things. Many of those come under the classification of fetishes. And although lots of them can be photographed or painted, I'm sure that there are others like the Tai-me which are not to be represented in that way. But the dolls that I'm working with are based upon actual dolls which are not fetishes, and so I don't feel any restraints.

CLW What are their origins? These dolls that you're working on?

MOMADAY The catalog that I've used as a model for several of my paintings is an exhibit of dolls from all over South America and Central America and North America.[27] Some of them are playthings, some of them are power dolls, and some of them are masks. They're very interesting.

CLW Were there, to your knowledge, any imagistic restrictions in traditional Kiowa culture besides restrictions in regard to the Tai-me? Things that weren't represented pictorially? Could not be?

MOMADAY Well, there were other medicine bundles. There were other things like the Tai-me which I'm sure one could not open. The contents of those things were pretty much secret and protected. They were available to view only on very special occasions. My father has told me of things like that. Secret Kiowa societies like the Ka-itsenko Society had many secret activities, and perhaps they had totems or fetishes or objects that were not to be looked upon by people outside the societies.[28] But specifically I don't know of anything beyond that.

CLW Were the Kiowas as apprehensive about photography as were some other cultures?

MOMADAY Not to my knowledge. I think they were more willing to be photographed than some other tribes, but I can't really be sure of that. I know that there are a lot of photographs of Kiowas. Nineteenth-century photographs by Soule and other people.[29] One of my kinsmen who was quite an accomplished photographer had a wonderful archive of Kiowa photographs, including some fairly old ones. And there were no restrictions that I know of.

CLW We've talked about the sense of play in your writing. How is it manifested in your painting and drawing?

MOMADAY In various ways. For example, I've done a painting of a woman who is seated in a blue chair.[30] She is someone I saw sitting at a bus stop in Switzerland. She has orange hair. She's very plump, and she's sitting in a condition of repose. In her midsection I have drawn a face. It is unmistakably a human face about the size of her abdomen. And it's a joke. It's a play with images. Another example is a painting called *Marriage at Huerfano.* It is a large acrylic painting of two people who are virtually one figure. A woman and a man. And the man is very austere and he's looking down. His bride is a woman with a very

Marriage at Huerfano, 1985, etching, 23 inches x 30 inches

large nose, and her head is tilted up, as if she's looking into the sky. There's something very funny about the conjunction of the two figures, and it is, as I think of it, a wonderful idea of the marriage itself. A melding of the figures. There is a foot in the painting, and you cannot say to which figure it belongs. So it's a humorous rendering of marriage itself, it seems to me, but accurate as well as humorous. I like to do things like that in my paintings, and I think I could probably give you a number of other examples.

CLW There's also a considerable amount of playfulness in some of your quick sketches.

MOMADAY Yes. Many of those are the consequence of playful impulses. Mischievous images appear.

CLW Why haven't you painted landscapes? There are dramatic landscapes in your writings. Descriptions which are very visual—prose paintings.

MOMADAY That's true, isn't it? And I don't suppose that I have a good and ready answer to your question. Maybe the answer is that landscape is not generally the information of Indian painting. And I think that my painting, more than my writing, derives in certain ways from Indian traditions. My father did not paint landscapes. Very few Indian artists paint landscapes, although there are some obvious exceptions. But describing landscapes in words comes quite naturally to me. I love to do that, and landscape descriptions inform much of my writing. Yet not my painting. It's an interesting question, and I'm not confident that I know the answer to it.

CLW Perhaps it does have something to do with tradition. There's no Kiowa writing tradition out of which to proceed. But there is a painting tradition, one which does not include the depiction of landscapes.

MOMADAY Yes. Another consideration is that when I describe a landscape in writing, I can be extremely precise. I can describe it in great detail. I don't think you can paint a landscape in the same detail. What you can do is what I do. You can take a detail in the landscape and define it as a precise image, or an image more or less precise. But that's a different thing, after all.

CLW Could you give me an example of such a detail?

MOMADAY Well, consider that mountain out there. With words, I can make that mountain extremely definite. But if I were to paint it, it would be vague. I could not get the same precision into the painting, but I could paint a tree or a rock on the mountainside with great precision. So there is an intrinsic distinction between painting with words and painting with pigments. If you look closely at most landscape paintings, the precision in them is illusion. What you really have are vague representations which from a given point of view seem to be precise. If you come close enough to them, you see that they aren't. Whereas with a paragraph of description, you can come almost as close as you want and be almost absolutely precise.

CLW In describing landscapes, you speak sometimes of the quality of light on them. Does that quality influence your painting?

MOMADAY Yes. I'm always conscious of special light. One of the things I like about watercolor is that it reflects light in a way that no other paint does. Well, it doesn't reflect light so much as it absorbs it. I learned a lot about light when I was beginning to work with watercolors. I was amazed to see what happened when you held such a painting up against the light. The painting itself was full of light. You see that with watercolors, but you don't with oils or acrylics or other color that I know of.

CLW Have your widely varied landscape experiences—all the places you've been—informed you in certain ways about light?

MOMADAY I think so. Yes. I think I have that kind of eye. I'm conscious of the effects of light upon landscape. I've been in a good many different landscapes, and I think I've always been aware of the light, consciously or subconsciously.

CLW Can you recall any particularly dramatic lighted environment?

MOMADAY Well, the greatest light upon landscape that I know of is in the Southwest. I have never seen light such as one sees in northern New Mexico anywhere else. It is purely distinctive. Georgia O'Keeffe knew that and talked about it. It's just a remarkable light. And I've seen wondrous light in Russia. I've been in Soviet central Asia, where in the foothills of the Himalayas there is wonderful light. I've also been in the Virgin Islands, where there is another kind of light, and in the Arctic, where there is yet another kind of light. So all of these are interesting to me. But if I'm thinking of painting, and I want the most wonderful light, I will probably point to San Cristobal, New Mexico, or Galisteo, or Taos, or Tres Piedras. Light that you cannot imagine!

CLW Do you go to those places regularly?

MOMADAY More or less regularly. Yes. I just came up from Taos and Tres Piedras. I love to get into that northern New Mexico country. Arizona, too. Monument Valley has wonderful light and space. Maybe space that has not its like anywhere.

CLW Do such places still surprise you?

MOMADAY Oh yes. They always seem fresh to me. I've been in Santa Fe thousands of times. I used to live there, so it ought to be known to me. But the mornings still surprise me. It is wonderful to wake up there and to observe the light filtering down through the leaves of trees. That surprises me every time. You're not expecting it, and you open a door and there is this crystalline quality to the air. It is wonderful. I have written a good deal about New Mexican mornings, and they are probably even better than I can say.

CLW Do you get homesick for that environment?

MOMADAY Very much. I miss it, and I have to get into that landscape periodically just to restore myself.

CLW You've mentioned doing portraits of Sitting Bear, Set-anyga. Why does he interest you so?

MOMADAY Well, he was Kiowa, and he was one of the most interesting of historical figures. He was the leader of the Ka-itsenko Society, and he was the man who recovered the bones of his son and carried them around. And of course, he foretold his death in a fascinating way and then brought it about.

CLW He attacked with a knife and then his guard shot him.

MOMADAY Yes. So he fascinates me. And Soule's photograph of him is wonderful. He's an old man at the time it's taken, and he's looking full face into the camera. He is wearing strange garb. It looks like maybe a buffalo robe off one shoulder, and there's a bandolier across his chest. One eye pierces the camera, and the other is like a slit. Anyway, it's a wonderful photograph, and I've painted four or five likenesses from it.

CLW In creating such images, are you looking to discover the people behind them the way you discovered the old woman Ko-sahn when you were writing about her? Hoping that those people you are painting will in some sense emerge from the page?

MOMADAY Yes. Although I don't think that is as highly developed in my painting yet as it is in my writing. But yes, it's the same thing. I hope that in the process, my subjects will reveal themselves. Emerge. Yes.

Set-anyga, 1984, watercolor, 11 inches x 14 inches

CLW You've said that living in Russia was a very good thing for your writing and your painting. Why do you think that was?

MOMADAY I think that the isolation had something to do with it. When I went to Russia, I really did not know what to expect. Literally. Nobody had told me what I was going to be doing there, for one thing. I knew that I was to teach American literature. But that's a very vague assignment and I didn't know what my schedule was going to be like, and I didn't know what my living conditions were going to be. But it turned out well. I had a very agreeable teaching schedule. I taught one course, which met once a week, so I had a lot of time, and my living conditions were very comfortable. One of the effects of having so much time was the sense of isolation. The sense of being very far from my native land. So there grew up in me in Russia a loneliness such as I have not known at other times or places in my life. And that turned out to be creative. I wrote. And I began to draw in a way that I had not done before. And something clicked. I just kept drawing. And it has blossomed into a larger thing. Russia was stimulating for me. But it would be hard to say exactly how. I think my sense of being emerged, because I was so very far away from my familiar world. There is a loneliness in such isolation that sparks creativity.

CLW You admire Georgia O'Keeffe a great deal and have written about her several times. Is your work similar to hers in any ways?

MOMADAY Not really. Certainly there are a few similarities, but I don't think that they're very important. I think of Georgia O'Keeffe as being a landscape painter. Obviously, she did things other than landscapes. But what I like best in her work is the evocation of the landscape of the southwestern canyon country.

CLW In "Forms of the Earth at Abiquiu," a poem you dedicated to O'Keeffe, you spoke of her beautiful objects. You described them as "clean and precise in their beauty, like bone."[31] That strikes me as something that you emphasize a great deal in your writing. I think, for instance, of the old man in "The Colors of Night," who transported the beautiful polished bones of his son.[32]

MOMADAY Yes!

CLW There are other such clean particulars throughout your writing. Descriptions with images similar to the objects painted by O'Keeffe.

MOMADAY There are those similarities, now that you mention it. In the poem you mentioned, I was commenting particularly upon the objects in her home. She loved stones and rocks. She had window boxes full of polished stones. And she had skulls of cows and sheep around, and even the skeleton of a snake in her living room. So that's what I had in mind when I said "clean and precise like bone." Certainly I strive for that kind of purity in my writing, and I suppose one could say that I strive for it in my painting too. I hadn't thought of that as a connection, but it may well be there. Maybe O'Keeffe's work and mine are closer than I realized.

CLW In *Set*, you are writing about a man who is an artist, a painter. Is that solely for the purposes of the novel, or are you thinking more of yourself as a painter these days?

MOMADAY I'm thinking of myself more in those terms, because I'm becoming more active in art. I've been gathering momentum over some years, and I've developed my art in certain ways, so it's becoming a larger part of my life.

CLW How has your art evolved?

MOMADAY Well, I think moving from one medium to another indicates progression and growth. I started out drawing, and still like to draw, but I think when I went from drawing to painting, that was a growing toward something. Each step of the way, I have become more confident. I have become more successful too. I'm becoming known for my paintings as well as for my writings, and I see that as progress. I think that my talents are becoming steadily more nearly equal. I have a long way to go, and I get some resistance. There are people who don't want to believe that I can paint, because they have already accepted me as a writer, and there is in human nature, I think, a tendency to resist new definitions. I have a friend in Germany who came to an opening of my work at Heidelberg. After we had looked at the paintings, she said, "Scott, I like your paintings. They're very nice. But you are a great writer and you're wasting your time." [Laughing.] And I'm sure that that's not an uncommon reaction.

CLW And a deflating experience for you?

MOMADAY How do you take a compliment like that?

CLW How did you take it?

MOMADAY I coughed, as I remember it. And changed the subject. [Laughing.]

But that's getting away from your question. I see a steady progression from the time I began painting about twelve years ago to where I am now with watercolor, and it seems to me that I've gained a great deal of confidence along the way. I really have invested myself in my painting, and I enjoy it very much. I have high hopes for it.

And Infinity

In the story of the arrowmaker, Momaday's favorite story, the arrowmaker reacts to the possible danger on the outside of his tipi by first speaking reassuringly to his wife, and then by significant action:

He took up an arrow and straightened it in his teeth; then, as it was right for him to do, he drew it to the bow and took aim, first in this direction and then in that.

Then he speaks again, naturally, conversationally. But he speaks to reveal his enemy, and receiving no response, he releases the arrow he is pointing and saves himself and his wife.

The key to the arrowmaker's survival is appropriate behavior. He positions himself to destroy his enemy by acting "as it was right for him to do," and he discovers his enemy by using the right words. He is a man who understands himself and who therefore understands how he should behave. He understands exactly what is appropriate.

The idea of the appropriate is central to Momaday's philosophy of life. In many ways, it is a summary of his worldview. In an essay entitled "Singing about the Beauty of the Earth," he says,

To know, instinctively or otherwise, that which is truly appropriate, fitting, worthy, and to act and react accordingly, that is to exist in the full realization of our humanity.[1]

As his statement suggests, right action is not necessarily a matter of societal etiquette, or of conforming to formally established rules and regulations. In another essay, "Graduation Brings Memories," there is this anecdote:

A couple of years ago, when I was the commencement speaker at a college in California, one of the graduates broke from the ranks, so to speak, went out of her way to greet me and shake my hand there on the stage in front of hundreds of people and in clear violation of rules and rehearsals. It was a beautiful, spontaneous, and altogether human gesture, and I shan't forget it.[2]

Here is important difference between spirit and letter. The young woman of this story knew "instinctively" what was appropriate, and she acted on that knowledge.

The contrast between appropriate and inappropriate attitudes and behavior appears throughout Momaday's work. It is, for example, central to *House Made of Dawn*. Father Olguin, the priest of the village, is alienated from the realities of his environment at the beginning of the narrative by his peculiarly limited theology and by his white arrogance and pride. His insensitivity is dramatized by his enthusiasm for the journal of his predecessor, Fray Nicholas. The journal reveals the old priest as almost incredibly selfish and self-serving, yet Olguin believes that in the journal he has discovered a model for his own behavior:

Father Olguin was consoled now that he had seen to the saint's heart. This was what he had been waiting for, a particular glimpse of his own ghost, a small, innocuous ecstasy. He was troubled, too, of course; he had that obligation. But he had been made the gift, as it were, of another man's sanctity, and it would accommodate him very well. He replaced the letter and closed the book. He could sleep now, and tomorrow he would become a figure, an example in the town. In among them, he would provide the townspeople with an order of industry and repose. He closed his good eye; the other was cracked open and dull in the yellow light; the ball was hard and opaque, like a lump of frozen marrow in the bone.[3]

The inappropriateness of Olguin's attitude is, of course, summarized in the terrible image of the blind eye, with the concluding reference to deadened life, the "lump of frozen marrow in the bone."

At the end of the narrative, Olguin feels that he has, after considerable turmoil through the years, "come to terms with the town." He is proud of his accomplishments and confident that he has at last achieved an almost total understanding of his circumstances. But then Abel comes to him in the predawn darkness to announce the death of his grandfather:

> *"What in God's name—?" he said.*
>
> *"My grandfather is dead," Abel said. "You must bury him."*
>
> *"Dead? Oh . . . yes—yes, of course. But,* good heavens, *couldn't you have waited until—"*
>
> *"My grandfather is dead," Abel repeated. His voice was low and even. There was no emotion, nothing.*
>
> *"Yes. Yes. I heard you," said the priest, rubbing his good eye. "Good Lord, what time is it, anyway? Do you know what* time *it is? I can understand how you must feel, but—"*
>
> *But Abel was gone. Father Olguin shivered with cold and peered out into the darkness. "I can understand," he said. "I understand, do you hear?" And he began to shout, "I understand!* Oh God! I understand—I understand!*"*[4]

But of course he does not. Blinded by his ethnocentric clock-time conditioning, Olguin does not understand at all. The opportunity to behave appropriately, feelingly, has again been lost.

In dramatic contrast to that is Abel's rediscovery of his native sense of the appropriate through the experience of his grandfather's death. After years of inappropriate behavior precipitated by the disorienting experience of war, Abel finds his way back through the spiritual legacy of his grandfather. In the end he is running sacrificially in the dawn, investing himself in the natural world to become one with it, as it is right for him to do.

In his essay entitled "A First American Views His Land," Momaday summarizes this matter of appropriate relationships that is so central to his thinking:

> *One afternoon an old Kiowa woman talked to me, telling me of the place in Oklahoma in which she had lived for a hundred years. It was the place in which my grandparents, too, lived; and it is the place where I was born. And she told me of a time even further back, when the Kiowas came down from the north and centered their culture in the red earth of the southern plains. She told wonderful stories, and as I listened, I began to feel more and more sure*

that her voice proceeded from the land itself. I asked her many things concerning the Kiowas, for I wanted to understand all that I could of my heritage. I told the old woman that I had come there to learn from her and from people like her, those in whom the old ways were preserved. And she said simply: "It is good that you have come here." I believe that her word "good" meant many things; for one thing it meant right, or appropriate. *And indeed it was appropriate that she should speak of the land, and an ancient perception of it, a perception that is acquired only in the course of many generations. It is this notion of the appropriate, along with that of the beautiful, that forms the Native American perspective on the land. In a sense these considerations are indivisible; Native American oral tradition is rich with songs and tales that celebrate natural beauty, the beauty of the natural world. What is more appropriate to our world than that which is beautiful?*[5]

Momaday condenses this philosophy, in his essay "I Am Alive," into "a number of equations" that he calls "the idea of the self":

You see, I am alive.
You see, I stand in good relation to the earth.
You see, I stand in good relation to the gods.
You see, I stand in good relation to all that is beautiful.
You see, I am alive, I am alive.[6]

In this sequence, being alive is both cause and effect. Because one is alive, one has these relationships, and when one lives appropriately in response to these relationships, one is most fully alive. Standing in good relationship is right action.

Finally, in "Four Notions of Love and Marriage," Momaday particularizes his philosophy of the appropriate for friends on the occasion of their wedding:

I.
Formerly I thought of you twice,
as it were.
Presently I think of you once
and for all.

2.
I wish you well:
that you are the runners of a wild vine,
that you are the roan and russet of dusk,
that you are a hawk and the hawk's shadow,
that you are grown old in love and delight,
I wish you well.

3.
Be still, lovers.
When the moon falls away westward,
there is your story in the stars.

4.
In my regalia,
in moccasins,
with gourd and eagle-feather fan,
in my regalia
imagine me;
imagine that I sing
and dance at your wedding.[7]

In the first stanza, it is now appropriate to think of the two people as one. In the second, it is appropriate also to think of the two as separate yet complementary and as both loving and delighting in their love. In the third, it is appropriate to think of the two as a part of the created world, and appropriate for them to respond to that world with a respectful attitude. In the final stanza, it is appropriate for the couple to imagine the singer of their song, appropriately dressed in ceremonial clothing and carrying ceremonial objects, appropriately commemorating in language and motion, through his full being, their sacred vows. Taken as a whole, the poem is a skillful integration of images that both celebrates an occasion and summarizes a distinctively native worldview.

CLW Years ago, when we first met, you told me that you thought of Yvor Winters as something of an absolutist and yourself as more of a relativist.[8] Do you still feel that way?

MOMADAY Hmm. I probably am not as inclined to think of myself as a relativist as I grow older. I am becoming more certain of some things. And I always admired Winters for his stance. He was a man of very strong conviction, and the absolute for him was very important, especially as it pertained to poetry. He worked this out beautifully in a short essay called "Preliminary Problems."[9] In that essay, he makes his point not only with conviction but very convincingly. He declares exactly what poetry is. He declares that it is not whatever anybody says is poetry. I believe that. He is right. His absolutism in that instance is entirely justified.

CLW So your attitudes have evolved from relativism to Winters's position?

MOMADAY Well, I'm rather surprised that I even classified myself as a relativist, because I don't think that I ever was in any real sense. I may have thought there was some place for relativity in literature. I may still think so. I'd have to sleep on that.

CLW Perhaps you said that to me back then as a cautious response to a graduate student question. [Both laughing.] But you do feel more and more inclined to declare yourself, don't you? As you mature as a writer?

MOMADAY I do. I used to be more defensive in my attitudes than I am now.

CLW The bear is emerging. [Both laughing.]

MOMADAY Yes.

CLW Tell me about your enthusiasm for J. V. Cunningham's poem "On the Calculus." I've heard you call it a masterpiece.

MOMADAY Well, it's a magnificent poem. It goes: "From almost naught to almost all I flee, / And *almost* has almost confounded me; / Zero my limit, and infinity."[10] I admire the poem very much because it's perfectly constructed. It's abstract. To me it exemplifies one of the highest uses of language. I wish I had written it. It speaks volumes and yet it's very precise. I don't know of a statement that is more precise than that one. And it's beautiful in its rhyme and construction. Its symmetry. It's a lovely poem. It and Emily Dickinson's "Farther in Summer Than the Birds" are the two examples that come readily to mind when I think of what a poem ought to be. They are exemplary poems—models. Poems to hold up to people who want to know what poetry should be.

CLW Does Cunningham's poem reflect your enthusiasm for the exact equation? For precision and symmetry?

MOMADAY That's certainly part of my appreciation of it. It is a wonderfully exact statement.

CLW How do you interpret the poem?

MOMADAY The rational statement of it is that life is a progression from here to there—from zero to infinity—and one never completely spans that distance, of course. Life is always a question of "almost," and "almost" is the thing that is confounding. "*Almost* has almost confounded me." But nonetheless, I understand that my destiny is "to run to the edge of the world and off into the darkness," as Thomas Aquinas said. The poem says the same thing. It bespeaks the infinite possibility of life. It's the knowledge of the unreachable which is inspiring to me. The unlimited potential of the universe.

CLW What does time mean to you?

MOMADAY Well, I like to say that I don't believe in time. Nabokov said that too. There's a wonderful chapter in his *Speak, Memory*, in which he begins a passage by saying, "I confess that I do not believe in time."[11] I share his disbelief in time on a certain level and in a certain way. Obviously, there is a dimension which we call time, and we live our lives according to an idea of time, but in a deeper sense, time is perhaps not relevant to our real being. That's a very complicated subject. I don't know how to get at it, exactly.

CLW Are you saying that it's not so much that you don't believe literally in time as it is that time is subordinate to a more important reality?

MOMADAY In a sense, yes. Time as we know it defines a very close dimension of our existence. We set alarm clocks and we wear wristwatches and we keep appointments according to the clock. But if you go outside that immediate dimension, you have timelessness. It behooves us, I think, to project our beings out into the dimension beyond our time. That's where the greater reality exists. In timelessness. Why confine ourselves to minutes and hours? Let's inhabit eternity. Now, I say that with the full realization that inhabiting eternity is not so easy to do, but nonetheless, it seems to me to be a worthy aspiration.

CLW How do we approach the possibility?

MOMADAY Well, in one sense we already take dimensions, or parts, or aspects of eternity and incorporate them into our daily lives. There is some-

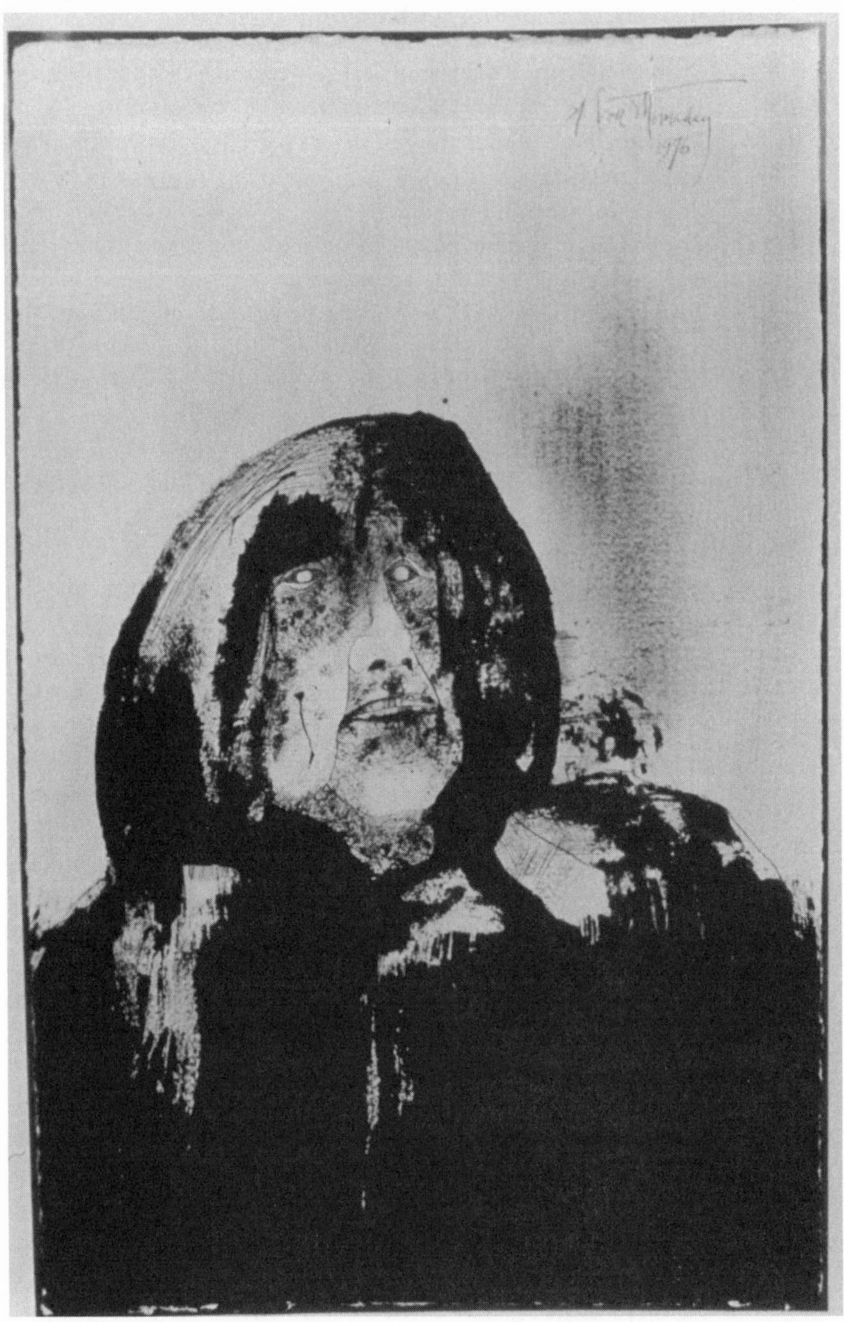

Cristobal, 1976, ink, 23 inches x 30 inches

thing eternal about stories. As I suggested earlier, I think the story of the arrowmaker exists outside our ordinary dimension of time. It's in some other dimension, and that's one of its best features. The arrowmaker is timeless. He's not born, he does not grow old, he does not die. He's there. He's there. He has perpetual being. He is somewhere in the dimension that is timeless.

CLW As are Keats's urn figures.[12]

MOMADAY Yes. That's what makes storytelling—mythmaking—so interesting. Through storytelling, we can project ourselves outside the confinement of time.

CLW What do you think is the most negative human quality?

MOMADAY Hmm. Selfishness.

CLW In *The Way to Rainy Mountain*, you say of your grandmother: "Without bitterness, and for as long as she lived, she bore a vision of deicide."[13] How do you imagine she accomplished that? Bearing a vision of deicide, without bitterness?

MOMADAY She possessed absolute dignity. And therefore, she could stand fast in the throes of chaos. She was capable of that. She was a remarkable woman. That quality of absolute dignity is a trait in the Indian world. Some of the sufferings and tragedies of American Indians stagger the imagination. One of the most impressive things to me is how they have dealt with those tragedies. How they have borne them—how they have reacted to them. They have done so with great equanimity and dignity. My grandmother lived through a time which was very hard. She lived through the ending of her way of life. That must have been a terrible thing, but she lived her life well in the face of it.

CLW Why do you suppose the migrating Kiowa were befriended by the warlike Crow people?

MOMADAY Ah. I don't know. It was a very fortunate thing. But it's not a unique story. The same thing happened when the Kiowas came into the southern plains. They were at war for a time with the Comanches, but then they became allies. Why did the Crows accept the Kiowas and teach them how to do certain things? We don't know.

CLW Yet the Crow people fought tenaciously against other intrusion.

MOMADAY Yes. The Crows and the Kiowas must have seen something in each other—a common denominator—and that caused them to see the desirability of alliance. But perhaps more than that. Perhaps friendship. Deep friendship. The Crows and the Kiowas continue even to this day to be friends beyond the ordinary.

CLW Is there something intuitive about their responses to each other?

MOMADAY I would say so. I don't understand it, but it seems so. You know, the last time I was at the Crow Agency in Montana, there was a delegation of Kiowas there playing a hand game.

CLW Are we less intuitive these days? And less intuitively responsive to each other?

MOMADAY I think as peoples we are. I'm not sure about individuals. But that intuitive strength—that tribal power—I think that would be hard to find now.

CLW Simply because the shared experiences are not as continuous? The tribal bonds are not as strong?

MOMADAY I think so. Yes. That would certainly be part of it. We do not journey together as we once did.

CLW What are your hopes for these conversations?

MOMADAY Oh, I hope that I will read them having forgotten everything that we've discussed and find that they are a fascinating probing of my intelligence. [Both laughing.]

CLW What part of yourself is a mystery to you?

MOMADAY My bear power is a mystery. And I think we all are mystified by things within us all the time. I cannot account for my actions sometimes. I surprise myself endlessly. There are many things in me which are mysterious to me and perhaps to others. That's probably how most of us feel about ourselves. I don't know. I can't get to the question the way I'd like to.

CLW What does the word *appropriate* mean to you?

MOMADAY That's an extremely important word to me. *Appropriate.* Right behavior. Something that is fitting and suitable. The ideal way to live one's life is to adhere to the appropriate. I think that's a strong concept in the Indian world. Things are done because it is appropriate to do them. What better motive can there be for behavior?

CLW How does the Indian sense of what is appropriate differ from majority-culture attitudes?

MOMADAY I think there's a great difference. When I use the word *appropriate,* I think of one of Vine Deloria's stories, in which there is a woman whose child has died. A priest comes to her thinking to console her. He tells her that the child has gone into a better state and one should not weep or feel grief, because after all, the child is in heaven. And the woman says no, it is appropriate that I should grieve. Anything else would be untrue to myself and to my child.[14] So there is that distinction, which I think is probably a very basic one. The dominant society doesn't seem as concerned about the appropriate.

CLW I think there is a contemporary tendency to reject grief, or to at least curtail it. Compress it.

MOMADAY Yes. In the modern world, there's not nearly as much interest in process as there once was.

CLW Because of the acceleration of things? The technological progression of events?

MOMADAY Probably. Probably. We live at such a rate that the question is no longer what is appropriate, but what is efficient.

CLW It would have been appropriate for me to spend a half hour eating breakfast this morning. Instead, I spent ten minutes. Our schedules compel us, don't they?

MOMADAY We are strapped to wristwatches.

CLW Do you view the modern world as an intrusion?

MOMADAY Well, there are things in the world today that interfere with my peace of mind. But the world doesn't really intrude upon my idea of myself. I don't feel threatened.

CLW As an American Indian, you favor certain accommodations to the majority culture, don't you?

MOMADAY Well, it's just that I think that the Indian has no choice in the matter. He must accommodate himself to what we call the dominant society. That is his future. By so doing, he will be able to grow and adjust to the wider world. He must do that. The question is how. How to do it without sacrificing the valuable parts of one's traditions and heritage. It's a delicate situation. A delicate matter. For example, I think the reservation system is necessary in our time. The reservations give certain societies necessary land bases, and upon those bases their whole heritages are defined. But eventually the reservations will be obsolete and outmoded—useless. One has to take a lot of questions into consideration and proceed very cautiously.

CLW You hope the reservations will be rendered obsolete?

MOMADAY There's no question. It will be a good thing when that time comes. It will be a good thing when the reservations are disposed of, because they keep the Indian isolated and imprisoned in certain respects. But it would certainly be a mistake to dissolve the reservations at this moment.

CLW What is your idea of the university? Ideally.

MOMADAY The university is the place where learning is preserved and secured and made available to the world. I've been associated with several universities, and they are fine institutions in our lives. They are good institutions. They are important to our civilization.

CLW How might they be improved?

MOMADAY In ways too numerous to mention. They could be much more responsible. Each university could be much more responsible to its community than universities tend to be, it seems to me. Some of them are getting better in terms of increasing their facilities for preserving knowledge—their scientific facilities. But in general I think *learning* is the word that should define the university, and it's easy for us to lose the central idea of the university now. Universities have become so diversified and involved in areas outside of learning itself. I'm concerned, as are a great many people, about the way in which the government, the federal government, has taken control of universities. Universities have become more and more dependent upon federal funding. That dependency is dangerous.

CLW You believe that your dreams are very powerful. Do you draw from them as you write or paint?

MOMADAY Yes. Dreams are very important to me. I believe that they are intrinsically powerful and creative. I don't dream as much as I'd like, or I don't remember my dreams as often as I'd like. But when I do dream, I try to make use of those dreams, because I think that they are priceless subject matter. They give you insights into experience that you don't get otherwise.

CLW You often say that language is "sacred." How do you define the term?

MOMADAY The sacred is a dimension of moral integrity. I don't know that I can define it quickly. Sacred is that which exists apart from the ordinary. Its existence is in one sense inviolable. The sacred is that which defines or determines the richest and deepest part of our being. It is holy. Now you ask, How do you define "holy"? Holy is that which is apart from ordinary existence, something on a higher level—a level that demands different attitudes, different conceptions, a greater and more serious attitude, a greater respect, a greater devotion. Sacred is that which is informed with spirit. The deepest spirit.

CLW And "spirit"?

MOMADAY Spirit is the best part of our lives. The highest expression of ourselves.

CLW Is the sacred eternal? Do you conceive of divinity?

MOMADAY I don't have a conception of divinity that is defined sufficiently so that I can give it to you in a sentence or two.

CLW Who is the God of whom you speak in that dramatic sequence in *The Names*? The one involving Jimmy on the road?[15]

MOMADAY Well, in that passage I'm using God in the way that Jimmy is thinking of him. I don't think his is the ordinary concept of God. Neither is mine. But when I use the term "God" there, I attribute the use to Jimmy. And what Jimmy thinks of God is not necessarily what I think of God. "God," to me, is a fairly imprecise term. When I think of God, I certainly don't see a bearded man in the sky. God and divinity for me are real, but I would not presume to define them. "Great Spirit," which is a concept that we hear a lot in connection with the Indian, is probably a more precise term than "God," as I see it. And yet I don't know exactly what "Great Spirit" means either. However, those words are more explanatory than "God," in my opinion.

CLW Why?

MOMADAY Well, I think they get closer to the reality of a supernatural agent. But I don't know. I haven't really spoken to that point in any of my writings, and I haven't really thought about it much.

CLW I think that there is a spiritual quality to what you write—a quality which is typical of your writings.

MOMADAY I hope so. But it's not a spiritual quality that I would call "God"—or even divinity.

CLW Or even "Great Spirit"?

MOMADAY Or even "Great Spirit." Even that doesn't quite say what I have in mind. I believe that spirit is something that is of a higher vitality than mere human life. I think that it is a quality that pervades the world. That is an Indian point of view. My grandfather thought that way. Spirit is everywhere. It informs all of nature. It is a higher order of vitality than we are given in ourselves. So it is incumbent upon us to share in the spirit of nature and in the spirit of the universe. Everything is alive. The mountains are alive, the sun is alive, the stars are alive, the stones are alive. That whole network of spiritual vitality is there to be entered into by us creatures.

CLW Then isn't what we're up to now in the modern world a cruelly reductive thing? Aren't we relentlessly reducing environmental possibilities?

MOMADAY Oh, yes. Absolutely.

CLW It's a spirit-killing sequence?

MOMADAY We are a spirit-killing race. Our civilization is a spirit-killing entity, in my opinion.

CLW Still, you retain a sense of optimism, don't you?

MOMADAY There is hope.

CLW What do you hope?

MOMADAY I hope that we two-leggeds will come to a better understanding of the spiritual realities of the world and the universe. I hope that before we pass away we will come to an understanding of the universe that is worthy of us. I really don't think that man is terribly important in the scheme of things. We are a highly evolved and very special species, but we cannot exist indefinitely, and I think that the universe can. Or at least it can exist far beyond us, and I find that not uncomfortable to live with. It is exciting to be Scott Momaday, alive at this time and presented with stimuli all around me. In fact, it is wonderful. But I don't delude myself into thinking that the human race is destined to outlive nature.

CLW The basis for your hope is that the world will survive us?

MOMADAY Absolutely. I think that the spirit which informs the landscape is more important than the rise of civilization. That spirit is really what matters. We certainly have the power to kill ourselves, but we do not, in my opinion, have the power to kill the universe. I find great consolation in that. I like the idea that my star sisters will be there long after I'm gone, and very likely long after any human existence on this earth.

CLW Isn't it depressing to think of no long line of descent?

MOMADAY No, I don't find that discouraging or depressing. I think that if I can meld my spirit with the spirit of the mountain, that's as much of eternity as I can know. It's enough to satisfy me. My relationship to the world is something apart from procreating my own species. Of great importance is that part of me which will survive in the mountain in a thousand years or a million years. Of much less importance is my reproducing an image of myself in flesh and blood.

Momaday at the base of Devils Tower (Photograph by Kevin Woster)

CLW You aren't concerned by the possibility that the recognition which is uniquely human will eventually be tragically lost?

MOMADAY What do you mean by "recognition"?

CLW Human understanding. Aren't you bothered by the thought that human awareness might cease? Wouldn't you prefer to believe in a long line of descent?

MOMADAY Well, I would like to think that I will be followed by people in whose veins my blood runs and who will take the same delight in life that I take now. But the spirit of which I speak will exist far beyond those beings, and that knowledge satisfies me.

CLW What is "evil"?

MOMADAY [Long pause] Evil is a negative force in the world. It is there. It has always been there. It always will be there. And it's a damn good thing it is.

CLW Why?

MOMADAY It is one of the means of maintaining a balance in the world. Without evil, life would be intolerably boring. This is just off the top of my head. That's a very deep question: What is evil? But I would say that it is a negative impulse that motivates us. We go out and deal with evil in various ways. Some of us try to ignore it. Some of us acknowledge it, and some of us confront it. It's a real part of life, I think.

CLW Do you imagine its origin or do you imagine it as preexistent in some way? In *House Made of Dawn*, you say, "Evil was."[16]

MOMADAY I think it is preexistent. I don't think of it as having an origin that one can point to, anyway. It did not come to be in the Garden of Eden. I think it's there like the concept of the appropriate. Evil is. There is evil in the world, and we are all threatened by it. If you're Ahab, you become obsessed with the idea of confronting it. If you're Billy Budd, it destroys you.

CLW You've said in a number of contexts that existence is illusory. Is evil part of the illusion?

MOMADAY I think to the extent that existence is illusory, evil is illusory, too, but you must not take that to mean that it does not exist. It is real. It simply exists behind masks. As everything does. And it must be identified according to its masks.

CLW How literally do you mean your statement that existence is an illusion? On the one hand, you say that we create our world in words. That idea is dominant in what you say. We create the world. Existence is made of words. We have a world of words. So if human consciousness dies out, and with it language, then where's the world? How can you also say that you're comforted by the fact that the universe exists beyond us?

MOMADAY Well, it exists, but not in human terms. We perceive the world through our intelligence. And so, as you say, if we cease to exist, then there is no longer that perception. But the world continues. The universe remains. The stars remain in the sky. To what purpose I don't know. Do they exist for our sake? That's a legitimate question. We think they do. At least, I suppose we think they do. But there is the other possibility that we're deluding ourselves. I think that the human species is doomed. I think that there will be a time when human beings no longer exist. I think we're threatened on many fronts and that we will, if nothing else, simply evolve out of existence. But we share with the universe just a miniscule part, a negligible part, a grain-of-sand part, of time. And there is some consolation, it seems to me, in the belief that long after we do cease to exist as a race, the planet will probably still revolve around the sun. The sun will still burn and the stars will still shine.

CLW So that part of the universe which is us is what's illusory? The universe is real?

MOMADAY Yes. Yes. I would say that. We can impose illusion upon the universe too, but that's beside the point. It is indifferent to us.

CLW But there's a reality beyond us? Beyond our imaginings, beyond our language, beyond everything that we construct verbally?

MOMADAY I think there is. The question is, what is the value of that reality? Inasmuch as we are human and we must perceive the world in human terms, that reality has no meaning for us. The reality that has meaning for us is that which we can produce by means of our own intelligence through our own perceptions.

CLW What of some traditional Native American philosophy? The idea of the purer form? The preexistent, purer form of the shadow world which exists here?

MOMADAY Well, that is a real part of the Indian way of thinking. The song of the Ka-itsenko. The sun and the moon will live forever, but Ka-itsenko must die. To me that is not a profound revelation. It seems quite obviously true. But that truth is important, and one can base his life upon it. There is the idea of the infinite on the one hand, and the human condition on the other hand. And the human condition is nothing close to infinite. Now, lots of people will disagree with me there, and say that I overlook the whole concept of religion—the idea that man is immortal. I don't want to argue the point, particularly, but it seems to me that there is a great value in making the distinction between the universe on the one hand and the human experience on the other. The whole idea is how the human can accommodate himself to that tremendous opposition of the universe. That's the whole reason for being, I think.

CLW If there is a truer essence outside human existence, then is there any possibility that the best storytelling is somehow attuned to that?

MOMADAY Hmm. I like that idea.

CLW Perhaps storytelling is even an intuitive recollection of that essence?

MOMADAY Yes. I think that you can say that all of literature is that. That is one of its functions, and maybe its essential function. By means of our imaginations, we can establish a link between us and that which is apart from us. We can bridge the gap by means of the imagination. Literature, art, is a bridge to essence.

CLW Does that reduce the artist by making him a transmitter rather than an originator?

MOMADAY No. No. That fulfills his greatest function, I think. That privilege is what ennobles him.

Tsoai, Tsoai-talee

As is typically the case with creative people, N. Scott Momaday is often mysterious, and he is still in various interesting ways mysterious to me. He is periodically mysterious to himself, as he has suggested several times in the course of our conversations. One celebrates the creative energy of such mystery, and learns from it. Therefore, whatever has been revealed through these conversations and essays, much more remains to be learned from and about this complicated man, the subject, the story, of this book.

Yet I also know more of N. Scott Momaday than I do of most other people, because of his commitment to discovering and revealing his individual and tribal identity, and because of the quality of his expressions of himself. And I know more experientially, because we have traveled together. Travel, as he has suggested in our conversations, as I have suggested, is natural to him. He is energized by it, and perhaps he is most fully himself in motion across landscapes.

Our recent, long journey together, in October of 1987, was across a particularly informative landscape: the Black Hills of South Dakota and then west-northwest along the centuries-old migration route of his Kiowa people. The landscape of much of his identity.

Of those days, I will remember especially our approaches to Tsoai, Devils Tower, in changing weather and times of day, riding, walking. Tsoai is the story place of Momaday's bear identity; and his attitude, his manner of being, becomes singular there. He is clearly concentrated on that rock. Standing back from it, he is not apart from it. His manner and the memory of his words fix him to that

Rock Tree, 1987, graphite and wash, 11 inches x 14 inches

place. One imagines, remembers, the sorrowful circumstances of the story he tells, seeing him there.

I will also remember the details of our journey west from the Black Hills, across hundreds of miles, years of migration time, perhaps, and into the Big Horn Mountains. It was an unplanned journey, and it lengthened spontaneously as we moved.

The day began under an uncertain, clouded sky, but by late morning we were traveling in snow-brightened light, a full sun against the ground cover from the day before. Shortly thereafter, we left the interstate for a narrow road rising and falling across pastured hills. There were no other cars, and only occasionally a slow-moving pickup, and fewer and fewer occupied homesteads as we moved on. Into early afternoon we drove along like that, talking, occasionally about migration possibilities, or riding along in silence, studying the distances in all directions. Here was a creek along which people might have moved, there a sheltered place to camp, and beyond that, bending away into the distance, a low place between bluffs into which grazing animals might have been driven for a kill.

Approaching midafternoon, we moved into the foothills of the mountains and began to climb, now looking ahead for signs of our final destination, changing our pace because of the lengthening light, until we were slowed again by sharp, climbing turns. Then we moved back and forth through shadows for an hour or more, ascending the eastern slopes, until the road suddenly straightened out across the top of the world.

When we reached our turnoff, an increasing wind was sweeping light snow before us. A wooden sign difficult to read indicated our direction and the three miles left for us. The road was immediately formidable—deep ruts in a mud-and-gravel surface softening with the wet, falling snow—deepening slopes on either side of the narrow way—and we proceeded very slowly.

Then suddenly there were deer, before and above us. A heavily antlered buck stood momentarily in the road, looking into the car, and smaller deer, does, stood on a high bank, looking down. We stopped, then moved slowly on, not talking.

Ahead there was a fork, and above and beyond that a large dome on what looked to be the highest ground. We turned toward the dome and moved up a long, precarious incline—a thin cut along the steep mountainside. At that height there were drifts in the road, and at a hairpin turn I stopped the car to see if we could go on. We walked around the bend into icy wind and snow, and decided to hike on to the dome—a radar station sealed tight behind warning signs. The man who finally came to the door pointed across the way, to the end of the other road, to our destination, to the medicine wheel.

As we returned to the car, an old Volkswagen bus approached, swaying through the mud and snow. We were surprised to encounter anyone else at that time and place, and again surprised to learn that the bearded young man who stepped out of it was Swiss, and also looking for the medicine wheel. He had come a great distance to find it, he said in hesitant English, because people in western Canada, Indians, had told him that it was a spiritual place. He was there on the strength of the story he had been told. He had been traveling through Canada and the Americas for several years, he said.

I have never had a better first impression. It was immediately obvious that he was an uncommonly gentle being. There was kindness in his voice and eyes. His name was Jürg.

We decided to go to the medicine wheel together, and with some difficulty we reversed the vehicles on the slightly wider hairpin turn and drove back down to the fork, Jürg following. The new road was even worse than the other—narrower, with heavier drifts on that unprotected side of the mountain—and we had to go faster to push through. The car lurched as we struck drifts.

When we reached the saddle between the radar mountain and the mountain on which the medicine wheel was located, we decided to hike the rest of the way. The medicine wheel road was steep, straight up instead of diagonal, with no visible turnoffs. Jürg had not yet appeared around the last bend, and we thought momentarily that he had decided against the last, hazardous way.

Then he was there, waving, and joined us.

The climb up was surprisingly easier than the other climb had been, and the wind seemed to have lessened. Over the last rise, centered on level ground, was the medicine wheel. I was briefly disappointed at the need for a barbed wire fence around it and a locked gate, until I noticed the pieces of cloth, prayer bundles, fastened to the wire. They fluttered in the small breeze.

The wheel, which by some accounts could be Kiowa in origin, is fashioned of stone.[1] Stone piles on the outer circle mark the main spokes, and there is a stone cairn in the center. From any point on the circle one can see indistinct distances, great sweeps of earth and sky. The only partial obstruction is the mountain on which the radar dome is built.

We were at the wheel for some time, mostly in silence. I could not have anticipated Jürg's silence. His calm manner. He must have been very curious and thought of many questions, having come so far to this place. But he was quiet, deferential, and never between us and the stones.

Later, on the way down the slope, and over tea Jürg brewed for us on a camp stove behind his bus, we told him what we knew of the place, and why we were there. As we sat drinking tea, the setting sun suddenly reappeared. It was the peculiar reappearance of late, golden light on a storm-clouded day.

Then we presented Jürg with a gift, and told him good-bye. It was an unusually congenial parting, considering the brief time we had been together. And we were sorry to see him go. Then we were gone, too, in the other direction, riding in silence down the mountain, into darkness, the deer again everywhere on both sides of the road.[2]

The next morning, Momaday and I had this conversation about the experience:

CLW — How are you informed by the Wyoming landscape we traversed yesterday? By our journey from Devils Tower to the Big Horn Mountains?

MOMADAY — That landscape represents to me, in the best sense, the cultural memory of the migration of the Kiowas. I look at it and I wonder who before me in my own line of descent has looked upon it. And what did it mean to that person. That is a very exciting thing to think about. And thinking about it in such a way is an appropriation, too. You know, I take possession of the landscape when I look at it in that way. I feel that I'm gathering it into my experience and I'm becoming richer because of it. Yesterday I was struck by what that landscape represents to me now. It is a point of contact between me and my ancestors. At the medicine wheel in the Big Horns, I was impressed by the tracks in the snow and by the little bundles that were tied to the wire. And I was struck by the difference in the air there, as opposed to the air at the radar site a little higher up.

CLW What was the difference?

MOMADAY At the medicine wheel, the air was warmer. And much more serene. There was no anger in the air at that wheel, as there was at the radar dome. It was a remarkable difference. [Pause.] And the vistas. Particularly to the north and west. Wonderful vistas.

CLW What of the many deer we saw? There were unusual numbers of deer moving about, even for that time and place.

MOMADAY I'm sure that they were there for a reason. They were there because we were. It was a meeting of some kind. That struck me most as we turned off the highway to drive up to the wheel. There was that very large buck with great antlers crossing the road, and then as we approached, others became visible, and three or four were standing on the embankment above us looking down. Standing still. That was a very strange and powerful thing to me. I felt that I was coming into the presence of something. It was very special.

CLW What will you remember of the young Swiss man we met there?

MOMADAY I will have very good memories of him. I mentioned him to Reina on the phone. He was a very congenial young man who I grew to like very quickly. He was so gracious to us and I think we responded in kind, and it was a good thing that he was there. I count our meeting him as good fortune.

CLW I was struck by how instinctively appropriate his behavior was. He didn't have our cultural or even geographic frame of reference. But he mostly said and did the right things. Did you notice that about him?

MOMADAY Yes. Of course. He was a very gracious human being.

At this point, Momaday paused, smiling. Then he spoke again.

MOMADAY And of course, Saynday was there.

CLW He was, wasn't he?

MOMADAY Yes. I think he heard the eagle-bone whistle and he knew I was there. It was a good thing.

CLW He chose to make his presence known?

MOMADAY Oh, beyond any shadow of a doubt. Of course, he kept to the edge of vision.[3] [Both laughing.]

Then I thought again of our walk down the shadow side of the medicine wheel mountain, the three of us, side by side. I had been watching my footing until Momaday spoke, pointing.

There beneath us, near the bottom of the opposite slope, was a coyote, seeming almost to drift in that curious sideways trot of his kind, head down, going along. We stood in silence as he passed from light into his own shadows, and was gone.

Notes

INTRODUCTION

1 Momaday often uses this phrase in discussing one of his Kiowa legends, "The Story of the Arrowmaker," and he used it as the title of his March 1970 assembly presentation at Princeton University. That presentation was published in Rubert Costo, ed., *Indian Voices: The First Convocation of American Indian Scholars* (San Francisco: Indian Historian Press, 1970), pp. 49–84.

2 For example, in a recent interview with Joseph Bruchac, Momaday said: "In a sense, I'm not concerned to change my subject from book to book. Rather, I'm concerned to keep the story going. I mean to keep the same subject, to carry it farther with each telling" (Joseph Bruchac, ed. and comp., *Survival This Way: Interviews with American Indian Poets* [Tucson: Sun Tracks and the University of Arizona Press, 1987], p. 187). In this excellent compilation, Bruchac and other leading contemporary Native American writers discuss many of the same questions and issues addressed in this volume. Bruchac's book also reveals the importance of Momaday's work to other Native American writers, and the affinities between Momaday and these contemporaries. For example, see Paula Gunn Allen, p. 11; Elizabeth Cook-Lynn, pp. 68–69; and James Welch, p. 319.

THE CENTER HOLDS

1 In *The Names: A Memoir*, Momaday recounts and discusses the Devils Tower story and the ceremonial presentation of his Kiowa name by the old man Pohd-lohk. See especially the introductory page and pages 55–57. These and subsequent page numbers refer to the 1976 Harper & Row edition.

2 Momaday wrote about Billy the Kid several times in his early columns for *Viva: Northern New Mexico's Sunday Magazine.* See especially "How It Began," Nov. 25, 1973, p. 2; and "Billy Offers a Kindness to an Old Man at Glorietta," Dec. 9, 1973, p. 2. See also "The Pear-Shaped Legend: A Figment of the American Imagination," *Stanford Magazine* 3, no. 1 (1975): 46–48; and "The Strange and True Story of My Life with Billy the Kid," *American West* 22, no. 5 (Sept.–Oct. 1985): 54–65. The latter volume also contains Momaday's Billy the Kid paintings.

3 N. Scott Momaday, "A Vision beyond Time and Place," *Life,* July 1971, pp. 66–67.

4 *The Way to Rainy Mountain,* p. 8. This and subsequent page numbers refer to the 1976 University of New Mexico Press edition.

5 N. Scott Momaday, "Thoughts on Jemez and Billy the Kid," *Viva,* Nov. 18, 1973, p. 2.

6 N. Scott Momaday, "He Encounters a Player at Words," *American West* 22, no. 5 (Sept. –Oct. 1985): 61.

7 See Maurice Boyd's *Kiowa Voices: Myths, Legends, and Folktales,* vol. 2 (Fort Worth: Texas Christian University Press, 1983) for the Saynday stories of Kiowa storytellers. See also Alice Marriott's *Saynday's People: The Kiowa Indians and the Stories They Told* (Lincoln: University of Nebraska Press, 1963).

8 *House Made of Dawn,* p. 84. This and subsequent page numbers refer to the 1969 Signet and 1977 Perennial paperback editions.

9 Kay Bonetti, "N. Scott Momaday Interview," the American Audio Prose Library, Inc., Columbia, Mo., Mar. 1983. The interview took place in Momaday's home in Tucson. A companion tape of readings features excerpts from *House Made of Dawn, The Names, The Gourd Dancer,* and *Set.* The tape is an excellent example of Momaday's compelling voice.

10 See especially Momaday's essay "A First American Views His Land," in the Bicentennial issue of *National Geographic Magazine* (105, no. 1 [1976]: 13–18).

11 *The Way to Rainy Mountain,* p. 3.

12 On November 14, 1987, at the Oklahoma Heritage Association's annual banquet in Oklahoma City.

INTO THE SUN

1 *The Way to Rainy Mountain*, p. 83.

2 Ibid., p. 12.

3 *The Names*, p. 142.

4 *The Way to Rainy Mountain*, p. 8.

5 In *The Way to Rainy Mountain*, Momaday says: "I came to know that country, not in the way a traveler knows the landmarks he sees in the distance, but more truly and intimately, in every season, from a thousand points of view. I know the living motion of a horse and the sound of hooves. I know what it is, on a hot day in August or September, to ride into a bank of cold, fresh rain" (p. 67).

6 Ibid., p. 60.

7 Samuel Taylor Coleridge, "The Rime of the Ancient Mariner."

8 Momaday made this comment in February of 1986 during a panel discussion on "Seeking and Confronting Self-Identity through Adversity." The discussion was part of a series entitled "Significant Literature and the Plains Experience," conducted by the South Dakota Committee on the Humanities. The interviewer was Richard Muller, SDPTV, Vermillion.

9 *The Way to Rainy Mountain*, p. 77.

10 Mildred Mayhall, *The Kiowas* 2d ed. (Norman: University of Oklahoma Press, 1971), p. 34.

11 "Wreckage" is forthcoming in a book of poems now entitled *Earth, Pray My Days*.

12 Mayhall, *The Kiowas*, p. 274. Fuller accounts are found on pp. 237–43 of Boyd's *Kiowa Voices*, vol. 2. These accounts were given to Susie Peters by Kiowa storytellers Charley Buffalo and Yellow Wolf. Another version is found in Evan Connell's *Son of the Morning Star* (New York: Harper & Row, 1985), pp. 147–48. Satank, or Set-anyga (Sitting Bear), being transported to prison in irons, began to chant his death song, freed himself, and attacked one of his guards with a knife. The other guards shot him.

13 "The Story of Satanta (White Bear)" (*Kiowa Voices*, 2:226–32) was compiled by Susie Peters from conversations with Satanta's grandson, James Auchiah, and T'owyhawlmah (Laura Dunmoe).

14 "Men must endure / Their going hence, even as their coming / hither: / Ripeness is all" (*King Lear*, act 5, sc. 2).

15 *The Way to Rainy Mountain*, p. 59.

16 Ibid., p. 39.

17 Ibid., p. 73.

18 "Headwaters" begins *The Way to Rainy Mountain.*

19 N. Scott Momaday, "Singing about the Beauty of the Earth," *Viva*, June 4, 1972, p. 2.

20 See especially Momaday's essay "A Vision beyond Time and Place," p. 67; and *The Way to Rainy Mountain*, p. 47.

WORDWALKER

1 N. Scott Momaday, "Plainview: 1," *Angle of Geese and Other Poems* (Boston: David R. Godine, 1974), p. 15.

2 N. Scott Momaday, interview with the author, Stanford University, Nov. 20, 1974.

3 *House Made of Dawn*, p. 89.

4 *The Way to Rainy Mountain*, p. 33.

5 Franciscan Fathers, *An Ethnologic Dictionary of the Navajo Language* (1910; reprint, St. Michael's, Ariz.: St. Michael's Press, 1968).

6 *House Made of Dawn*, pp. 88–89.

7 The fourth of five Crow charms in John Bierhorst, ed., and Robert Lowie, trans., *In the Trail of the Wind: American Indian Poems and Ritual Orations* (New York: Noonday, 1977), pp. 92–93.

8 This story is clearly one of Momaday's favorites. It was first published as No. 6, "Blue," in his prose poem sequence "The Colors of Night." The sequence was published in *Sequoia* 19, no. 1 (1974): 22–23; in *The Gourd Dancer* ([New York: Harper & Row, 1976], pp. 44–47); and as a separate volume, *The Colors of Night* (San Francisco: Arion, 1976). A version of "Blue" will also appear in *Set.*

9 *House Made of Dawn*, p. 29.

10 In Momaday's November 20, 1974, interview with the author, he said: "I have in mind an autobiographical narrative . . . after *The Way to Rainy Mountain*, dealing with my lifetime and people I have known—people who are contemporary. I don't want to bring that up to date. I see that as coming to an end about 1965." Momaday finished his degree work at Stanford University in 1963.

11 In "The Story of the Arrowmaker," an essay in the *New York Times Book Review* of May 4, 1969, Momaday says of the storyteller, "It must occur to us that he is one with the arrowmaker and that he has survived, by word of mouth, beyond other men" (p. 2).

12 Satanta's speech was delivered at the Medicine Lodge Council of October 19–20, 1867, on Medicine Lodge Creek in Kansas, and first published in the November 20, 1867, *New York Times*. It is included in W. C. Vanderwerth, comp., *Indian Oratory: Famous Speeches by Noted Indian Chieftains* (Norman: University of Oklahoma Press, 1971). Its title in that volume is "I Love the Land and the Buffalo and Will Not Part with It."

13 Originally published in Frances Densmore, *Teton Sioux Music* (Bureau of American Ethnology Bulletin 61, 1918), p. 394.

14 From the poem of that title.

15 Margot Astrov, *The Winged Serpent: An Anthology of American Indian Prose and Poetry* (New York: John Day, 1946). In Chapter 1, "The Power of the Word," Astrov writes: "Wherever the value of the word deteriorated, turning into a cheap weapon and an easy coin, the intrinsic meaning of silence was also lost. We, indeed, live in a period of an alarming inflation of the word, and nothing is more symptomatic of it than our aversion to silence and quietude that amounts to phobia" (p. 39).

16 In "The Dreamers," a story in *Seven Gothic Tales*, Dinesen's first book, the character of Lincoln makes this preparatory statement before telling a story: "But as to names and places, and conditions in the countries in which it all took place, and which may seem very strange to you, I will give no explanation. You must take in whatever you can, and leave the rest outside. It is not a bad thing in a tale that you understand only half of it" ([New York: Random House, 1934], p. 279).

17 Donald Hall, *The Pleasures of Poetry* (New York: Harper & Row, 1971), p. 4. Hall also refers to "the collision of words that makes the poem."

18 The buffalo story is in *The Way to Rainy Mountain*, p. 54.

19 *The Way to Rainy Mountain, p.* 46.

20 Jorge L. Borges, *Book of Sand*, trans. Norman T. Di Giovanni (New York: Dutton, 1979).

21 Chapter 51, Herman Melville's *Moby-Dick*.

22 *House Made of Dawn*, p. 25.

23 Ibid., pp. 85–91.

24 For informative speculations about the case to which Momaday may be referring, see Lawrence J. Evers, "The Killing of a New Mexican State Trooper: Ways of Telling a Historical Event," *Wicazo Sa Review* 1, no. 1 (Spring 1985): 17–25. Evers also discusses the extent to which the event in question was the source for Leslie Silko's "Tony's Story" and Simon Ortiz's "The Killing of a State Cop." Those stories appear in Kenneth Rosen, ed., *The Man to Send*

Rain Clouds: Contemporary Stories by American Indians (New York: Viking, 1974).

25 During a reading at the Aspen Writers' Conference, Aspen, Colorado, in August 1986. The poem was "The Great Fillmore Street Buffalo Drive," forthcoming in *Earth, Pray My Days.*

26 From Momaday's *Viva* column entitled "Way Down Yonder in the Pawpaw Patch," Dec. 17, 1972, p. 2.

27 Peggy Whitman Prenshaw, ed., *Conversations with Eudora Welty* (Jackson: University Press of Mississippi, 1984), p. 53.

28 In presenting Momaday with an honorary degree in 1971, Thomas S. Smith, president of Lawrence University, said: "The writer is the intelligence of his soil. There is a corollary to such a statement: only art which is supremely local has any chance of becoming universal."

29 The working title for the book was *The Furrow and the Glow,* from the fourth stanza of Emily Dickinson's "Farther in Summer Than the Birds": "Remit as yet no grace, / No Furrow on the glow, / Yet a druidic difference / Enhances nature now" (*The Complete Poems of Emily Dickinson* [Boston: Little, Brown, & Co., 1924], pp. 102–3).

30 The friend of whom Momaday speaks is Gaetano Prampolini. Cather's emblematic description of the plow against the setting sun is at the end of Chapter 14 of *My Ántonia.*

31 Edward Abbey, "Memories of an Indian Childhood," *Harper's,* Feb. 1977, p. 94.

32 Howe made this statement in 1962 in a Stanford University seminar on Henry James in which Momaday was enrolled.

33 *The Gourd Dancer,* pp. 2, 21–23.

34 A person whose name Momaday does not recall made this comment while introducing him at a conference.

35 *The Gourd Dancer,* pp. 16, 17, 31, 11, 12.

36 Ibid., pp. 11, 31, 48, 50, 30, 28.

37 Ibid., pp. 31, 12, 16, 25.

38 From the third stanza of Cunningham's poem "For My Contemporaries": "Despise me not, And be not queasy / To praise somewhat: / Verse is not easy" (*The Collected Poems and Epigrams of J. V. Cunningham* [Athens, Ohio: Swallow Press, 1971], p. 43).

39 "The Hotel 1829," "Concession," and "Sonnet for a Mottled-Breasted Girl," *Paris Review* 28 (Spring 1986): 160–62.

40 Kenneth Lincoln's excellent essay entitled "Word Senders: Black Elk and N.

Scott Momaday" is an extensive discussion of the creative language of the two men. The essay appears in *Native American Renaissance* (Berkeley: University of California Press, 1983), pp. 82–121.

THE VISION PLANE

1 N. Scott Momaday, "A Garment of Brightness," *Viva*, July 29, 1973, p. 2.

2 N. Scott Momaday, "Angle of Geese," *Angle of Geese and Other Poems*, p. 28. The poem first appeared in the *New Mexico Quarterly*, n.s., 1 (1965).

3 N. Scott Momaday, "Approaching the Intricate Topic Obliquely," *Viva*, Dec. 24, 1972, p. 2.

4 N. Scott Momaday, "I Am Alive," in *The World of the American Indian*, ed. Jules B. Billard (Washington, D.C.: National Geographic Society, 1975), p. 26.

5 Ibid., p. 14.

6 Momaday, interview with the author, Nov. 20, 1974.

7 N. Scott Momaday, "The Horse That Died of Shame," *Angle of Geese and Other Poems*, p. 21.

8 N. Scott Momaday, "The Burning," *Pembroke Magazine* 6 (1975): 31; reprinted in *The Gourd Dancer*, p. 58.

9 N. Scott Momaday, "New World," *The Gourd Dancer*, pp. 38–40.

10 N. Scott Momaday, "Winter Holding off the Coast of North America," *The Gourd Dancer*, p. 49.

11 N. Scott Momaday, "Before an Old Painting of the Crucifixion," *The Gourd Dancer*, pp. 28–29.

12 N. Scott Momaday, "North Dakota, North Light," *The Gourd Dancer*, p. 48.

13 N. Scott Momaday, "For the Old Man Mad for Drawing, Dead at Eighty-nine," *The Gourd Dancer*, p. 55.

14 N. Scott Momaday, "Abstract: Old Woman in a Room, *The Gourd Dancer*, p. 56.

15 N. Scott Momaday, "Wide Empty Landscape with a Death in the Foreground," in *Carriers of the Dream Wheel: Contemporary Native American Poetry*, ed. Duane Niatum (New York: Harper & Row, 1975), p. 90. This volume contains an impressive variety of representative writings.

16 N. Scott Momaday, "Unholy Sights," *Viva*, Sept. 9, 1973, p. 7.

17 Yvor Winters, *Forms of Discovery: Critical and Historical Essays on the Forms of the Short Poem in English* (Denver: Alan Swallow, 1967), p. 290.

18 *Running Coyote*, 1986, watercolor, 11" x 14".

19 Winters, *Forms of Discovery*, p. 290.

20 Lincoln, "Word Senders," p. 99.

21 *House Made of Dawn*, pp. 177–78.

22 Lincoln, "Word Senders," p. 98.

23 See especially *The Way to Rainy Mountain*, pp. 86–87.

24 Ibid., p. 12.

25 The working title is *A Round of Shields.*

26 N. Scott Momaday, *The Journey of Tai-me* (Santa Barbara: Privately published, 1967).

27 Mary Jane Lenz, *The Stuff of Dreams: Native American Dolls* (New York: Museum of the American Indian, 1986).

28 The Ka-itsenko Society is an elite Kiowa warrior society.

29 A large collection of the William S. Soule photographs is included in Wilbur S. Nye's *Plains Indian Raiders: The Final Phases of Warfare from the Arkansas to the Red River* (Norman: University of Oklahoma Press, 1968).

30 *Woman at a Bus Stop*, 1984, watercolor, 11" x 14".

31 N. Scott Momaday, "Forms of the Earth at Abiquiu," *The Gourd Dancer*, p. 60.

32 In "White," the first story in the sequence "The Colors of Night."

AND INFINITY

1 N. Scott Momaday, "Singing about the Beauty of the Earth," p. 2.

2 N. Scott Momaday, "Graduation Brings Memories," *Viva*, June 10, 1973, p. 2.

3 *House Made of Dawn*, p. 52.

4 Ibid., p. 190.

5 Momaday, "A First American Views His Land," p. 17.

6 Momaday, "I Am Alive," p. 14.

7 N. Scott Momaday, "Four Notions of Love and Marriage," *The Gourd Dancer*, pp. 18–19.

8 In a November 19, 1974, interview with the author at Stanford University, Momaday said of Winters: "I admired him a great deal. He could seem gruff, even intolerant, but he wasn't really that, I don't think. But he was something of an absolutist, and I think I am more of a relativist."

9 Yvor Winters, "Preliminary Problems," in *In Defense of Reason* (University of Denver Press, 1947), pp. 361–73.

10 J. V. Cunningham, "On the Calculus," *The Collected Poems and Epigrams of J. V. Cunningham*, p. 113. Reprinted with the permission of Ohio University Press / Swallow Press.

11 Vladimir Nabokov, *Speak, Memory* (New York: Wideview/Pedigree, 1979), p. 139. Nabokov adds: I like to fold my magic carpet, after use, in such a way as to superimpose one part of the pattern upon another. Let visitors trip."

12 John Keats, "Ode to a Grecian Urn."

13 *The Way to Rainy Mountain*, p. 10.

14 Vine Deloria, *Custer Died for Your Sins: An Indian Manifesto* (New York: Macmillan, 1969), pp. 119–20.

15 *The Names*, pp. 79–80.

16 *House Made of Dawn*, p. 96.

TSOAI, TSOAI-TALEE

1 For example, see Maurice Boyd's *Kiowa Voices: Myths, Legends, and Folktales*, vol. 1 (Fort Worth: Texas Christian University Press, 1981), pp. 13–14. The wheel is in northern Wyoming between Dayton and Lovell.

2 Momaday's account of the experience appears in the *New York Times Magazine: The Sophisticated Traveler*, pt. 2, March 13, 1988, pp. 28–30, 81.

3 On p. 55 of *House Made of Dawn*, Momaday says, "Coyotes have the gift of being seldom seen; they keep to the edge of vision and beyond, loping in and out of cover on the plains and highlands."

For a thorough listing of writings by and about N. Scott Momaday, see Matthias Schubnell's *N. Scott Momaday: The Cultural and Literary Background* (Norman: The University of Oklahoma Press, 1985,) pp. 299–323.

Index